Approaches to Marx

Approaches to Marx

Edited by

MARK COWLING AND
LAWRENCE WILDE

OPEN UNIVERSITY PRESS
Milton Keynes • *Philadelphia*

Open University Press
12 Cofferidge Close
Stony Stratford
Milton Keynes MK11 1BY

and
1900 Frost Road, Suite 101
Bristol, PA 19007, USA

First Published 1989

British Library Cataloguing in Publication Data

Approaches to Marx
  1. Marxism. Theories
  I. Cowling, Mark II. Wilde, Lawrence
  335'.4'01
  ISBN 0–335–15622–3
  ISBN 0–335–15621–5 (paper)

Library of Congress Cataloging-in-Publication Data

Approaches to Marx / edited by Mark Cowling and Lawrence Wilde
          p. cm.
     "This collection ... originated in the proceedings of the
Political Studies Association (UK) Marxism Specialist Group"— Pref.
     Bibliography: p.
     Includes index.
     ISBN 0–335-15622–3 ISBN 0–335-15621–5 (pbk.)
     1. Marx, Karl. 1818–1883—Congresses. I. Cowling, Mark.
II. Wilde, Lawrence. III. Political Studies Association of the
United Kingdom Marxism Specialist Group.
HX39.5.A5596 1989
335.4—dc20
                                        89–32079
                                          CIP

Typeset i

Printed i

Contents

List of Contributors

Mark Cowling is a Senior Lecturer in Politics in the Department of Humanities at Teesside Polytechnic. He is the author of a number of articles on Marxism and epistemology, Marxism and the welfare state and on housing policy. He is the current convenor of the Political Studies Association Marxism Specialist Group.

Lawrence Wilde is Senior Lecturer in Political Theory in the Department of Economics and Political Administration at Trent Polytechnic. He is the author of a number of articles on Marx and on Sorel, and a book, *Marx and Contradiction* (Aldershot, Gower, 1989).

Terrell Carver is Lecturer in Politics at the University of Bristol. His books include *Marx's Social Theory* (Oxford, Oxford University Press, 1982), *Engels* (Oxford, Oxford University Press, 1981) and *Marx and Engels: The Intellectual Relationship* (Brighton, Wheatsheaf, 1983). He has also published a number of translations of texts by and about Marx. He is currently working on a major biography of Engels, and a volume on Marx's later writings for the series 'Cambridge Texts in the History of Political Thought'.

Joseph McCarney is Senior Lecturer in Philosophy, South Bank Polytechnic. He is the author of *The Real World of Ideology* (Brighton, Harvester, 1980), and of a number of papers on Marxism, philosophy and social science.

Peter Jowers lectures at Bristol Polytechnic.

John Cunliffe is Senior Lecturer in Politics in the Department of Government and Economics at Birmingham Polytechnic. He is the author of articles on

Marx's theories of the party and Marx's politics, and on mutualist views of exploitation.

Paul Smart is Lecturer in the Department of Politics, University of Edinburgh. He is working on Marx and individualism.

Christopher J. Berry is Lecturer in the Department of Politics, University of Glasgow. He is the author of *Hume, Hegel and Human Nature* (Martinus Nijhoff, The Hague, 1982), *Human Nature* (London, Macmillan, 1986) and *The Idea of a Democratic Community* (Brighton, Wheatsheaf, 1988), together with some 18 articles on political theory and the history of ideas.

Ian Forbes is Temporary Lecturer, Department of Politics, University of Southampton, and Executive Director of the Political Studies Association. His thesis, 'The Individual in Marx's Social and Political Thought', won a prize in the Political Studies Association 1986 thesis competition. He edited *Politics and Human Nature* with S. Smith (London, Frances Pinter, 1983) and has published a number of articles on Marx, Nietzsche, human nature and socialist philosophy.

Michael Levin is Principal Lecturer in Politics, Department of Social Science and Administration, Goldsmiths' College, University of London. His book, *Marx, Engels and Liberal Democracy*, is to be published by Macmillan in 1989. He is the author of several articles on Marxism.

John Hoffman is Senior Lecturer, Department of Politics, University of Leicester. His publications include *Marxism and the Theory of Praxis* (London, Lawrence and Wishart, 1975), *Marxism, Revolution and Democracy* (Amsterdam, B.R. Grüner, 1983), *The Gramscian Challenge* (Oxford, Basil Blackwell, 1984) and a textbook for undergraduate students of political theory, *State, Power and Democracy* (Brighton, Wheatsheaf, 1988).

Christopher Pierson is Lecturer in Political Studies and Sociology, University of Stirling. He is the author of *Marxist Theory and Democratic Politics* (Cambridge, Polity Press, 1986) and of articles on Marxism, the state and democracy. A book entitled *Beyond the Welfare State* is scheduled to be published by Polity Press at the end of 1989.

Alan Carling lectures in the Department of Interdisciplinary Human Studies at the University of Bradford. He is the author of several articles on problems of rational choice Marxism. His book, *Rational Choice and Social Division* is to be published by Verso in 1989.

Preface

This collection of papers originated in the proceedings of the Political Studies Association (UK) Marxism Specialist Group. The group was founded in 1983. Since then it has been running a one-day conference each September and one or more sessions at the Political Studies Association Annual Conference. The group is a loose body which is not committed to any political line. It discusses papers concerning the interpretation of classic Marxist texts, and also the possible application of Marxist theories to particular political issues. The papers in this volume are thus a small selection of the group's output, specially revised and edited. To find out more about the group, please contact Mark Cowling at Teesside Polytechnic.

The editors would like to thank Ray Cunningham of the Open University Press for suggesting this volume, and for his assistance and encouragement in getting it into print. Other staff at the Open University Press have also been unfailingly friendly and helpful. We would like to thank the contributors, who have been very supportive, and (almost) universally very prompt in returning revised drafts. We would like to thank the staff at the Computer Centre at Teesside Polytechnic, who have assisted with some typing. They have also dealt with such arcane matters as the transfer of material from assorted micro-computers to the Polytechnic's Prime computer; sending a file electronically from Bradford University to Teesside via a facility charmingly called Postman Pat (it only took him about a month!); and repairing a terminal used for the book when it was indirectly struck by lightning. Finally we would like to thank the staff in our respective Departments at Teesside Polytechnic and Trent Polytechnic for providing a congenial atmosphere, especially those at the Department of Humanities at Teesside, who provided Mark Cowling with a sabbatical Summer Term in 1988.

Mark Cowling and Lawrence Wilde

Acknowledgements

The editors and publishers gratefully acknowledge the kind permission of the publishers to reprint the following articles:

Imprint Academic for Christopher J. Berry, 'Need and Egoism in Marx's Early Writings', from *History of Political Thought*, vol. 8, part 3 (Winter 1987); *New Left Review* for Alan Carling, 'Rational Choice Marxism' from *New Left Review*, no. 160 (November–December, 1986).

Butterworth Scientific Ltd., for Terrell Carver, 'Marx, Engels and Dialectics', from *Political Studies*, vol. 28, part 3 (June 1980), and also for John Cunliffe, 'Marx's Politics – The Tensions in the Communist Manifesto', from *Political Studies*, vol. 30, part 4 (December 1982).

Basil Blackwell for John Hoffman, 'The Problem of Coercion and Consent in Marx and Gramsci', which summarizes some of the arguments in Hoffman, J., *The Gramscian Challenge* (Oxford, Blackwell, 1984).

The Macmillan Press Ltd. and St. Martin's Press Inc. for Mike Levin, 'Marx, Engels and the Parliamentary Path' which appears as Chapter 5 of Levin, M., *Marx, Engels and Liberal Democracy* (London, Macmillan, and New York, St. Martin's Press, 1989).

Routledge and Kegan Paul for Joe McCarney, 'Recent Interpretations of Ideology', from *Economy and Society*, vol. 14, no. 1 (February 1985).

The editors and publishers also gratefully acknowledge the kind permission of Lawrence and Wishart for the use of quotations from their translations of the writings of Marx and Engels as listed under *References*, to Penguin for the use of quotations from their translations of Marx in the Pelican Marx Library, again as listed under *References* and to Random House, Inc. for the use of quotations from *Early Writings* by Karl Marx, edited by Quintin Hoare, translated by Gregor Benton and Rodney Livingstone. Copyright ©1975 by New Left Review; from *Grundrisse: Foundations of the Critique of Political Economy* by Karl Marx, translated with a foreword by Martin Nicolaus. Translation copyright ©1973 by Martin Nicolaus.

References

All references are given in the notes, collected at the end of each contribution. For most works a full title and publication details are given the first time the work is mentioned in any contribution, citations being abbreviated thereafter.

A special system has been employed for editions of Marx and Engels. Ideally all references would be to one agreed edition, such as the *Collected Works* from Lawrence and Wishart, but unfortunately this edition was incomplete at the time of writing. In addition, some of the authors prefer the Penguin translations. Less commonly cited works of Marx and Engels are referred to in the normal way, but for the more frequent references we have used the following abbreviations (in alphabetical order):

Marx

1	*Capital*	*Capital*, vol. 1, trans. B. Fowkes (Harmondsworth, Penguin, 1976)
2	*Capital*	*Capital*, vol. 2, trans. D. Fernbach (Penguin, Harmondsworth, 1981)
3	*Capital*	*Capital*, vol. 3, trans. D. Fernbach (Penguin, Harmondsworth, 1981)
	Early Writings	*Early Writings*, trans. R. Livingstone and G. Benton (Harmondsworth, Penguin 1974)
	Grundrisse	*Grundrisse*, trans. M. Nicolaus (Harmondsworth, Penguin, 1973).
1	*TSV*	*Theories of Surplus Value*, Part 1, trans. E. Burns (London, Lawrence and Wishart, 1969)
2	*TSV*	*Theories of Surplus Value*, Part 2, trans. R. Simpson, (London, Lawrence and Wishart, 1969)

3 *TSV*   *Theories of Surplus Value*, Part 3, trans. J. Cohen and S.W. Ryazanskaya (London, Lawrence and Wishart, 1972)

Marx and Engels
AOB   *Articles on Britain* (Moscow, Progress, 1975).

CW   *Collected Works* (London, Lawrence and Wishart, 1975–) referred to as 1 *CW* for vol. 1 etc.

MESC   *Marx–Engels Selected Correspondence*, (London, Lawrence and Wishart, 1975) – this is the only currently available English translation of the later correspondence.

MESW   *Marx and Engels Selected Works in One Volume* (London, Lawrence and Wishart, 1970).

1 *MESW* or   *Marx and Engels Selected Works in Two Volumes*
2 *MESW*   (Moscow, Progress, 1962) – vol. 1 and vol. 2 respectively. This edition has been generally avoided, but is the best source in English for some later pieces.

Werke   *Werke* (Berlin, Dietz Verlag, 1956–62) – main works of Marx and Engels in German in 43 volumes.

Introduction

Mark Cowling

The papers in this book have been collected together in order to provide an introduction to some of the main concerns of researchers currently interested in the links between the work of Marx and Engels and politics. Our particular aim is to enable students to sample approaches other than those of their lecturers, and to find some direction in the massive literature on Marx and Engels.

After a relatively dormant period in the 1950s, the volume of literature on Marx increased enormously in the next decade. A major reason for this was the translation into English in 1959 of Marx's *Economic and Philosophical Manuscripts,* which raised the problem of how the philosophical account of alienation found there could be reconciled with the apparent scientific determinism of *Capital.* The publication of the *Grundrisse* in an easily-accessible German edition further increased the problems of interpretation. The student rebellions of the late 1960s, culminating in Paris in May 1968, suggested that perhaps there might still be practical applications for Marxism in the West. The theoretical debate was heightened by the much-disputed claims of Althusser that the *Economic and Philosophical Manuscripts* were juvenilia, and that he had a method of reading which would uncover the scientific achievements of the later Marx. New books propounding general interpretations of Marx appeared in the review pages of the quality newspapers at the rate of about two per week. There was a widespread assumption on the Left that if only the appropriate method of understanding Marx could be discovered (or accepted by unbelievers) it should be possible to build a successful revolutionary movement in Western Europe.

In the later 1970s and 1980s the New Right has become the intellectual fashion; what socialist successes there have been in Western Europe and Australia and New Zealand have been achieved by moderate socialists rather than Communists or those further to the left; and students of Marx and Engels have generally become more cautious, sceptical and diversified. The careful study of one or another aspect of Marx, including comparisons with non-Marxist theory, is now more typical than the sweeping claim to have found *the* key to his work.

Several theoretical criticisms and practical problems have all pushed contemporary approaches to Marx in the same direction. The idea that Marxism could provide a scientific guide to the proletariat and thus bring nearer an inevitable revolution, and then offer an adequate guide to the running of a classless society, has been increasingly discredited. Instead the emphasis is much more on the relationship between class, gender and ethnicity, and between the working class and other classes, and on the need for democratic politics to reconcile these different interests. Thus in one way or another many current Marxist concerns lead to a – relatively favourable – reassessment of liberalism, which is a major theme of many papers in this book.

One criticism of Marxism as a science concerns less Marx himself than Althusser: as is briefly outlined in the paper by Cowling in this volume, Althusser himself and others attacked the claim made in *Reading Capital*[1] that the key scientific feature of *Capital* is structural causality.[2] Althusser's British followers have become sceptical of any general claims for scientific certainty, and also of the particular claim of Marxism that the economy determines the other features of society in the làst instance but that these other features have relative autonomy. They say that there is no way of telling whether relative autonomy or determination in the last instance will operate in any particular event.[3] They therefore argue that there are an indefinite number of conditions of existence of capitalist production relations, and there is no sure way of telling in advance whether or not they will be secured.[4] In addition they object to treating economic classes as straightforward political actors in the traditional Marxist manner, arguing that the effects of economic position on political action are much more indirect and oblique than this suggests.[5] Having abandoned so much of Marxism as traditionally defined, it is arguable that they have stepped outside this tradition, but their origins within it are undeniable.[6]

A second problem concerns Marx's economics. Although commentators willing to defend the labour theory of value and the doctrine of the falling rate of profit can be found,[7] the criticisms of these doctrines by commentators such as Steedman, Hodgson, Morishima, and, from their different perspective Hindess and Hirst *et al.*,[8] have been widely influential. The upshot is that Marx's attempt at demonstrating scientifically that capitalist economies are doomed or at least highly unstable is now widely regarded as having failed.[9]

Thus, writers on Marx in the 1980s, much more than those of the early 1970s, tend to be sceptical of economic tendencies 'working themselves out with iron necessity'.[10]

Two further concerns stem from discussions of the state and class. As Jessop shows in *The Capitalist State*,[11] a view of the capitalist state as *simply* the instrument of the ruling class, devoid of internal struggles and uninfluenced by parliamentary democracy is not really plausible. Various lines of research are suggested by the criticisms which Jessop summarizes, and the question of the role of liberal democratic politics is certainly one of them. Again, with industrial manual workers as a shrinking minority in the advanced capitalist countries, a Marxist politics founded on them alone looks increasingly hopeless. On the other hand, a majority of economically active adults in such countries sell their labour power in order to live. The question addressed by authors such as Carchedi, Olin Wright and Poulantzas is thus how far the interests and behaviour of various groups are compatible with socialist politics.[12] Liberal democratic politics are obviously an issue in bringing these groups together.

Another line of criticism concerns features of Marx's picture of life under communism. Two interrelated arguments have commanded much attention. One concerns Marx's slogan for communism: 'From each according to his abilities, to each according to his needs'.[13] If 'needs' here means basic needs for food, shelter, warmth, medical attention and education, giving people opportunities to read, write poetry or discuss philosophy, Western capitalism satisfies them sufficiently to raise serious doubts about whether a communist revolution in these countries would be worth the inevitable disruption. But if 'needs' is interpreted generously it is soon apparent that no society could give *all* its members the resources to meet their needs – say, to make an epic film, to enjoy space travel using the most advanced vehicles of the day, to do scientific experiments requiring the use of the whole of Australia. But all of these activities are in principle legitimate human aspirations. The obvious requirement for a socialist society is to have some sort of collective rationing procedure for activities needing massive resources – to ask, for example, which people or groups of people would make the best epic films. This leads to a second argument: that the 'withering away of the state' and its replacement by the 'administration of things' must be questioned, as some sort of political procedure for securing a just allocation of scarce resources would be needed in any society.[14]

Criticism of Marx's ideas on the 'withering away of the state' is also provoked by two further important concerns. The record of communist states on human rights has generally been worse than that of capitalist democracies, so that there is a concern to find some road to socialism which preserves pluralist democracy and individual rights. In addition, there seem to be major political issues concerning – notably, but not only – ethnicity, gender and the environment which are not directly reducible to class politics, and it is debatable whether communism as defined by Marx would entirely resolve them.[15]

This sketch of the background to the papers in this volume allows the two major general themes approached by the authors to be seen. One substantial theme is the ongoing attempt to make sense of the writings of Marx and Engels, and in various – conflicting – ways the papers by Cowling, Wilde, Carver, McCarney and Cunliffe try to advance this. Obviously new interpretations of Marx and Engels should not be seen in a vacuum; they are liable to affect the uses to which the theories are put. These historical papers are generally not primarily concerned with methodological issues, and that by Jowers attempts to remedy this.

The other main theme concerns in various ways the interrelation between Marxism and liberalism. All the lines of criticism of Marx's theories outlined above point in this direction, for they undermine the certainty of a revolution leading to a completely harmonious society. Instead they point towards the continuing value of democratic politics, including a role for opposition parties, under communism, and alongside this suggest that liberal values such as individualism, free speech and assembly, rights, justice, and so on, might all have some role to play both before and after the revolution. Obviously this approach conflicts greatly with the aspects of Marxism most prominently found, for example, in Lenin, and considerable debate and analysis are needed to see which liberal and Marxist positions are compatible. This is all the more apparent as neither doctrine is internally simple and unambiguous. All the remaining papers in one way or another address this set of problems. Those by Smart, Berry and Forbes look in various ways at the relationship between Marxism and individualism. Hoffman and Levin look at the relationship between Marxism and liberal democratic politics; Pierson looks at the question of rights, and Carling at some recent attempts to import fundamentally liberal ideas into the reorientation of Marxism. Let us see in a little more detail how each paper relates to the wider debate.

The paper by Cowling, 'The Case for Two Marxes Restated', attempts to make some sense of Althusser's claim that there is a break in Marx's work between 1845 and 1847. Before 1845 we find the young humanist Marx whose theories are focused on alienation; after 1847 the scientific Marx of *Capital* develops. Cowling argues that although many features of Althusser's work have rightly been dismissed, the basic claim that there is a break in Marx's work is valid. Cowling's claim is that the alienation theory is replaced in the later Marx by the theory of the mode of production. He briefly offers some reasons for the appearance of the term 'alienation' in Marx's work after 1847. Apart from offering a view of the issue which is opposite to that held by most British commentators on Marx, Cowling's article also necessarily involves a helpful overview of many of Marx's theories. Cowling's conclusion is relatively modest: his paper does not claim to rule out the fairly restricted view of basic human nature in Marx found in Geras's *Marx and Human Nature: The Refutation of a Legend.*[16] He simply claims – and Geras does not contest – that the works of the later Marx do not have alienation at their core. Further, Cowling's view that the mode of production is central to the older Marx's work could lead either towards the kinds of criticism made by the neo-Althusserians described above or to the sort of defence of Marx made by Cohen.[17] He does, however, offer an alternative to the usual position of Anglo-Saxon commentators, which combines a strong emphasis on the importance of alienation in the older Marx with a reluctance to discuss its detailed significance.

Cowling's paper is part of a project which looks at the dialectic in the older Marx. Wilde in 'The Early Development of Marx's Concept of Contradiction' is also interested in Marx's dialectic, and concurs with Cowling that the role of alienation (or the lack of it) in Marx's work generally is very significant for our understanding of what Marx's dialectic is all about. Wilde assumes broad continuity in Marx's work and is therefore particularly interested in the role of the dialectic in the younger Marx, which he hopes will give indications about Marx's work in general. He therefore rejects the view in Cowling's article that

Marx from 1843 to 1845 broadly accepted Feuerbach's view of the dialectic.

Wilde focuses on contradiction, an important but ambiguous term in Marx's writings. He argues that a clear concept of essential contradiction is to be found in the 1843 *Critique of Hegel's Philosophy of Right*. An example of such a contradiction might be that between pole and non-pole or human and non-human; no underlying connection or mediation is assumed between the two terms. He then argues that a concept of the human essence as creative activity is central to both the Marx of the *1844 Manuscripts* and the older Marx. The negation of this human essence under capitalism is the essential contradiction which underpins the other major contradictions which Marx describes, and which are analysed by Wilde in his recent book, *Marx and Contradiction*.[18] Thus what is absolutely central in Marx for Wilde is dropped in Cowling's version.

Those who wish to argue that Marx dropped the concept of alienation in 1847 tend to argue that Marx and Engels had differences of emphasis and perhaps, indeed, unexamined differences on some minor issues, but that they were generally in harmony. There is, however, a long tradition of disagreement with this view, particularly among those who emphasize humanist themes in the older Marx, and therefore reject Engels's willingness to see Marxism as a natural science.[19] If any one issue is central to this question it is Marx's attitude to Engels's *Anti-Dühring* and *Dialectics of Nature* in which Engels tries to present a materialist version of Hegel's *Philosophy of Nature*, complete with the three laws of dialectics. Carver in 'Marx, Engels and Dialectics' shows that there is little evidence that Marx actively endorsed Engels's project. Instead he suggests there was general encouragement, support for reasons of political tactics, and a little rewriting of intellectual history by Engels after Marx's death. Carver's case, elaborated in *Marx and Engels: The Intellectual Relationship*,[20] is largely circumstantial: the positive evidence of Marx's active endorsement of Engels is not strong. On the other hand, it can be argued that Marx had a history of vigorously opposing theories when he disagreed, that he had the opportunity of doing so, and that he failed to take it. Carver's argument was disputed by Welty, who claims there is historical evidence that Marx was more familiar with, and sympathetic to, Engels's *Dialectics of Nature* than Carver argues.[21] Stanley and Zimmerman argue that Marx and Engels were agreed on the dialectics of nature and that supposed differences between them are largely 'an intellectual contradiction within their commonly held theory'.[22] One comment of Carver's which might be a useful foundation for further work is that, at minimum, there is no solid evidence that Marx's method incorporates Engels's dialectics of nature, whatever Marx thought of it. That said, the obvious procedure is to examine closely the details of Marx's *own* theories, without presuppositions on this issue.[23]

From the fundamentals of Marx's view of man and his dialectics we move on to his theory of ideology. In his book *The Real World of Ideology*,[24] Joe McCarney argues that ideology is, as Marx puts it in the Preface to the *Critique of Political Economy*, the 'legal, political, religious, artistic or philosophic – in short, ideological – forms in which men become conscious' of the class struggle and fight it out. He is concerned to deny a number of other popular views about ideology. It is not *determined* by class interests (anyone can adopt any ideology). It is not, as theorists who are influenced by Gramsci or by Marx's ideas about the fetishism of commodities tend to argue, a form of cement which holds societies together.[25] It is not defined as 'false' or 'inverted' consciousness; Marx makes no special cognitive claims about its status, and the passage comparing it to a *camera obscura* in *The German Ideology* has been mistranslated.[26] These are all contentious claims, and some might feel at minimum that if Marx did not develop these contested views of ideology it was a failing, not a merit. In 'Recent Interpretations of Ideology' in this volume McCarney takes issue with Jorge Larrain's *Marxism and Ideology*[27] and Bhikhu Parekh's *Marx's Theory of Ideology*.[28] In so doing, McCarney offers an introduction to a number of current issues in the interpretation of Marx's theories: whether Marx had a 'negative' concept of ideology; whether ideology serves the ruling class alone; the idea of ideology as the 'displacement of contradictions'; the question of whether bourgeois ideology can have only a formal definition such as 'defending the bourgeoisie' or whether it can be substantively identified as unjustifiably universalizing and dehistoricizing the social order; the relationship between a proletarian class position and a scientific approach to theorizing about society.

McCarney's paper and the authors he criticizes stick fairly closely to Marx's original conceptions. In recent years ideology has, of course, attained considerable importance as a topic in its own right. One major line of development has been 'discourse theory'. In brief, this is developed from Althusser's idea that the subjects of ideology are constituted in ideological discourse; the neo-Althusserian idea that no external epistemological checks on discourse are available; and the Althusserian idea that one of the dangers of Marxism is the reduction of the social totality to any sort of essence. In this approach ideological discourses are examined as such rather than reduced to a class or economic base. Important protagonists of this approach have been Laclau and Mouffe.[29] Starting from a version of Althusserian Marxism, this approach is prone to move on to deconstruction and Post-Marxism, as in Laclau and Mouffe's latest book.[30]

Apart from Ryan's *Marxism and Deconstruction*,[31] relatively little has been specifically written on the use of deconstruction as a technique for approaching Marx's texts. Peter Jowers's article 'Defending Theoretical Openness: Deconstruction and Post-Marxism' provides a relatively straightforward exposition of deconstruction and sympathetically examines the possibilities it offers. Many students of Marx approach deconstruction with anxiety because of its implicit relativism, but it would be unfortunate automatically to dismiss an approach which has been found so productive elsewhere.

John Cunliffe's paper on 'Marx's Politics – The Tensions in the *Communist Manifesto*' is a rigorous attempt to analyse Marx's political strategy. The problem Cunliffe tackles is easy to state in general terms and well known: initially in the *Communist Manifesto* and, indeed, elsewhere (notably in the Preface to the *Critique of Political Economy*), Marx appears to regard proletarian revolution as the product of a mature capitalism. In Part IV of the *Communist Manifesto* and elsewhere (notably in the March 1850 Address to the

Central Committee of the Communist League) he apparently accepts the possibility of proletarian revolution in a backward capitalist country, such as the Germany of 1848. Cunliffe carefully considers five possible versions of what Marx might be asserting, and argues that the two positions are in fact compatible. He also offers his readers references to authors who put forward a variety of alternative interpretations. Given that actual communist revolutions have all happened in underdeveloped countries, Cunliffe's work offers a significant link between Marx's texts and communist politics.

With Paul Smart's paper we start to look at Marx's view of the major liberal theme of individualism. Smart argues that Marx's *Grundrisse* combines for the first time his idea of alienation, his materialist dialectic (as found explained in his Introduction to the *Critique of Political Economy*) and a detailed examination of capitalism. Individualism for Marx is founded on the vast increase in productivity developed by capitalism, which produces the possibility of free time and resources for individual development. Under capitalism, however, both these appear potentially, as properties of capital, which dominates the worker. Once capitalism has been replaced by communism the realization of the individual through labour as a member of the community becomes the aim of work. Smart's paper gives a good introduction to Marx's views about individualism and its preconditions. These views, however, leave us with a lot of problems. What about the idea that some labour at least will be socially necessary but unfulfilling?[32] How much can individually fulfilling labour and an economic plan be harmonized – might not everyone want to do ploughing or engine-driving? Might not some of the new individual energies go into (non-class) politics (say feminism, animal liberation, and the like?). Is there *any* connection between the isolated individualism fostered by capitalism and communist individualism – and if so, what? And, on the exegetical level, if Cowling's paper is to be believed, something *must* be wrong with Smart's.

The major theme of Chris Berry's work up to now has been the concept of human nature and its implications for political thought.[33] His paper on 'Need and Egoism in Marx's Early Writings' in this collection is part of a project aimed at understanding the concept of luxury. This is obviously logically connected to the idea of need, hence the interest in Marx's analysis of need. He starts by pointing out that in following Hegel's conceptualization of society into Family, Civil Society and State, Marx is following Hegel's theoretical innovation in seeing civil society as apolitical and distinct from the state. He then points out the parallels between (a) Marx's idea of production for need as a confirmation of authentic, communal human nature; (b) Hegel's idea of marriage as a special contract which transcends the egoism which is the normal foundation of contracts and which achieves a realization of our 'substantive self-consciousness'; (c) Marx's notion of the relationship between men and women as the index of the extent to which society has transcended egoism. Further, Hegel's view of the way in which civil society multiplies 'needs' in its search for profits, while generating poverty amongst the propertyless, is broadly similar to Marx's. The difference, chiefly, comes in the evaluation of this process – Hegel seeing it as the liberation of mankind from nature, Marx (in 1845) as an additional manifestation of dehumanization. Berry's paper implicitly raises a variety of interesting problems which it could not possibly answer. The older Marx, as we see in Smart's paper, looked less to the dehumanization of capitalism than to the potential it develops for individuals under communism. How much is this merely a shift of emphasis rather than a reassessment of the historical role of capitalism? Can the links between the analysis of the *Economic and Philosophical Manuscripts* and Hegel which Berry traces be expanded, diminishing the role of Feuerbach in the young Marx? Or can they actually be explained away by, say, a common interest in the political economists, on the one hand, and a limited coincidence between Fourier, Hegel and Marx, on the other? Finally, to anticipate further stages of Berry's project, does the analysis of need here offer any new perspective on the recent upsurge of interest in the issue of needs and socialism?[34]

Smart and Berry are both chiefly concerned to establish Marxian views on aspects of individualism which can then be related to other thinkers. Forbes, in his paper on 'Marxian Individualism', is mainly concerned to go further and relate Marxian individualism to other variants of it. He starts by pointing out that the meaning of 'individualism' is heavily dependent on its context. Although liberalism tends to be associated with the defence of capitalism, one can find liberal individualist criticisms of capitalism; and some collectivists are critical of Stalinism and 'contempt for concrete people'. Individualism certainly asserts the moral primacy and autonomy of the individual, but is faced with methodological problems when it is asked whether the needs of the individual are socially determined. This leads to the development of political, economic, epistemological and methodological individualism. Turning to this last form, Forbes follows Bhaskar in suggesting that human actions might be explained by methodological individualism, but that changes in social structure might require something more.[35] Forbes dismisses full-blown Althusserian anti-humanism in that it fails adequately to tackle the sorts of issue raised by Bhaskar. He then moves on to consider Marx's claim that communism facilitates individuality, and argues that this must have its roots in capitalist individualism. Moreover, individualism may prove disruptive of such socialist values as solidarity. Forbes argues for a dialectic between the individual and society as the foundation of Marxian individualism. Forbes's argument is very compressed, and readers may wish to turn to some of his references to explore the very large issues involved.

We now move on to two contributions which look more specifically at Marxism and political practice. In 'Marx, Engels and the Parliamentary Path', Mike Levin sketches the implications of Marx and Engels's various statements on parliament, concluding that they were fairly flexible on tactics, and took parliaments on their perceived merits, so that the notorious Frankfurt Parliament of 1848 was dismissed as a talking shop, while the British and US democracies – at least – were seen as offering real possibilities of advances towards socialism. Obviously this issue of the relative role of parliament and other possible strategies ties up with the question of the need for rights and democracy under communism discussed earlier; and it still forms a focus of live debate between political groups on the Left, on the *Guardian*'s Agenda page, in the writings of Coates and Miliband, and so on.[36]

John Hoffman's 'The Problem of Coercion and Consent in Marx and Gramsci' forms part of a more general project on Gramsci, in which Hoffman is particularly concerned with his originality. Gramsci has become popular with Marxists in the West because he thought at length about the problems of Marxism in a society where political authority is much more extensively bolstered than by Lenin's 'special body of armed men with prisons, etc.': the state is surrounded by a whole range of supporting institutions such as political parties, the education system, churches, trade unions and so on. Working-class politics therefore becomes a matter of winning ideological hegemony within a range of these institutions before moving on to attempt to take state power, a 'war of attrition' rather than a 'war of manoeuvre'. The attractions of this for Western Marxist intellectuals are not hard to find: it seems more directly applicable to Western European realities than undiluted Leninism; it shows that ideological struggle conducted by intellectuals is important; and it also offers a route to some sort of revisionist politics which has a better Marxist pedigree than the overt espousal of Bernstein's positions.

In his paper Hoffman is concerned with the claim that Gramsci, unlike Marx, recognized that politics involves not just coercion but also consent. He argues that their views are closer than is usually acknowledged. Gramsci, he says, is specifically *supplementing* the classical view rather than supplanting it, and certainly thought that violence is necessary for the construction or destruction of states. Second, Marx himself recognized an ideological dimension to politics, although he perhaps emphasized it less than he should have. Third, significant comments of Engels suggest a (relatively) autonomous role for politics.

There are, however, hints in Gramsci that the struggle for consent is the more important one, perhaps with a coercive struggle against the state as the struggle for consent is brought to a successful conclusion. These are reinforced by a tendency in Gramsci to see the political will as undetermined rather than relatively autonomous.

Hoffman's book *The Gramscian Challenge*[37] develops and explores the significance of these last two points. He argues against Gramsci's tendency to see consent as an add-on extra to coercion; for example, in Marx's political economy abstract labour appears as a commodity and thus coercion in the labour process can appear as consent.[38] Having shown how Gramsci's phenomenalist philosophy facilitates the idea of an autonomous will, Hoffman argues that actually all forms of consent involve the active recognition of coercion, and are not free-standing as Gramsci appears to think.[39] Hoffman links the Gramscian idea of a war of attrition with Bernstein and Kautsky[40] and argues that Marx and Engels see a war of attrition and a war of position as complementary parts of the same process.[41] While Gramsci recognized in theory that coercion and consent were linked, the Eurocommunists use his thought as a way of detaching them from each other and concentrating on consent.[42] The coup in Chile shows the limitations of the democratic road if not backed up with coercion.[43] He then turns to the dictatorship of the proletariat in the socialist states and argues that coercion over individual members of the the proletariat is a necessary feature of the dictatorship.[44] Stalinism is thus to be seen as in part a product of the nature of the dictatorship of the proletariat rather than an individual aberration.[45] What thus emerges is a critique of Gramsci and a realistic recognition of the coercive side of Marx's politics.

If Hoffman's arguments lead towards an unfashionable emphasis on coercion, Pierson's, in his paper 'Marxism and Rights', lead in the opposite direction. He starts with a straightforward exposition of Marx's account of rights in his youthful writings, and then does the same for the older Marx. Particularly in the later Marx there is some tendency to see rights as a bourgeois sham, and as an underpinning of capitalism. In both the older and the younger Marx there is the view that bourgeois rights are a poor substitute for full human emancipation or communism. Pierson presents a vigorous challenge to these claims. Some important rights, notably of association and combination, have been won *from* the capitalists rather than *by* them, and many capitalist societies run efficiently without them. In addition, he gives several cogent reasons why rights would be necessary under a communist (or near-communist) society if resources are scarce: if free movement of labour ceases to exist; if individuals need to contest the plan's allocation of resources; in relation to non-class interests.

Pierson's paper is related to the larger project in his *Marxist Theory and Democratic Politics*.[46] Here he looks at the differing views on democracy of Kautsky, Bernstein, Lenin and Luxemburg. He notes that throughout the disputes between Kautsky, Lenin and Luxemburg on the Russian Revolution there is a lack of thought about autonomous politics, although there are very important differences in how each of them treats democracy. He then looks at the Italian and Swedish roads to socialism as possible examples of a democratic version of Marxism, noting both promising features and weaknesses in each. He then turns to an extensive review of recent socialist writing on democracy and rights, in which the line of thinking found in the paper is more fully developed.

The last paper is Alan Carling's 'Rational Choice Marxism'. Carling argues that a new Marxist paradigm has arisen in the work of Cohen, Elster, Roemer and others. Perhaps all the contributions to this volume are analytical in the sense that they value the precise use of language, but rational choice Marxism, says Carling, is supremely so in that it subjects each individual Marxist assertion to careful and critical analysis. Rational choice Marxism particularly involves 'the reinstatement of the subject', the individual faced with structural inequalities. Rational choice Marxism generally assumes individuals to be rational unless their behaviour cannot be explained using this assumption, and claims to be able to explain much more behaviour in this way than hitherto thought. Cohen's *Karl Marx's Theory of History: A Defence* is seen as the defence of a view of human history as a pattern generated by human deliberation in the face of scarcity. Roemer's *A General Theory of Exploitation and Class* [47] is seen as the analysis of exploitation and class on the basis of increasingly complex models of rational individuals possessing different resources. A precise definition is given of exploitation as: taking unfair advantage of a situation in which another person is placed by lack of access to resources. Questions of power are introduced only after this initial analysis. The general effect is a downgrading of analyses based on hierarchical descriptions of capitalist society and on ideology. Although some major features of Marx's economic analysis have to be abandoned in Roemer's reworking, we are left with precise definitions of capitalist, socialist, feudal, status and needs exploitation, forms which probably coexist in varying degrees in most real societies.

If Carling is right we are faced here with a crucial development within Marxism. Obviously there will be numerous criticisms of such a wide-ranging approach, and Carling himself refers to some of them. Not all rational choice Marxists agree that they are such; the assumptions in rational choice Marxism about basing explanations on rational individuals are challenged, notably by Hindess in articles to which Carling refers and by Hirst in *Marxism and Historical Writing*. Rational choice Marxism has generally been blind to gender and ethnicity as possible sources of oppression or exploitation, a deficiency which Carling himself is attempting to remedy in his book, *Rational Choice and Social Division*.[48] Rational choice Marxism works by taking Marxism apart, and it is not clear what is left when the pieces are reassembled. None the less, it is clear that Carling is pointing to some very interesting and powerful new theories which merit the closest attention.

Notes

1. L. Althusser, and E. Balibar, *Reading Capital* (London, New Left Books, 1970).
2. See ibid., pp. 186 L. Althusser, *Essays in Self Criticism*, trans. G. Lock (London, New Left Books, 1976); T. Benton, *The Rise and Fall of Structural Marxism* (London, Macmillan, 1984).
3. A. Cutler, B. Hindess, P.Q. Hirst, and A. Hussain, *Marx's 'Capital' and Capitalism Today* (London, Routledge and Kegan Paul, 1977), vol. I, p. 42.
4. Ibid., vol. I, pp. 172, 208–9.
5. Ibid., vol. I, pp. 237, 242.
6. For an account of some of these developments by one of the leading protagonists see P.Q. Hirst, *Marxism and Historical Writing* (London, Routledge and Kegan Paul, 1985). For a more general review from the outside see Benton, *The Rise and Fall of Structural Marxism*.
7. For example, with qualifications, B. Fine, *Marx's 'Capital'* (London, Macmillan, 1975); J.F. Becker, *Marxian Political Economy* (Cambridge, Cambridge University Press, 1977).
8. I. Steedman, *Marx after Sraffa* (London, New Left Books, 1977); G. Hodgson, *Capitalism, Value and Exploitation* (Oxford, Martin Robertson, 1982); M. Morishima, *Marx's Economics* (Cambridge, Cambridge University Press, 1977); M. Morishima and G. Catephores, *Value, Exploitation and Growth* (London, McGraw Hill, 1978); Cutler *et al.*, *Marx's 'Capital' and Capitalism Today*, vol. I, p. 42.
9. For a good summary of the criticisms mentioned here, see J. Elster, *Making Sense of Marx* (Cambridge, Cambridge University Press, 1985), ch. 3.
10. K. Marx, Preface to first German edition, 1 *Capital*, p. 91.
11. B. Jessop, *The Capitalist State* (Oxford, Martin Robertson, 1982).
12. G. Carchedi, *The Economic Identification of Social Classes* (London, Routledge and Kegan Paul, 1979); idem, *Problems in Class Analysis* (London, Routledge and Kegan Paul, 1983); E.O. Wright, *Class, Crisis and the State* (London, New

Left Books, 1978); N. Poulantzas, *Classes in Contemporary Capitalism* (London, New Left Books, 1978).

13. K. Marx, 'Critique of the Gotha Programme' in K. Marx and F. Engels, *MESW*, p. 321.

14. The arguments of this paragraph can be found elaborated in N. Geras, 'The Controversy about Marx and Justice', *New Left Review*, no. 150 (March–April, 1985), pp. 47–85.

15. For an excellent discussion of these points, with numerous references to additional literature see C. Pierson, *Marxism and Democratic Politics* (Cambridge, Polity Press, 1986).

16. N. Geras, *Marx and Human Nature: The Refutation of a Legend* (London, Verso, 1983).

17. G. Cohen, *Marx's Theory of History: A Defence* (Oxford, Oxford University Press, 1977).

18. L. Wilde, *Marx and Contradiction* (Aldershot, Gower, 1989).

19. For example, N.O. Levine, *The Tragic Deception: Marx Contra Engels* (Oxford and Santa Barbara, CA, Clio, 1975).

20. T. Carver, *Marx and Engels: The Intellectual Relationship* (Brighton, Wheatsheaf/Harvester, 1983).

21. G. Welty, 'Marx, Engels and the *Anti-Dühring*', *Political Studies*, vol. 31, no. 2, (June 1983), pp. 284-94.

22. J. L. Stanley, and E. Zimmerman, 'On the Alleged Differences between Marx and Engels', *Political Studies*, vol. 32, no. 2, (June 1984), pp. 226–48.

23. For Carver's extended answer to his critics, see his 'Marx, Engels and Scholarship,' *Political Studies*, vol. 32, no. 2 (June, 1984), pp. 249–56.

24. J. McCarney, *The Real World of Ideology* (Brighton, Harvester, 1980).

25. Ibid., p. 54.

26. Ibid., ch. 3.

27. J. Larrain, *Marxism and Ideology* (London, Macmillan, 1983).

28. B. Parekh, *Marx's Theory of Ideology* (London, Croom Helm, 1982).

29. For example, E. Laclau, *Politics and Ideology in Marxist Theory* (London, New Left Books, 1977); E. Laclau and C. Mouffe, *Hegemony and Socialist Strategy* (London, Verso, 1985).

30. For an explicitly unsympathetic critique see N. Geras, 'Post Marxism?', *New Left Review*, no. 163 (May–June 1987), pp. 40–82. Laclau and Mouffe responded in E. Laclau and C. Mouffe, 'Reply to Norman Geras', *New Left Review*, no. 166, (November–December 1987), pp. 79-106; for a further comment see N. Mouzalis, 'Marxism or Post-Marxism?', *New Left Review*, no.167 (January–February 1988), pp. 107–23.

31. M. Ryan, *Marxism and Deconstruction* (Baltimore, MD, and London, Johns Hopkins University Press, 1982).

32. See Marx, 3 *Capital*, pp. 958–9.

33. See, for example, C. Berry, *Human Nature* (London, Macmillan, 1986); idem, *Hume, Hegel and Human Nature* (The Hague, Martinus Nijhoff, 1982).

34. See A. Heller, The *Theory of Need in Marx* (London, Allison and Busby, 1974); K. Soper, *On Human Needs* (Brighton, Harvester, 1981); P. Springborg, *The Problem of Human Needs and the Critique of Civilization* (London, Allen & Unwin, 1981); L. Doyal and I. Gough, 'A Theory of Human Needs', *Critical Social Policy*, vol. 4, no. 1 (Summer 1984), pp. 6–38.

35. R. Bhaskar, *The Possibility of Naturalism* (Sussex, Harvester, 1979), p. 35.

36. See, for example, D. Coates, *The Labour Party and the Struggle for Socialism* (Cambridge, Cambridge University Press, 1975); R. Miliband, *Capitalist Democracy in Britain* (Oxford, Oxford University Press, 1982); idem, *Marxism*

and Politics (Oxford, Oxford University Press, 1977); idem, *The State in Capitalist Society* (London, Quartet, 1973); B. Hindess, *Parliamentary Democracy and Socialist Politics* (London, Routledge and Kegan Paul, 1983); G. Hodgson, *Socialism and Parliamentary Democracy* (Nottingham, Spokesman, 1977).

37. J. Hoffman, *The Gramscian Challenge* (Oxford, Basil Blackwell, 1984).
38. Ibid., p. 85.
39. Ibid., p. 127.
40. Ibid., p. 140.
41. Ibid., pp. 141–2, 148–9.
42. Ibid., pp. 140 ff.
43. Ibid., pp. 158 ff.
44. Ibid., p. 183.
45. Ibid., p. 193.
46. C. Pierson, *Marxist Theory and Democratic Politics* (Cambridge, Polity Press, 1986).
47. J. Roemer, *A General Explanation of Exploitation and Class* (Cambridge, MA, Harvard University Press, 1982).
48. A. Carling, *Rational Choice and Social Division* (London, Verso, 1989).

1
The Case for Two Marxes Restated

Mark Cowling

Introduction

The question of whether or not Marx's works form a fairly continuous whole has been discussed ever since the first publication of the *Economic and Philosophical Manuscripts* (*EPM*) in 1932. The general conclusion has been that Marx's work *does* form a continuous whole, despite the intervention of Althusser.[1] Some writers who have taken this general position are Avineri, Cornu, Garaudy, Howard, Hyppolite, Kamenka, Korsch, McLellan, Maguire, Mandel, Mészáros, Plamenatz, Ollman, Tucker, Lewis, Cornforth, Kolakowski, Thomas, and, in a limited way, Geras.[2] The issue is an important one, for two reasons. First, if Marx's works *are* continuous, then their core must be the ethical condemnation of alienation found in the *EPM*, and not the attempt at a scientific theory found in the later work. Attempts to revise or apply or test Marx's work would have to bear in mind that they are dealing with an ethic and not an attempted science. Second, the interpretation of much of Marx's work is greatly affected by how one resolves the question whether interpreters should be seeking an account of alienated man under the apparently scientific or practical political appearance of Marx's later work. Thus, for example, Marx's view of the state as an apparatus for maintaining class rule would have to be integrated with a view of the state as the alienated essence of man or of some classes. And *Capital* would have to be seen as an exposition of alienation in the capitalist economy, or in the work of the classical political economists.

The aim of this paper is to show that Marx's work is not continuous, and that there is a break between 1845 and 1847 on roughly the lines Althusser suggested. To be more specific, I see Marx as a Young Hegelian from 1837 to 1842; as a Feuerbachian from his *Critique of Hegel's Philosophy of Right* (1843) to *The Holy Family* (1845); and I regard these periods together as constituting the young Marx; I regard the *Theses on Feuerbach* and Parts II and III of *The German Ideology* as being transitional works; and I consider everything from the first part of *The German Ideology* onwards as the mature Marx, although there are some quite important developments within this framework up to the *Grundrisse* in 1857.[3] I take it that the core of the continuity problem is the alienation theory. It cannot be denied that the Marx of 1844 was, like the Marx of 1847, communist, revolutionary, atheistic, a believer in the abolition of the state and in the importance of economic conditions. However, this is a rather superficial continuity. In the same way both Edward Heath and Tsar Nicolas II were anti-communist, anti-revolutionary, theistic, concerned to maintain the state, and conservative, but their underlying approach to politics is obviously profoundly different. What I want to argue is that the communist views of the Marx of 1844 are developed from a theory of alienation taken from Feuerbach, the main point of his writings being to condemn capitalism using this theory. All aspects of the social whole are explained as products of alienated man. In contrast, the starting point for the mature Marx is the mode of production, of which man is only the bearer. For the mature Marx there is no essence of man to become alienated, no generic man with which to contrast capitalist man. From the theory of the mode of production a whole series of different theories is developed; for these theories, the young Marx's account of alienation is at best an irrelevant psychological hindrance and at worst a logically contradictory theory.

The periodization of Marx's work for which I am arguing is basically the same as Althusser's. However, so much of Althusser's work has been subjected to well-aimed criticism that it would be foolhardy to accept anything he says on trust. In particular, nowhere does he present the case for a break in Marx's work systematically.[4] His periodization of Marx depends on his theory of reading, which no one seems able to apply, and which depends on circular definitions. He fails to distinguish the question 'What are Marx's theories?' from the question 'Are Marx's theories scientific?'.[5] (I am, of course, concerned here only with the former question.) He gave the keystone of Marx's new science in *Capital* as 'structural causality', but this concept has subsequently been argued to be vacuous by various critics, not least Althusser himself. He takes no account of the *Grundrisse*, which is frequently cited as evidence that there is one Marx, whose theories are founded on alienation.[6]

In contrast to Althusser's elaborate methodology, I depend on two commonsense assumptions. First, I assume that words must be taken in context, so that the mere appearance of the word 'alienation' in the later Marx should not be taken as a vindication of the one-Marx theory without an analysis of how it is used. Second, I assume that authors may not be fully aware of the implications of their theories, and may thus contradict themselves by using incompatible theories in the same text. In particular, this means that the fairly occasional appearances of the full-blown concept of alienation in the older Marx may be treated as irrelevant interspersions if they do not properly fit in the context in which they appear.

These considerations lead me to reject the approach of Lewis, who argues that the *word* alienation appears over 300 times in the *Grundrisse*[7] without stopping to consider that the bulk of these uses simply mean 'selling' and have no obvious connection with the theories of the young Marx;[8] and that of Mészáros, who quotes passages from the later Marx which sound somewhat similar to the *EPM*, but without seriously discussing whether and how these fit into the later Marx's theoretical framework.[9]

'One-Marx' theorists take various approaches besides the simple quotation of passages where the word 'alienation' appears, and it is necessary to clarify what I am arguing against. I would not dispute the idea that the alienation theory remained for Marx a *motive* throughout his life. This view can be reconciled with the 'two-Marx' approach, provided it is accepted that this motive had no impact on Marx's later *theories*. Indeed, a plausible explanation for such appearances of the alienation *concept* as we do find in the later Marx could be that an inconsistent but underlying ethical theory occasionally bursts out. In the same way one might find occasional passages in praise of rabbits as friendly and easygoing in the work of a biologist whose *theories* treat rabbits as sophisticated machines.[10]

It is not Marx's motives which concern me but rather the substantive content of his theories. A valid one-Marx approach would, in my view, show *either* that the ethical alienation theory found in the young Marx functions as a sub-theory in the later Marx, similar to the theory of surplus value or the theory of the declining rate of profit, *or* that it is in some way an essential presupposition of all the later Marx's theories. The former alternative is not usually pursued. The latter is what I regard as my main target. Frequently what occurs is that textual and logical evidence which warrants the ascription of the alienation theory as a *motive* is presented as if it warranted this latter theory, but the precise connections are not drawn out. What I want to suggest in this paper is that these connections do not exist, because Marx's later work is founded on the *rejection* of the alienation theory and its replacement by the theory of the mode of production.

Norman Geras's *Marx and Human Nature: Refutation of a Legend* is cited elsewhere in this volume as a vindication of the continuity thesis. In my view the book is a very useful clarification of the debate. Geras shows conclusively that the older Marx does have a theory of human nature. To be more specific: he shows that implicitly, and to some extent explicitly, the older Marx accepts that there is a universal underlying human nature. This includes needs such as other human beings, sex, food, water, clothing, shelter, rest, and healthy conditions.[11] Also, there are human capacities: language, purposive activity, the ability to produce, to formulate and follow norms.[12] Human nature sets limits to the productivity of labour, the length of the working day, the lowering of wages.[13] Capitalism is said to squander labour power, the labourer's life and health.[14] Socialism facilitates the full and free development of people's artistic and scientific potential.[15] To fulfil human needs makes for human happiness, and, *ceteris paribus*, human needs should be fulfilled.[16]

Geras leaves no room for doubt that the older Marx does have a concept of human nature. What he does not show, and does not claim to show, is that the later Marx's discussion of human nature is closely tied to an account of alienation which continues that in the young Marx, nor that such a theory is central to or underlies the older Marx's view of historical materialism. Certainly Geras shows that the older Marx makes moral judgements, but no general moral theory is implied beyond an acceptance that human happiness is important: from what Geras says the older Marx could as well subscribe, say, to some general version of utilitarianism as to the alienation theory. Almost everyone accepts that human happiness is important; by no means everyone accepts (or knows about) the young Marx's theory of alienation.

The Young Marx

The issue of continuity in Marx is complicated by the fact that it is not totally clear to what extent the *EPM* are Feuerbachian and to what extent they are Hegelian.[17] I do not think this question is capable of final resolution, and I think the two-Marx case can be vindicated whichever alternative is taken. To state the major differences baldly, the denial of abstraction, the idea of the reversal of subject and predicate, the idea of a loving, communal species-being, are indicators of a Feuerbachian approach, and the use of rational abstractions and the idea of history as the necessary presupposition of the present are indicators of Hegelianism.

There is no serious contention that the Marx of the 1837–42 period is other than a Left Hegelian, and he could hardly be argued at this stage to have developed more than some very distant precursors of his later views. Let us therefore consider aspects of Marx's work from 1843 to 1845, contrasted with features of his later work.

Theory of Abstraction and Ideal of Man

Even those critics who wish to minimize the influence of Feuerbach on Marx are forced to admit that the first text of the 1843–5 period, the *Critique of Hegel's Philosophy of Right* is wholly Feuerbachian in character. As McLellan puts it, the influence of Feuerbach's method is evident 'on every page'.[18] Marx makes continual use of the notion of the reversal between subject and predicate in formulating a critique of both the actual state and Hegel's account of the state.[19]

Moving on to the *EPM*, in the Preface Marx writes: 'It is hardly necessary to assure the reader conversant with political economy that my results have been obtained by means of a wholly empirical analysis based on a conscientious critical study of political economy.'[20] Now I would want to argue that both Marx's analysis of political economy and Feuerbach's theory of alienation involve very thoroughly philosophical and non-empirical assumptions about human nature; but it is clear that Marx thought that he had completely avoided abstraction. As we see from the discussion of communism in the *1844 Manuscripts*, the ideal, non-alienated man who emerges when he has reappropriated his essence from the economy, the state, and so on, is the Feuerbachian communal, loving man.[21]

Again, in the last part of the *EPM*, the 'Critique of the Hegelian Dialectic and Philosophy as a Whole', we find a conscious avowal from Marx that he is following Feuerbach in his critique of the Hegelian dialectic: the achievements Marx here attributes to Hegel are not really Hegelian but results which can be taken as anticipations of Feuerbach, mainly in a 'mystified' form.[22] In *The Holy Family*, too, Marx provides a lengthy Feuerbachian parody of the method of speculative philosophy in the fruit example, in which real fruit is made to appear as the predicate, the semblance, of a ghostly 'substance' of fruit, which is supposed to be the abstracted essence of all real fruits.[23] Marx claims that his characterization of Hegelian method in the fruit example will work against *all* of Hegel, together with his Left Hegelian disciples, the Bauers and Strausses, and the treatment by them of history, which becomes 'a person apart, a metaphysical subject of which humans are but the bearers'; only Feuerbach has provided the basis of a critique of speculation and metaphysics.[24] Speculative idealism is condemned in the first sentence of *The Holy Family* as the most dangerous enemy in Germany for 'real humanism', which is later identified in Feuerbachian fashion with materialism and communism.[25]

The Theory of the State

In this period Marx's theory of the state was that the state comprises the alienated essence of the citizens which has come to dominate them.[26] Precisely how this process occurs is not made clear. Marx proposes two remedies for this alienation. The first is universal democracy,[27] but this is rapidly discarded in favour of proletarian revolution. In the Introduction to the *Critique of Hegel's Philosophy of Right*, the proletariat is seen as the only class which embodies the 'complete loss of humanity' and could only be redeemed by the 'total redemption of humanity'. Thus the proletariat would fulfil the demands of Feuerbach's philosophy, that is, that man should take back into his collective self his alienated essence.[28] The mature Marx's theory is that the state is the instrument used by the ruling class or their representatives to guarantee the continuance of their class rule. As such it is not in any sense the alienated essence of the proletariat and the bourgeoisie united in order to crush the proletariat. For the later Marx the first aim of the proletariat is to take over the state, which, following the defeat of the revolutions of 1848, is seen as a relatively difficult undertaking. The young Marx depicts political revolution as a narrow act by an excluded class or as a minor preliminary to socialist reorganization, 'man's protest against a dehumanised life', against isolation from 'man's true community'.[29]

The Theory of 'Ideology'

There is no theory of ideology as such in the period 1843–5. What I am concerned with here are the theories of art, law, religion, and so on, *later* covered by the term 'ideology'. Marx's view in his mature work is that ideology is determined by the economic. In the 1843–5 period his view is that economic productive activity *and* ideological production *and* the state are all products of alienated *man*. He thus does not subscribe to his mature view, which gives the economic the determining role with regard to other social phenomena. The closest he gets to the idea of economic alienation determining all the other forms is the idea that 'the whole of human servitude is involved in the relationship of the worker to production, and that the return from economic estrangement is a return from general alienation'.[30] The central role of economic alienation seems to be that of a kind of summing up rather than a thought-out pattern of determination. Thus all Marx's analyses of 'ideology' in 1843–5 conform to the Feuerbachian pattern: human activity projects itself into another sphere where it takes up an independent existence. This applies to Marx's analysis of religion, the only ideological phenomenon discussed in any depth at this period, although two incompatible accounts of religion, as a reflection of egoism and as illusory happpiness, are given.[31] The mature theory of ideology is strikingly missing from the comments of Marx on radical bourgeois materialist philosophers such as d'Holbach, Helvétius, Bentham, and so on: he regards communism as an *extension* of the materialism of these philosophers.[32] From *The German Ideology* onwards these philosophers are regarded as the epitome of bourgeois thought, their individual atomism and egoism reflecting the interests of the bourgeoisie.[33] Again, in the 1843–5 period political economy is regarded as simply reflecting the interests of the bourgeoisie,[34] whereas after 1846 Marx considered that Ricardian political economy *as such* was dangerous to the bourgeoisie once the first general trade crisis had signalled the doom of capitalism.[35]

Economic Analysis

The contrast between the 1843–5 economic analysis and that of *Capital* is more revealing than anything else. The mature Marx in *Capital* was seeking the law of motion of the capitalist mode of production, which would be crucial to the analysis of societies where this mode was dominant.[36] In the *1844 Manuscripts* economic activity is treated as the *expression* of the alienated essence of man in capitalist society, and the aim is to show how man alienates himself in his economic activities in the same way as in religion by showing how all the results produced by the political economists – James Mill and Smith particularly – presuppose alienated man. The aim in the *1844 Manuscripts* is not, in fact, to analyse capitalist production but to *condemn* it, using the theories of the economists as material in which to 'recover' Feuerbach's account of alienation.[37] The four well-known dimensions of alienation in labour – my forced productive activity expresses my essence in alienation from me; alienation from my product; alienation from my species-being; alienation from my fellow man – are the result of the application of Feuerbach's search for alienated abstractions from man to the new area of labour.[38] Alienated labour, egoism, the division of labour and private property are clearly related concepts which Marx develops together.[39] In Marx's theory at this stage, there is no standard of fairness or value in the exchange of commodities and labour. Those who continually come out on top in exchanges are eventually able to purchase the *labour* of others, and thus become capitalists. Those with only their labour to sell become the proletariat: the capitalists can almost always get the better of the bargain with them so that two processes occur.[40] First, the less successful capitalists become proletarians – polarization.[41] Second, the losers of the social war of all against all continue to lose in almost all exchanges and get absolutely and relatively poorer – immiseration.[42] In the end they are driven by their misery and dehumanization to revolution. In revolution man's alienated essence is reappropriated.[43] The main points to note about the above, standard, account of the young Marx's economic theories are as follows.

First, there is no labour theory of value in the young Marx or the young Engels: hence, whatever names are given to the social classes they are effectively only rich and poor.[44] No mechanism is given to explain how the bourgeoisie *exploit* the proletariat in any sense other than that in which a corn merchant exploits his customers in a famine: 'the capitalist and the worker defrauding each other is ... the normal relationship'.[45] Hence also there are none of the consequences of the labour theory of value found in the mature Marx – no theory of surplus value; no theory of the deceptive nature of the wage form, with its consequent distinction between trade union and revolutionary politics; no theory of the role of the capitalist state as an organ which permits but does not carry out the extraction of surplus value. Many of the major theories which characterize the later Marx are thus absent.

Second, the analysis of alienated labour in the *1844 Manuscripts* is not specific to capitalism. It would hold perfectly well in a society of independent commodity producers. The key feature is that labour is related to the competitive market and not directly to other men; the intervention of the capitalist is more or less incidental.[46] The analysis of labour in *Capital* is, of course, specific to the capitalist mode of production once the labour versus labour-power distinction has been introduced.

Third, almost all Marx's analysis in the *EPM* is drawn from Adam Smith; the analysis of *Capital* is almost invariably developed from Ricardo. The main exception to this provides a good example of my next point. Whereas the older Marx vindicates a much modified version of Ricardo's theory of rent,[47] the younger Marx distorts Ricardo's theory to prove that 'the landlord has become in essence a *common* capitalist'.[48] Ricardo's point, of course, is precisely that the landlord is *not* in essence a capitalist.[49]

Fourth, the detailed way in which Marx uses Smith reveals an ethical rather than a scientific intent. For example, for Smith the market price of a commodity is the long-term average price.[50] By definition, fluctuations around this price will not give anyone a long-term advantage or disadvantage, yet Marx argues that in such fluctuations 'it is the worker who loses most of all and necessarily'.[51] Again, Smith discusses the possibility of a stationary state where a country had attained 'a full complement of riches'. In this state both wages and profits would be very low.[52] Marx distorts this by saying that the stationary state has almost arrived, whereas for Smith it is only a distant possibility; and by asserting that the 'surplus labourers' (unmentioned by Smith) 'would have to die'.[53] Marx correctly gives the political economists' view of a subsistence wage as that needed for the subsistence and reproduction of the labourer, and then goes on to cite Smith's discussion of this concept. Smith himself is not too definite about what the subsistence level is. He cites an argument by Cantillon that if the race of labourers is to reproduce itself, and if half of the children born die before manhood, then the wages of a man and his wife must be sufficient to attempt to rear four children.[54] Smith himself is not too struck on this argument, and goes on to illustrate the conditions of labour in four societies. In China, a static society, wages are at 'the lowest rate which is consistent with common humanity', and there the 'poverty of the lower ranks of people ... far surpasses that of the most beggarly nations in Europe'. In Bengal wages are *below* this level, and the numbers of workers are being reduced by starvation; in Britain, and even more so in North America, wages are well above the 'lowest rate consistent with common humanity'.[55]

This optimistic analysis of successful capitalist societies reappears in Marx as: 'The ordinary wage, according to Smith, is the lowest compatible with common humanity, that is, with cattle-like existence.'[56] Smith's rock-bottom reproduction level becomes the statement that 'at the best of times' the worker earns 'so little, that of four children of his, two must starve and die'.[57] The later Marx, in contrast, takes great care not to distort the political economists in this manner, which is obviously intended to 'demonstrate' the acute alienation of the worker.

Fifth, in the *EPM* Marx states that the alienation of the serf is obscured (by political relationships), but that of the wage labourer is transparent. In *Capital* the relations of exploitation are said to be clear under the obviously coercive system of feudalism, but obscured under 'free-contract' capitalism.[58]

Sixth, Marx's criticism of Proudhon in the *1844 Manuscripts* is that he is a pioneering investigator of the premises of political economy who did not fully understand Marx's ideal of dealienated man; in the mature Marx, for example in *The Poverty of Philosophy*, Proudhon is presented as an ignorant petty bourgeois moralist.[59]

Seventh, in the *EPM* there is a theory of the *absolute* immiseration of the proletariat; in *Capital* there is a more qualified theory.[60]

On my analysis all these differences between the young Marx's economic analysis and *Capital* make sense. They *should* cause problems for one-Marx theorists, but in general they are ignored.

The Theory of Communist Revolution

The mature theory of communist revolution attributes a crucial role to the propagation of correct communist theories, and emphasizes the importance of the political organization of the working class. There is no need for such a role to be played in the youthful theory because the dual processes of immiseration and polarization will ultimately force the proletariat to revolution or starvation. The chief revolutionary tactic would apparently be general arson.[61] Again in the youthful theory, capitalists are also alienated and could participate in the revolution;[62] in the mature theory Marx is sceptical of this happening. Note also the comment above on revolution starting in the workshops, not against the state.

The Theory of History

My case so far has been that the young Marx is a Feuerbachian who extends Feuerbach's method to cover labour and society. Most one-Marx commentators emphasize this new subject matter as what distinguishes Marx from Feuerbach and as the germ of the later theories. However, there is another one-Marx interpretation of the young Marx which places much more emphasis on his continued Left Hegelianism, in contrast to my argument that he was a Feuerbachian. This theory, associated with the Frankfurt School, and advocated in varying forms by Lukács, Marcuse, Mészáros, and Howard,[63] claims that Marx remained a Left Hegelian all his life. For them Marx's problem from 1839 onwards was how reason would realize itself – the problem of the Left Hegelians.[64] In the *Critique of Hegel's Philosophy of Right* Marx thought that universal democracy would mediate between reason and the world, but this solution was rejected and Marx's final solution was found in the Introduction to the *Critique of Hegel's Philosophy of Right*: 'As philosophy finds its *material* weapons in the proletariat, the proletariat finds its spiritual weapons in philosophy.'[65] This quotation is seen as crucial by Howard, Marcuse, Lukács, Korsch and Mészáros.[66] The emancipation of the proletariat is communism, which is the goal of world history, that is, of reason, too.[67]

The rest of Marx's work is then presented as an attempt to find increasingly detailed mediations between philosophy and the world. This thesis is comparable to the view that alienation provided Marx with a *motive*: any empirical analysis can be said to be a mediation, just as it can be motivated by a belief that man is alienated. Almost any reference to Hegel is evidence for this 'Left Hegelian' view, especially Marx's comments on his own and the Hegelian dialectic,[68] and Engels's assertion that '[the] German working class is the inheritor of German philosophy'.[69]

Advocates of this Left Hegelian interpretation maintain that the theory of alienation remains central to the mature Marx, and that Marx rapidly rejected in 1844 his espousal in 1843 of an abstract, Feuerbachian ideal of man in favour of a Left Hegelian position in which the morally ideal man of communism is seen as the teleological goal of history, as a figure by which the current social institutions can be morally judged.

In my view, the textual evidence does not support their interpretation of the works of the young Marx. First, there are only isolated remarks in the young Marx to the effect that he is seeking mediations between philosophy and the world. For example, the most straightforward interpretation of the crucial quotation above is that Marx thought proletarian revolution would realize

Feuerbach's philosophy. Second, the idea of finding mediations between philosophy and the world contradicts the evidence we have seen on pp. 17–18 above that Marx rejected abstraction at this stage. Third, the Hegelian idea of history as a *necessary presupposition* of the present or future is largely absent from the *EPM*, and the view of capitalism as having this relationship to communism emerges only in *The German Ideology*. In the *EPM* Marx twice mentions history in discussing communism, but in one case communism seems to be the solution of a Feuerbachian 'riddle';[70] in the second the context is a Feuerbachian analysis of man and nature.[71] Fourth, Marx ought to give an account *somewhere* in either his young or his mature works of how moral judgements can be made by reference to a dealienated future, but in the young Marx moral judgements are made in relation to an ideal of dealienated man which is not clearly founded anywhere. In the older Marx we have a mixture of the condemnation of attempts to found socialism on moral judgements and various apparent moral judgements, but no systematic discussion.[72]

The Left Hegelian interpretation does not find much support in the works of the older Marx, either. First, the mature Marx nowhere claims to demonstrate the *inevitability* of communism, as opposed to the inevitability of crises, and he does not seem concerned to show that communism is *the* morality of *the* future. Second, in *The German Ideology* Marx makes it clear he is opposing all Hegelian-type philosophy in terms which would condemn his own theories if the Left Hegelian interpretation were correct.[73] Third, consistent with their Hegelian approach, the commentators I am criticizing turn Marx into an idealist philosopher.[74] In contrast, the mature Marx treated nature as a reality independent of and prior to man or thought.[75]

In addition their claims about ethics are naive in the extreme: the guiding ethical theme of the Frankfurt School interpretation of Marx is, I maintain, refuted by some not particularly original remarks by Popper, pointing out that it is an ethical judgement that the future state of man is good.[76]

The central feature of the work of the young Marx is the alienation of man from his species-being. What I have tried to show above is that the main theories of the young Marx result directly from this concept. The central concept of the mature Marx is that of the mode of production. I want now to give a brief account of the theories of the mature Marx which illustrates that this is the central feature. The other differences which I have mentioned and will mention between the young and the old Marx are ultimately made possible by this difference: they are important because they are all indications of the break which occurred in 1845.

The Mature Marx

Whether or not there is a break in an author's work must ultimately be decided by an examination of the concepts he uses, but his own ideas about his work are a helpful guide, and Marx and Engels thought (at least at some times!) that there was a break in their work. At the beginning of *The German Ideology*, written in the second half of 1846, we find the following clear statement:

> German criticism has, right up to its latest efforts, never quitted the realm
> of philosophy. Far from examining its general philosophic premises, the
> whole body of its enquiries has actually sprung from the soil of a definite
> philosophical system, that of Hegel. Not only in their answers but in their
> very questions was there a mystification.[77]

This would appear to indicate that Marx and Engels considered that they were
no longer philosophers, and that they thought they had the basis for explaining
the illusions of philosophy. Second, we may cite Marx's comment in the Preface
to the *Critique of Political Economy* (1859) that he and Engels in *The German
Ideology* aimed to 'settle accounts with our former philosophical conscience'.[78]
Third, we can look at the attitude of the mature Marx and Engels to their work.
Marx never published the *EPM* or anything like it, although he could certainly
have done so. Marx indicates in his *Marginal Notes on Wagner* that it was not
his intention that *Capital* should be read as a work with a concept of man at its
centre.[79] Engels rejected his own and Marx's youthful writings as scientifically
incorrect on several occasions, although, in the light of arguments such as
Terrell Carver's in this volume, some readers may not want to place too much
weight on this.[80]

Let us now consider some of the main theories of the mature Marx, referring
back to their equivalents in the young Marx.

The Theory of Abstraction

For the young Marx no abstractions were considered legitimate. While it is still
possible to find some statements condemning abstraction in the mature Marx, these
have in the main a polemical force and are intended to show that Marxism is not
idealist and finds its ultimate test in experience.[81] Marx's fullest statement of his
theory of abstraction in the Introduction to the *Critique of Political Economy*
(1857) makes it clear that he considers that knowledge as a whole is abstract: developed Marxist theory is termed here 'concrete-in-thought', in contrast to the
'concrete-real', which is what we would call the material, tangible, kickable. Moreover, Marx gives an account of why he considers his theory of political economy to
be scientific on the lines that it is developed from very abstract concepts by a quasi-
deductive process.[82] Without arguing about the validity of claims of this sort, it is
plain that they are irreconcilable with the theories of the young Marx.

The Theory of the Mode of Production and the Concept of the Social Whole

The theory of alienation is founded on a conception of the human essence from
which man is alienated: the theory of the mature Marx describes man as the
bearer of or personification of or actor in a mode of production.[83] Obviously the

bearers of a mode of production have to be able to act as bearers, and much of the concept of human nature which Geras shows to exist in the older Marx can be seen as the prerequisites of acting as bearers. The focus of theoretical interest is, however, the mode of production and its law of motion rather than the nature of its bearers. If the nature of man is largely constituted by his mode of production, then it seems to me that there is nothing from which he can become alienated. The condemnation – indeed the assertion – of man's alienation requires a model of non-alienated man as a standard of judgement. Why could this standard not be men, considered as the bearers of the communist mode of production? This line of argument leads us back to the alternatives in the young Marx. Man as a bearer of the communist mode of production must be seen either as an abstract, Feuerbachian-type ideal, or, in Left Hegelian fashion, as man's future, which serves as a standard by which to judge his present. It is generally agreed that the older Marx had advanced beyond the former version, and the latter is ruled out by my arguments on p. 23 above.

It is the fundamental position of the mode of production which is being emphasized in the famous dictum that man must have food and shelter before he can do anything else. Exactly how Marx analyses the mode of production has been much debated in recent years.[84] Here I simply want to show that some uncontroversial features of this analysis limit the possible application of an alienation theory.

The concept of a mode of production directs our attention to two sorts of relationship which exist between the direct labourer, the non-labourer (if any) and the means of production. These are a technical connection in production, concerning how much the labourers have to co-operate and how much the non-labourer organizes them, and a property connection, that is, who has legal ownership and/or use and enjoyment of the means of production.[85]

If we consider the application of this framework to capitalism, where the labourer neither organizes nor owns (legally or in the sense of use and enjoyment) the means of production, we find one source of the alienation vocabulary in the later Marx: it is a shorthand for these two types of separation. Whether or not there is *also* a reference to the youthful theory must depend on our general reading of the older Marx.

Engels summarizes the relations between the other areas or levels of society, notably politics and ideology, and the economic in terms of those unsatisfactory guidelines, determination in the last instance by the economy, and the relative autonomy of the different areas.[86] How one makes sense of this is contentious, but unless the other areas of society are reduced to epiphenomena of the economy, which is an implausible reading, the whole society cannot be seen as explained by alienation in the mode of production.

The idea that the social whole is fully determined from any one centre is further undermined by the fact that Marx's historical writings obviously accept that in any one society there may well be more than one mode of production.[87] Thus, although the economic aspects of the dominant mode of production presumably count as some sort of 'centre', the social whole is now much looser and more complex than in Hegel, Feuerbach or the young Marx.[88]

The Theory of the Capitalist Mode of Production

The first difference in this area is that in *Capital* Marx is plainly taking the Physiocrats, Smith and Ricardo, seriously, and using their theories to develop laws of the capitalist mode of production rather than simply regarding them as ideologists or trying to show from their work that man is alienated in the capitalist system. If *Capital* is 'obviously' an exposure of man's alienation, then it is odd that the earliest expression of this idea is in Lukács's *History and Class Consciousness*, written in 1922, over 50 years after the first volume of *Capital* was first published. Second, on most questions Marx's work is developed from Ricardo rather than Adam Smith. Third, unlike his position in the *EPM*, Marx accepts the labour theory of value from *The German Ideology* onwards.[89]

The major innovations Marx claimed to make in the classical form of political economy were first, the distinction between labour and labour power, and second, the distinction between surplus value and its forms – profit, interest and rent.[90] Neither of these changes relates in any obvious way to alienation. Both changes are linked to Marx's analysis of capitalism as one mode of production among others, rather than as a mixture of eternal economic features and the culmination of economic evolution, since both changes reveal that class exploitation is a feature of capitalism just as much as it is of other modes. This linking of capitalism with obviously exploitative modes such as feudalism has a clear political significance. The analysis of wage forms demonstrates that 'fair wages' are perfectly compatible with capitalist exploitation.

It might be thought that economic alienation and the appropriation of surplus value are different expressions of the same concept, but in fact the two concepts are not readily compatible. This is first of all because the assertion that I should be paid the value of what I produce leads to absurdities,[91] whereas the demand for the return of my alienated essence does not. Second, for the mature Marx a worker is *exploited* to the extent that he produces surplus value. However, workers in an industry with a low organic composition of capital, such as agriculture, will often tend to be less *exploited* (produce relatively less surplus value) than those in a modern industry with a high organic composition of capital. Yet the hours of work, working conditions and pay of agricultural workers are *worse* than those in the modern industry – that is, they are more 'alienated'. In other words, degrees of alienation and exploitation can be *inversely* related.[92]

The Theory of the State

The capitalist state is merely required to maintain the situation in which labour power may be bought and sold. It does not, unlike the feudal state, need to interfere directly in production. As capitalism can only be ended by ending the wages system,[93] and the role of the state is to guard against incursions on this system, the proletarian revolution must be directed in the first instance at establishing the 'revolutionary dictatorship of the proletariat'.[94] This account of the state, based on Marx's analysis of capitalist and other modes of production, differs from a one-Marx account in two ways. First, it hardly makes sense to say that the state as a 'committee for managing the common affairs of the whole bourgeoisie' is the alienated essence of the bourgeoisie *and* the proletariat, as does the young Marx: the 'essence' of the bourgeoisie is surely not 'alienated' in an institution which fully represents its interests. Second, this account stresses the need for political activity by the proletariat: given the multiplicity of classes and groups discussed, for example, in Marx's writings on France, it is plain that political strategy is *not* irrelevant for communists. This makes sense of the later Marx's intense concern with practical political strategy, which is a puzzling anomaly in accounts which present the later Marx's work as closely centred on one concept.[95]

The Theory of Ideology

Marx's first use of his theory of ideology is a break with his past, for in *The German Ideology* he condemns such former mentors as Bauer and Feuerbach as ideologists. Marx's initial theory of ideology *would* fit with a social whole which contained no 'relative autonomy', for ideology is merely 'phantoms', 'sublimates', 'muck' and 'humbug', and has no genuine independence.[96] It soon becomes apparent, however, that Marx thinks that ideology also acts back on the economic. This is evident in his condemnation of socialist ideologies which were based on non-proletarian interests, and which the scientific study of society showed to be false or impractical.[97] The implication of these attacks and Marx's own efforts at propaganda was that ideology *does* have non-ideological effects, even though it is based on the economic. The same point is clear from his discussion in *Capital* of 'The Trinity Formula', that is, of the way economic ideology assists the smooth running of the capitalist mode of production. A point made above about the state may be repeated here. If an ideology serves the interests of a class, then it is odd to say that it is the alienated essence of that class. Again, the idea of a social whole with just one centre cannot make sense of the later Marx.

Communist Strategy

Instead of the naive early view that communism would result rapidly and readily from crises, proletarian immiseration and polarization, the mature Marx realized that economic crises did not necessarily lead to political collapse, and that the laws of a 'pure' capitalist mode of production would not apply directly to the mixture of modes of production found in real societies. The immediate experience of capitalist society led the proletariat towards trade union demands, for the wage-form deceived them; true theories had to be introduced by 'bourgeois ideologists who have raised themselves to the level of comprehending theoretically the historical movement as a whole',[98] that is to say, who based themselves on the scientific achievements of the bourgeoisie.

These features of Marx's theories led to a much greater stress on developing and maintaining true theories about capitalist society, which could alone provide a scientific basis for proletarian strategy, and on avoiding theoretical compromise.[99] They also led to a much greater emphasis on the need for proletarian political organization and activity, and were responsible for Marx and Engels's role in the Communist League and the First International.

Conclusion

I hope that what I have shown in the above is that the theory of alienation is irrelevant, psychologically odd, or even, as in the case of 'bearers', logically contradictory within the theoretical framework of the mature Marx.

By way of conclusion I want briefly to consider Bertell Ollman, the author who, in my opinion, has given the most consistent reinterpretation of Marx's later work as a coherent development of the alienation theories found in the young Marx. *Capital*, for Ollman, is the tracing out of all the categories of political economy in terms of alienated labour,[100] yet no one realized this until Lukács. Classes, for Ollman, are the product of competition,[101] but Marx would surely want to enquire how this 'competition' arose. Again, the state, in Ollman's view of Marx, is the product of men's disposal of their freedom, but Marx would deny that 'men' have ever 'freely' created a state.[102]

Assuredly, Ollman's is not the only possible reinterpretation of the older Marx in terms of the alienation theory, but his rather strange views reinforce my case that a properly thought-out and consistent one-Marx account which is reasonably true to the original is very difficult to produce.

Notes

1. L. Althusser, *For Marx* (London, Allen Lane, 1969).
2. S. Avineri, *The Social and Political Thought of Karl Marx* (Cambridge, Cambridge University Press, 1972); A. Cornu, *The Origins of Marxian Thought* (Springfield, ILL, C.C. Thomas, 1957); R. Garaudy, *Karl Marx, The Evolution of His Thought* (London, Lawrence and Wishart, 1967); D. Howard, *The Development of the Marxian Dialectic* (Carbondale, ILL, Southern Illinois University Press, 1972); J. Hyppolite, *Studies on Marx and Hegel* (London, Heinemann, 1969); E. Kamenka, *The Ethical Foundations of Marxism* (London, Routledge and Kegan Paul, 1972); K. Korsch, *Karl Marx* (London, Chapman and Hall, 1938); idem, *Marxism and Philosophy* (London, New Left Books, 1970); D. McLellan, *Marx's 'Grundrisse'* (London, Macmillan, 1971); idem, *Marx Before Marxism* (Harmondsworth, Penguin, 1972); idem, *Karl Marx, His Life and Thought* (London, Macmillan, 1973), pp. 290–310; J. Maguire, *Marx's Paris Writings* (Dublin, Macmillan, 1972); E. Mandel, *The Formation of Marx's Economic Thought* (London, New Left Books, 1971), pp. 154–86; I. Mészáros, *Marx's Theory of Alienation* (London, Merlin, 1970); J. Plamenatz, *Karl Marx's Philosophy of Man* (Oxford, Clarendon, 1975); B. Ollman, *Alienation, Marx's Critique of Man in Capitalist Society* (Cambridge, Cambridge University Press, 1971); R. Tucker, *Philosophy and Myth in Karl Marx* (Cambridge, Cambridge University Press, 1967); J. Lewis, 'The Althusser Case', *Marxism Today*, (January

1972), pp. 23–8, (February 1972), pp. 43–8; M. Cornforth, 'Some Comments on Louis Althusser's Reply to John Lewis', *Marxism Today* (May 1973) pp. 139–47; L. Kolakowski, 'Althusser's Marx' in R. Miliband and J. Saville, eds, *Socialist Register* (London, Merlin Press, 1971), pp. 111–28; P. Thomas, 'Marx and Science', *Political Studies*, vol. 24, no. 1 (1976), pp. 1–23; N. Geras, *Marx and Human Nature: Refutation of a Legend* (London, Verso, 1983).

3. Cf. Althusser, *For Marx*, pp. 34–5.
4. The nearest is ibid., pp. 9–85.
5. Ibid., pp. 55–70; idem, *Reading Capital* (London, New Left Books, 1970), p. 14.
6. R. Dangueville, *Un Chapitre inédit du 'Capital'* (Paris, 10/18, 1971), p. 13, K. Kosik, *La Dialectique du Concret* (Paris, Maspéro, 1970), pp. 130–1, McLellan, *Marx's 'Grundrisse'*; idem, *Marx before Marxism*, pp. 275–83; idem, 'The Grundrisse in the Context of Marx's Work as a Whole' in P. Walton and S. Hall, eds, *Situating Marx* (London, Human Context Books, 1972), pp. 7–14; P. Walton, 'From Alienation to Surplus Value' in Walton and Hall, *Situating Marx*, pp. 15–35; Maguire, *Marx's Paris Writings*, Preface; Mandel, *The Formation of Marx's Economic Thought*, ch. 10. For an elaboration of some of these criticisms of Althusser see M. Cowling, 'Resolving the Contradictions of Althusser's Philosophy: Popperian Falsificationism as an Alternative to Hindess and Hirst's Anti-Philosophy', *Scottish Journal of Sociology*, vol. 4, no. 2, (May 1980), pp. 169–90.
7. Lewis, 'The Althusser Case', p. 26.
8. For example, K. Marx, *Grundrisse*, pp. 136, 192, 204, 226, 238, 266, 308, 322, 330, 475, 509, 515, 546, 547, 548, 551, 590, 608, 638, 643, 700, 709, 722, 758, 759, 836, 838; idem, *A Contribution to the Critique of Political Economy* (London, Lawrence and Wishart, 1971), pp. 43, 57, 58, 69, 92; idem, 1 *Capital*, pp. 182,.183, 212, 232, 271–2f., 277, 757; idem, 3 *Capital*, pp. 469–70, 938; idem, 2 *TSV*, p. 347; idem, 3 *TSV*, pp. 251, 255, 256, 455, 456, 457, 458, 475, 477, 492, 493, 498, 530, 537, 538. I include derivatives, for instance 'alien' and instances where Marx uses *Veräusserung* rather than *Entäusserung*, which is more usual in the young Marx; it could be argued that I am not sticking sufficiently to references to 'alienation'. If this is so then there is *a fortiori* a great problem in finding 'over 300' references to alienation.
9. Mészáros, *Marx's Theory of Alienation*, pp. 217–27.
10. The most plausible examples of the reintroduction of the *concept* of alienation in the mature Marx are: K. Marx and F. Engels, 5 *CW*, pp. 45, 86–7; Marx, 3 *Capital*, pp. 958–9; idem, *Grundrisse*, pp. 610–13. It is my view that other appearances can be interpreted in the later framework without distortion.
11. Geras, *Marx and Human Nature*, pp. 72, 83.
12. Ibid., pp. 80–2, 108.
13. Ibid., pp. 80–1.
14. Ibid., p. 84.
15. Ibid., p. 85
16. Ibid., p. 101.
17. See C. Arthur, *Dialectics of Labour* (Oxford, Basil Blackwell, 1986), for an extended and careful discussion of the *EPM* which assumes they are basically Hegelian.
18. McLellan, *Marx before Marxism*, p. 143.
19. On the relation of subject and predicate see Marx and Engels, 3 *CW*, pp. 39–40, 64, 83. On Hegel's 'recovery' of the idea in whatever he is dealing with, see ibid., p. 10; also pp. 7, 8, 12, 14, 15, 18, 19, 23, 37, 39, 40, 48, 62, 63, 84; cf. ibid., p. 346.
20. Ibid., p. 231.
21. Ibid., pp. 232, 295, 296, 297, 298, 302, 326, 336–8.

22. Ibid., pp. 328–9, 332–3, 334, 341–2, 344n.
23. Marx and Engels, 4 *CW*, Ch. V, Sect. 2.
24. Ibid., pp. 39, 92–4, 125, 139.
25. Ibid., p. 186.
26. Marx and Engels, 3 *CW*, pp. 29, 31, 39 ff., 72–3, 77–8, 83, 116, 297.
27. Ibid., pp. 30–2.
28. Ibid., pp. 186–7.
29. Ibid., pp. 204–6.
30. Ibid., pp. 280, 297.
31. Ibid., pp. 169–74, 175.
32. Marx and Engels, 4 *CW*, p. 131.
33. Marx and Engels, 5 *CW*, pp. 408–14; Marx, 1 *Capital*, pp. 758–9.
34. Marx and Engels, 3 *CW*, pp. 286–8.
35. Marx, 1 *Capital*, p. 97.
36. Cf. ibid., p. 92.
37. Marx and Engels, 3 *CW*, pp. 290–1.
38. Ibid., pp. 272–6, 220–8.
39. Ibid., pp. 220–1, 306–7.
40. Ibid., p. 270.
41. Ibid., pp. 251–2, 289.
42. Ibid., p. 270.
43. Ibid., pp. 293 ff.
44. Cf. Mandel, *The Formation of Marx's Economic Thought,* ch. 3. Mandel, however, fails to tie this together with his account of alienation.
45. Marx and Engels, 3 *CW*, pp. 84–5, cf. idem, 4 *CW*, p. 49.
46. Ibid., 3 *CW*, pp. 278–9, 227–8.
47. Marx, 2 *TSV*, chs 9 and 11; idem, 3 *Capital*, Part VI.
48. Marx and Engels, 3 *CW*, pp. 285–6.
49. D. Ricardo, *Principles of Political Economy and Taxation*, 3rd edn. (Harmondsworth, Penguin, 1971), ch. 2. On this and the point made in the next paragraph see the very thorough article by Mike Evans, 'Karl Marx's First Confrontation with Political Economy: the 1844 Manuscripts', *Economy and Society*, vol. 13, no. 2, (May 1984), pp. 115–52, esp. sections IV and V.
50. A. Smith, *The Wealth of Nations* (Harmondsworth, Penguin, 1970), p. 158.
51. Marx and Engels, 3 *CW*, p. 236.
52. Smith, *The Wealth of Nations*, p. 197.
53. Marx and Engels, 3 *CW*, pp. 239–41.
54. Smith, *The Wealth of Nations*, pp. 170–1.
55. Ibid., pp. 172–6.
56. Marx and Engels, 3 *CW*, p. 235.
57. Ibid., p. 240.
58. Ibid., pp. 266–8; Marx 1 *Capital*, p. 170; idem, 3 *Capital*, p. 928.
59. Marx and Engels, 4 *CW*, pp. 31–3; idem, 6 *CW*, pp. 105–212.
60. Cf. the above comments on Smith and subsistence, and R. Meek, 'Marx's Doctrine of Increasing Misery' in idem, *Economics and Ideology* (London, Chapman and Hall, 1967), pp. 113–28.
61. Engels in Marx and Engels, 4 *CW*, pp. 519, 581–2.
62. Marx and Engels, 3 *CW*, p. 282.
63. G. Lukács, *History and Class Consciousness* (London, Merlin, 1971); Korsch, *Marxism and Philosophy*; H. Marcuse, *Reason and Revolution* (New York, Routledge and Kegan Paul, 1967); Mészáros, *Marx's Theory of Alienation*; Howard, *The Development of the Marxian Dialectic*.
64. Cf. Marx and Engels, 1 *CW*, pp. 84–7; Howard, *The Development of the Marxian*

Dialectic, pp. 37, 38.
65. Marx and Engels, 3 *CW*, p. 187.
66. Howard, *The Development of the Marxian Dialectic*, pp. x–xii, 156–7, 167; Marcuse, *Reason and Revolution*, pp. 252–5, 258, 261, 275–6, 286, 291–3, 319, 321; Lukács, *History and Class Consciousness*, pp. 19, 20, 42, 142; Korsch, *Marxism and Philosophy*, pp. 34, 41–6, 66–8, 77, Mészáros, *Marx's Theory of Alienation*, pp. 88 ff., 163, 184.
67. Cf. Howard, *The Development of the Marxian Dialectic*, pp. xii, 134; cf. Marx and Engels, 3 *CW*, pp. 296–7.
68. Marx, 1 *Capital*, pp. 102–3; cf. Korsch, *Marxism and Philosophy*, pp. 34f8, 44f15.
69. Marx and Engels, *MESW*, p. 622.
70. Marx and Engels, 3 *CW*, pp. 296–7; cf. Preface to the second edition of *The Essence of Christianity* in L. Feuerbach, *Sämtliche Werke*, ed. W. Bolin, and F. Jodl, (Stuttgard Bad Cannstatt, Fromman Verlag, 1959–60), p. 280.
71. Marx and Engels, 3 *CW*, pp. 305–6, cf. Mandel, *The Formation of Marx's Economic Thought*, pp. 38–9; A. Hernandez, 'Marx's Formation: An Exchange', *New Left Review*, no. 72 (March–April 1972), p. 99.
72. See N. Geras, 'The Controversy About Marx and Justice', *New Left Review*, no. 150 (March–April 1985), pp. 47–85.
73. Marx and Engels, 5 *CW*, pp. 28–30, 55–7.
74. Mészáros, *Marx's Theory of Alienation*, pp. 84–7, ch.VI; Korsch, *Marxism and Philosophy*, pp. 76–8, 82–3; Howard, *The Development of the Marxian Dialectic*, p. 111; Marcuse, *Reason and Revolution*, p. 214.
75. Marx, *A Contribution to the Critique of Political Economy*, pp. 206, 207; idem, *Marginal Notes on Wagner*, in T. Carver, trans. and ed. *Karl Marx Texts on Method* (Oxford, Blackwell, 1975), pp. 190–1; cf. D.–H. Ruben, *Marxism and Materialism* (Brighton, Harvester, 1977).
76. K. Popper, *The Poverty of Historicism* (London, Routledge and Kegan Paul, 1969), p. 54; idem, *The Open Society and Its Enemies* (London, Routledge and Kegan Paul, 1966), vol. 2, ch. 22.
77. Marx and Engels, 5 *CW*, p. 28.
78. Marx, *A Contribution to the Critique of Political Economy*, p. 22.
79. Marx, *Marginal Notes on Wagner*, pp. 189–95.
80. See McLellan, *Marx before Marxism*, pp. 267–8; F. Engels, Preface to the English edition of *The Condition of the Working Class in England in 1844*, 11 January, 1892, in K. Marx and F. Engels, *Werke*, vol. 22, pp. 269–70. For further remarks in the same vein see O. Hamman, 'A Note on the Alienation Motif in Marx', *Political Theory*, vol. 8, no. 2 (1980), pp. 223–42.
81. Marx and Engels, 5 *CW*, pp. 28–31, 36–7, 49, 57, 61–2, 97–101, 181, 232–4, 262, 277, 446–7, cf. idem, 6 *CW*, pp. 162–5.
82. Marx, *A Contribution to the Critique of Political Economy*, pp. 205–8.
83. Cf. ibid., pp. 95, 188–9; idem, *Grundrisse*, pp. 297, 512, 541, 717; idem, 1 *Capital*, pp. 207, 643; idem, 3 *Capital*, pp. 914, 957–8, 960, 961, 963; idem, 1 *TSV*, pp. 170, 409; idem, 3 *TSV*, pp. 315, 514; Marx and Engels, 5 CW, p. 77.
84. See the discussion of the neo–Althusserians in my introduction to this volume, and Alan Carling's paper on 'Rational Choice Marxism'.
85. Marx, 1 *Capital*, pp. 643–4; idem, 2 *Capital*, p. 120; idem, *Grundrisse*, pp. 491–2; idem, 3 *Capital*, pp. 730, 925–7; Marx and Engels, 10 *CW*, pp. 120–2; K. Marx, *Pre-Capitalist Economic Formations*, ed. E. Hobsbawm (London, Lawrence and Wishart, 1964); cf. E. Balibar, *Reading Capital* (part, with L. Althusser) (London, New Left Books, 1970), pp. 207 ff.; M. Evans, *Karl Marx* (London, Unwin, 1975), pp. 62 ff.
86. Engels in K. Marx and F. Engels, *MESC*, pp. 495–507, 540–4, 548–51.

87. Marx and Engels, 6 *CW*, pp. 491–2, 494, 509; idem 11 *CW*, pp. 187–8, 192–3; idem 10 *CW*, pp. 61, 71, 118–19; cf. Y. Wagner and M. Strauss, 'The Programme of the *Communist Manifesto* and its Theoretical Foundations', *Political Studies*, vol. 22, (1974), pp. 470–84.

88. Cf. Althusser's notion of decentred totality in Althusser, *Reading Capital*, pp. 99–112.

89. See Marx and Engels, 5 *CW*, p. 399 cf. Mandel, *The Formation of Marx's Economic Thought*, ch. 3.

90. Marx and Engels, *MESC*, p. 232.

91. See K. Marx, *Critique of the Gotha Programme* in Marx and Engels, *MESW*, p. 318.

92. For Marx's definition of the rate of exploitation, see Marx, 1 *Capital*, p. 326.

93. Marx and Engels, *MESW*, pp. 226, 324–5.

94. Ibid., pp. 327, cf. idem, 6 *CW*, p. 504.

95. Examples of the type of account of Marx which I am attacking here are Popper, *The Open Society and Its Enemies*, vol. 2, pp. 104, 108–9, 119, 135, 142; Avineri, *The Social and Political Thought of Karl Marx*, p. 218; H.B. Acton, *The Illusion of the Epoch*, (London, Cohen and West, 1955) pp. 135–41.

96. Marx and Engels, 5 *CW*, pp. 45, 54.

97. See Marx and Engels, 6 *CW*, pp. 507–17; idem, *MESC*, pp. 315–31; idem, 38 *CW*, p. 105.

98. Marx and Engels, 6 *CW*, p. 494.

99. See, especially, Marx, *The Critique of the Gotha Programme*.

100. Ollman, *Alienation, Marx's Critique of Man in Capitalist Society*, pp. 174, 197.

101. Ibid., pp. 209–11.

102. Ibid., p. 216. For further criticisms of Ollman, see M. Evans, 'More Marx Studies', *Political Studies*, vol. 22, no. 2 (1974).

2
The Early Development of Marx's Concept of Contradiction

Lawrence Wilde

'Contradiction' was a concept of central importance in Marx's method, both in the formulation of his theoretical framework, historical materialism, and in the detailed analysis of the capitalist mode of production – the disclosure of the contradictions of capitalism. In this paper I will argue that the concept was imbued with a philosophical view of human essence which underpinned his entire social theory. It was an element of his philosophy of method which emerged from his intellectual struggle with the philosophies of Hegel and Feuerbach between 1843 and 1846. For clarity of presentation I will examine three aspects of the early development of Marx's original conception of contradiction. The first aspect is the idea of essential contradiction which he embraced in the 1843 *Critique of Hegel's Philosophy of Right*, and, linked to this, his comments on Hegel's method and his work on human essence contained in the *Economic and Philosophical Manuscripts*. The second aspect is the methodological consideration of the concept of contradiction which appeared in his criticisms of the Young Hegelians in *The Holy Family*, particularly his view of political contradictions and their relationship to the contradiction between human essence and human existence. The third aspect is the use of the concept in his early forays into political economy, first in the *Manuscripts* and later in *The German Ideology*, in which he set down for the first time his production-orientated theory of historical development.

Essential Contradiction and Essence

In the *Critique of Hegel's Philosophy of Right*, Marx analysed that part of the book which dealt with the state, and rejected the idealist method employed by Hegel. In doing so he adopted Feuerbach's fundamental criticism of Hegel's method which claimed that the 'subject–object relationship' was the wrong way round. For Hegel, the subject was the 'Idea', a mystical notion which he described in the concluding chapter of the *Science of Logic* as 'all truth' or as the 'totality' in the form of 'nature'.[1] In the *Philosophy of Right*, family and civil society were regarded as expressions (or objects) of the Idea,[2] so that, according to Marx, 'the Idea is made the subject and the actual relation of family and civil society to the state is conceived as its internal imaginary activity'.[3] Marx argued that this caused confusion in dealing with empirical relationships, the result being that Hegel, by effecting certain conceptual mediations, arrived at the conclusion that the existing Prussian state harmonized all the potentially antagonistic elements of society.

Feuerbach had already provided a materialist critique of Hegel's philosophy which demanded an inversion of the 'subject–object' relationship so that human beings became the subjects, and ideas (such as religious ideas) became the objects of human creation. Feuerbach's *Contribution to the Critique of Hegelian Philosophy* appeared in 1839, and his rejection of idealism permeated his most enduring work, *The Essence of Christianity*, published in 1841, an event greeted with enthusiasm by radical German intellectuals – Engels later commented that after its publication 'we all became at once Feuerbachians'.[4] Two important methodological pieces by Feuerbach appeared in February 1843, months before Marx's own critique of Hegel – the preface to the second edition of *The Essence of Christianity* and the *Preliminary Theses for the Reform of Philosophy*. In the latter he reiterated the 'transformative' method, stating that in order to find the 'unconcealed, pure and untarnished truth' it was necessary to reverse speculative philosophy by turning 'the predicate into the subject'.[5] In July of the same year he published another work which developed his methodological prescriptions, *Principles of a Philosophy of the Future*. Marx wrote to Feuerbach and expressed his admiration for his work,[6] and in the section of the *Manuscripts* dealing with Hegel, he wrote that Feuerbach, 'both in his *Theses* ... and, in detail, in the *Philosophy of the Future* has in principle overthrown the old dialectic and philosophy'.[7] A rejection of the *old* dialectic did not imply that dialectics as such was a redundant method, but merely that the *idealist* dialectic mystified rather than enlightened our understanding of social life. When Marx began to express his disappointment at the limitations of Feuerbach's philosophy, it was precisely because it lacked a dialectical approach and settled instead for an unhistorical, contemplative materialism.

Bhikhu Parekh has performed a valuable service by drawing attention to the significance of Marx's observations on the nature of opposition contained in the *Critique of Hegel's Philosophy of Right*.[8] Marx was unhappy with Hegel's attempts to draw a series of 'mediations' between the extremes of 'particularity', as embodied in the monarch, and 'generality', as embodied in civil society. In presenting real groups and their interrelationships as embodiments of concepts, Hegel presented the institutions of the Prussian state as the ideal means for conciliating oppositions. Marx considered that Hegel had simply masked the real divisions of interest which existed in society and which were reflected in the state. For Marx, 'real extremes cannot be mediated precisely because they are real extremes', nor did they require mediation because they were 'opposed in essence' and 'they do not need each other'.[9]

Marx identified three types of opposition in the passages in which he criticized Hegel's 'absurdity of mediation'. I will try to follow Marx's language as closely as possible by terming them *essential, existential,* and *illusory* oppositions.[10] Marx's chief criticism was that Hegel had not perceived *essential* oppositions, which occurred when entities with distinct essences opposed each other and could not be mediated precisely because their essences were different: 'the one does not have in its bosom the longing for ... the other'. The examples cited were oppositions between human and non-human, and between pole and non-pole (it should be pointed out that during the discussion in these passages the relationships between entities were described as either 'opposition' (*Gegensatz*) or 'distinction/difference' (*Unterschied*); a little further on, however,[11] Marx described the legislature as the manifestation of the 'essential contradiction' (*Widerspruch*) between the state and civil society). Marx had already acknowledged Hegel's 'profundity' in describing the separation of civil and political society as a contradiction, but he could not accept the conceptual mediations which purported to resolve the contradiction.[12]

Existential oppositions involved a 'difference of existence' within the same essence. As examples Marx cited north and south as opposite aspects of the polar essence, and men and women as opposite genders of the human essence. In these cases mediations were necessary, and Marx commented that in the case of man and woman 'man is born only through the unifying of their polar differences'. The qualitative distinction between the two kinds of opposition centres on the concept of essence, to which we will shortly return: 'the difference in one case is a difference of existence; in the other a difference of essence – between the two essences'.[13]

The third type of opposition is the most difficult to grasp, and is really a sub-species of the existential opposition, in the sense that Marx was adamant that the opposition occurred only *within* an essence. It is produced when a concept is taken in abstraction and then opposed by an equally abstract concept. He used the example of matter being opposed by spirit, and for him the single essence to which they both belonged was abstract materialism. Another example was between philosophy and religion, which did not form 'true opposites' because 'philosophy comprehends religion in its illusory actuality ... there is no actual dualism of essence'. The reduction of this apparent opposition to an illusion suggests *illusory* as an appropriate name for this type of opposition, a type which annoyed Marx when he saw it recurring in Hegel's work.

It is not surprising that there are 'loose ends' in a manuscript not prepared for publication, and we are left to ponder what Marx meant by 'essence' (*Wesen*). It is the sort of question a trained philosopher such as Marx might have been expected to confront in an analytical manner, but by this time he had developed a hostile attitude to the practice of abstract philosophizing. However, I would like to emphasize some themes which arose from the *Critique* and were developed in his subsequent writings. The first is his assertion that private property formed the basis of the contradictions reflected in the state. He accused

Hegel of confusing cause with effect when dealing with the relationship between private property and the state, condemning 'the *illusion* that the state determines, when it is being determined'.[14] Marx viewed the state as the expression of property relationships, of dominant economic interests, and Hegel's claims that it reflected the general interests of society were regarded as fallacious. Indeed, on the final page of the manuscript, Marx slammed Hegel's views on representation for the 'glaring' contradictions which they contained.[15] The significance of property relationships was recognized by Marx, a recognition which had been developing during his experience as a journalist over the previous 18 months, and from here he began his life-long excursion into political economy in order to understand the genesis of modern private property.

A second theme is the notion of essence, used to attack Hegel's formal mediations, which he derided as 'the fiction of harmony',[16] and to appeal to a 'reality' of social antagonisms. The direction which Marx took in order to understand social antagonisms was clearly presented in the Introduction to the *Critique*, written for publication after the *Critique* itself, later in 1843. In this he expressed his conviction that the proletariat, as the ultimately exploited class, would be the class which would emancipate society by achieving its own emancipation and escaping from its existence as the 'complete loss of man'.[17] This notion of the 'loss of man' echoed the consideration of human essence touched on in the *Critique* and in the final passages of *On the Jewish Question*,[18] which was written between the *Critique* and the *Introduction*.

A third theme is the search for a better methodology, which is usually implicit in his criticisms of Hegel, but which became explicit when he accused the Young Hegelians of identifying contradictions but being satisfied merely with the act of identification: 'the truly philosophical criticism of the present State constitution not only shows up contradictions as existing; it *explains* them, it comprehends their genesis, their necessity'.[19] While there is no doubt that at this stage Marx was keenly appreciative of Feuerbach, the methodological imperative which he had set himself brought him to the decision that Feuerbach was also unable to explain such contradictions.

These themes express different perspectives on method. The first, that the system of private property provides the basis for social and political contradictions, focuses on content – political economy – and was immediately developed in 1844 in the *Comments on James Mill* and the *Economic and Philosophical Manuscripts*. Marx's interest was undoubtedly stimulated by reading Engels's *Outlines of a Critique of Political Economy*, which appeared in the *Deutsch-Französische Jahrbücher* in January 1844 under Marx's editorship. The commitment to the study of political economy and the personal and intellectual friendship with Engels were to endure throughout his life. The second theme, however, is far more controversial, but I would argue that the centrality of the idea of 'essence' plays a key role in Marx's method. Here the focus is philosophical but the treatment is almost anti-philosophical with its exasperated impatience with abstract philosophizing and its desire to get to grips with 'real' relationships. The third theme, the striving for methodological correctness, was developed largely from the critiques which he made of Hegel, the Young Hegelians, and Feuerbach, and *The German Ideology* was its fruition.

The passages on alienated labour in the *Comments on James Mill* and the *Economic and Philosophical Manuscripts* made it clear that industrial workers were deprived of their essential humanity in the production process. Yet, as Norman Geras has pointed out, commentators have been reluctant to accept that Marx had a theory of human essence or human nature.[20] Possibly this is because 'essence' carries connotations of fixity which make it appear incompatible with the fluidity inherent in dialectics. Commentators intent on recovering the dynamic nature of Marx's account of human existence may have avoided the question of human essence for fear of giving the impression that Marx adhered to a form of 'spiritual determinism' in which the logic of history pointed to a return to 'true humanity'. Well, Marx *did* speak of communism as 'the appropriation of the human essence',[21] and the significance of the concept of essence for Marx *has* been noted by some writers, particularly Herbert Marcuse in his discussion of Marx in *Reason and Revolution*,[22] and, implicitly, in an earlier essay on the concept of essence.[23] Above all, Marcuse made it clear that the 'materialist dialectical' view of essence demanded an understanding of the historical development of the relationship between human essence and existence, that is, of historical change, whereas other conceptions were frequently invoked to demonstrate the impossibility of change (or certain kinds of change). Thus we often hear that communism is all very well in theory but it goes against the grain of human nature. Such conceptions, resting on a bleak notion of human nature similar to that which Hobbes described in *Leviathan*, serve not to understand the human condition but to justify its subservience. According to Marcuse (and this is true for Marx), 'essence is conceivable only as the essence of a particular "appearance", whose actual form is viewed with regard to what it is itself and what it could be (but is not in fact)', a relation which 'originates in history and changes in history'.[24]

Marx arrived at his conception of human essence via an analysis of human existence in industrial production, an existence which he considered would quickly become general in Western Europe and beyond. The loss of control or power which the workers suffered in alienated labour appeared to Marx to reduce the workers to little more than animals. What distinguished humans from animals was the human capacity for creative activity, the ability to produce according to a plan. Marx derived this view from observing the world around him, which, with the rapid development of capitalism that was taking place, particularly in Britain, was developing its forces of production at a faster rate than ever before. But if the world of *products* appeared to be the realization of the human essence of creative activity, the method of *production* was its very antithesis, depriving the mass of producers of all creativity. It was the process which produced the 'complete loss of man'[25] which Marx endeavoured to unravel, and this purpose set him apart from the sophisticated apologetics of classical bourgeois political economy.

When Marx compared animals and humans in the *Manuscripts*, he argued that the animal was 'one' with its life activity but that humans made their life activity the object of their will. It was this 'conscious life activity' which distinguished humans from animals.[26] Alienated production, which developed with private property and the division of labour, and was therefore most pronounced under capitalism, rendered the workers so powerless that they felt themselves freely active only outside the production process, in animal functions such as eating, drinking, and procreating, while feeling little more than animals at work.[27] Early in the first volume of *Capital*, when he tried to explain how surplus value was extracted, he wanted to state what was quintessentially human about the labour process, and again he had recourse to comparing human and animal life. Marx accepted that animals produced, and sometimes with great intricacy, and he compared the works of a spider with a weaver and a bee with an architect. But however poor was the work of the weaver or the architect, this work was created in their minds before production, a feat which was beyond the spiders and bees.[28]

It is possible to interpret Marx's commitment to the idea of the essential creativity of humans as an ethical basis for his scientific work. However, it is important to remember that Marx's conception of human essence arose only because, in an apparently free process of exchange, the worker remained enslaved. The righteous denunciations of capitalism throughout Marx's writings were not a substitute for the analysis of how alienated labour operated in the capitalist mode of production. The fact that alienation was systemic meant for Marx that even the owners of capital were alienated, although he commented in *The Holy Family* that the ruling class 'recognises estrangement as its own power and has in it the semblance of a human existence'.[29] But although the power of the bourgeoisie stemmed from alienated labour, the fact that the dominant class could not control the system as it wished was displayed by periodic economic crises. Already Engels had argued that periodic trade crises demonstrated the chronic instability of the capitalist system, and that they would increase in severity,[30] and now Marx talked about the 'headlong rush of over-production' followed by a slump.[31] The system may have invested the bourgeoisie with immense power, but that power did not extend to control of the further development of the system. This point was eloquently expressed by Marx and Engels in the *Manifesto of the Communist Party* when they likened the bourgeois to a magician who was overwhelmed by his own magic – 'a sorcerer who is no longer able to control the powers of the nether world whom he has called up by his own spells'.[32] The existence of systemic contradictions was the result of a process built on alienated labour, and alienation was regarded primarily as a fact of production.

Marx's view of human essence was also a social view, for it stemmed from his attempts to understand contemporary social processes, and demanded that social solutions be sought to resolve the radical disjunction between essence and appearance. This contrasts with the subjectiveness of formulations such as Descartes' 'I think therefore I am'. For Marx, the human essence of creative activity was a social essence, and in the *Manuscripts* he commented that the estrangement of the human species' nature 'is realised and expressed only in the relationship in which a man stands to other men'.[33] A year later he made a statement on the sociality of the human essence in the sixth of his *Theses on*

Feuerbach in which he wrote that 'the essence of man is no abstraction inherent in each individual. In its reality it is the ensemble of the social relations'.[34] However, this statement requires qualification, as it might be interpreted to mean that Marx held *no* view of human essence.[35] Marx did not arrive at his idea of the essence of humanity by contemplating an abstract individual, but by examining the predicament of human existence in contemporary society. But the predicament was not regarded as insoluble, a negation without prospects, to be opposed only by some romantic appeal to an abstract 'better life'. On the contrary, Marx arrived at his conception of human essence precisely from the real achievements of the 'ensemble of the social relations', despite the fact that those relations were alienated, for the achievements of alienated production pointed to the possibility of the producers gaining control over production and directing it in accordance with socially rational ends.

The evidence for Marx's conception of human essence was the world we had created, and the evidence for his theory of alienation was the misery and poverty which abounded in this world of potential abundance. It was the contradiction between the social nature of production and the private character of appropriation. The sixth thesis demonstrated only that Marx was no idealist or romantic, not that he rejected the idea of the human essence. This idea was at the heart of his theory of production and revolution, as he made clear in the following passages in *Theories of Surplus Value*, written in 1862, in which he defended Ricardo's support of production 'for the sake of production':

> To assert, as sentimental opponents of Ricardo's did, that production as such is not the object, is to forget that production for its own sake means nothing but the development of human productive forces, in other words the *development of the richness of human nature as an end in itself*.[36]

This adulation of production did not mean that Marx supported capitalism, of course, for he foresaw the fulfilment of the human essence as a 'historical process' culminating in an emancipatory revolution:

> although at first the development of the capacities of the human species takes place at the cost of the majority of human individuals and even classes, in the end it breaks through this contradiction and coincides with the development of the individual.[37]

The view of essence as creative activity did not disappear with the philosophical vocabulary of 1844, nor did it reappear sporadically in moments when Marx was nostalgic for his philosophical past. On the contrary, it was a conception central to his whole enterprise.

Political Contradictions and the Human Essence

Late in 1844, Marx and Engels collaborated in writing *The Holy Family*, a published work which attacked a variety of positions taken by the Young Hegelians, who had adopted the name of 'Critical Criticism'. One of the features of the Young Hegelian method was the identification of contradictions, but Marx and Engels wanted to expose the illusion that this method offered real penetration of the matters under examination. One example chosen was Bruno Bauer's analysis of the debates in the French Convention in 1793. Bauer, in a piece of honest self-criticism, admitted that he had previously failed to realize that the contradiction between theory and practice evident in the debates was a general contradiction of constitutionalism. Marx agreed, but he was not happy with Bauer's reason for failing to see this 'universal contradiction' in the first place.[38] Marx was making the point that it was not sufficient to recognize the general contradiction, but that it was necessary to specify what a resolution of the contradiction would look like in practical political terms, and what effect this would have on society. Marx argued that the contradiction lay between a system of limited monarchical rule and a democratic representative state, and that the latter should be supported because it represented *political* emancipation. However, he criticized Bauer for implying that *political* emancipation could be equated with *human* emancipation:

> Herr Bauer is committing a very serious oversight when he thinks he is rising from the political to the human essence by conceiving and criticising this contradiction as a 'general' one. He would thus only rise from partial political emancipation to full political emancipation, from the constitutional state to the democratic representative state.[39]

Marx considered that the alienation of the human essence occurred within civil society, and the emergence of a democratic political system provided no guarantee that this condition would be overcome. The constitutional issue was indeed the political essence of the debates in question, but the emergence of a democratic system would do no more than provide an arena in which the contradictions of civil society could be expressed.

The chief methodological point that can be drawn from these passages confirms the line of criticism which Marx had levelled earlier at Bauer in *On the Jewish Question*, in which he rejected Bauer's argument that the Jews should renounce their religion as a prerequisite for political emancipation. For Marx, what was at stake was a confusion of cause and effect. Political activity, the state itself, and religion, were *effects* of civil society, and would change their form as a result of struggles within civil society. Certainly it was possible to locate the essence of a political problem in the sphere of politics itself, but the genesis of that problem had to be sought in civil society, or, more specifically, in the way in which production is organized.

Marx produced another example of this inversion of cause and effect when he examined Bauer's explanation of the general state system, which allegedly 'must hold together the self-seeking atoms'.[40] Marx argued that although many self-seeking individuals would like to think of themselves as being like atoms, entirely independent and self-sufficient, their needs and desires made them social beings, whether they wanted to be or not. In order to protect individual or class interests in the social act of production, states exist, and Marx asserted that it was only 'political superstition' which imagined that civil life must be held together by the state, as 'in reality, on the contrary, the State is held together by civil life'.[41] It is important to note that Marx did not want to dissolve political contradictions by referring to causes outside the political sphere. On the contrary, he engaged in highly detailed political analyses in which he attempted to unravel the political contradictions and draw general lessons about the character of political events, a particularly fine example being *The Eighteenth Brumaire of Louis Bonaparte*.

Early Political Economy

In the Preface to *A Contribution to the Critique of Political Economy*, Marx recalled that his work on Hegel in 1843 had convinced him that legal relations and political forms were derived from the material conditions of life, or 'civil society', and that the 'anatomy' of civil society had to be 'sought in political economy'.[42] The detailed contradictions which he unearthed became clear only with the publication of the *Contribution* in 1859 and his subsequent writings in this field. However, the general contradiction of the modern system of production, the fundamental contradiction on which all the other contradictions developed, was set down in the *1844 Manuscripts* and the first part of *The German Ideology*. The theory of alienation was not simply an aspect of his social theory, it was the theoretical corner-stone of his political economy. As we have seen, the theory of alienation was also a theory of human essence, and the negation of that essence of creative activity in the capitalist mode of production was the theoretical starting point of his analysis. This is most clearly seen in the *Grundrisse* and the first three parts of the first volume of *Capital*. The analysis of the distinction between use value and exchange value (between 'concrete' and 'abstract' labour), and the presentation of his theory of surplus value, revealed the systemic contradictions which stemmed from the alienation of labour in the production process.

The earliest expressions of the contradictory nature of capitalism remained at a general level. In a passage in the *Economic and Philosophical Manuscripts* he referred to the relationship between capital and labour as a contradiction, emphasizing that it became a contradiction only at a certain stage of its development, prior to which it was merely an opposition (*Gegensatz*). He stated that the opposition between property and lack of property should not be regarded as a contradiction until it was seen as an active, internally related opposition between capital and labour, by which he meant that the contradictions occurred *within* capital and *within* labour as well as *between* them. By definition, the opposition between property and lack of property had existed for as long as private property itself, but only in capitalism had there occurred a contradiction which imperilled the very existence of private property. Labour created property yet possessed none, while capital transformed labour into objects and constituted itself as a powerful, impersonal *thing*:

> labour, the subjective essence of private property as exclusion of property, and capital, objective labour as exclusion of labour, constitute private property as its developed state of contradiction – hence a dynamic relationship driving towards resolution.[43]

The dynamic relationship between and within the elements involved contradiction, reciprocity, and change, and while operating within the 'totality' of the capitalist mode of production, it threatened to explode that totality. This was a dialectical formulation, for it involved a dynamic, internally related contradiction, but it was not a Hegelian formulation because the contradiction could be resolved only by abolishing the condition on which it arose, rather than by some sort of 'mediation' within the existing system. The formulation reappeared in the 1849 pamphlet *Wage Labour and Capital*, which was printed from talks given in Brussels in 1847. Here he stated that capital and labour 'reciprocally condition the existence of each other', but he insisted that 'the interests of capital and the interests of labour are diametrically opposed'.[44]

This formulation indicates that Marx's idea of essential contradiction did not represent a return to a non-dialectical position, such as that held by Kant, but had become part of a new kind of dialectical method, the materialist dialectic. The interests of capital and labour were diametrically opposed, based as they were on essences which could never be reconciled, but the interaction of capital and labour was seen as a dialectical process. In the third of the *Economic and Philosophical Manuscripts* he commented that bourgeois political economy acknowledged labour as 'the sole essence of wealth', but that the implications of its theory were 'anti-human in character'.[45] Writers such as Ricardo and James Mill appeared more cynical than Adam Smith simply because their scientific analyses came closer to identifying contradictions within the system, which they nevertheless defended. The capitalist system had labour as its essence, but it was dehumanized, alienated labour, and 'the contradiction of reality corresponded completely to the contradictory being which they accept as their principle'.[46] The bourgeois political economist used the phenomena of the division of labour and exchange to boast of the social character of his science, but 'in the same breath he gives unconscious expression to the contradiction in his science – the motivation of society by unsocial, particular interests'.[47]

The expression of the contradictory nature of capitalism in a general way in the *Manuscripts* is significant because it shows that Marx was concerned with the alienation of the human essence and the dialectical contradiction between capital and labour as aspects of the same problem. Philosophical and socio-economic perspectives were explicitly combined, and although in the bulk of his subsequent political economy the philosophical perspective was not so explicit, it was *immanent* in the various expressions of contradiction which appeared there. The clearest evidence of the persistence of the philosophical perspective is offered by the content of the *Grundrisse* and the beginning of *Capital*.

In *The German Ideology*, the general contradiction of capitalism was expressed in a more sophisticated way by incorporating it into the conception of historical development commonly known as the materialist conception of history, or historical materialism. Marx and Engels argued that the history of humanity 'must always be studied and treated in relation to the history of industry and exchange', and that consciousness itself was a social product.[48] Historically, with the development of a division between mental and material labour, consciousness assumed an independence from its social basis and proceeded to 'the formation of "pure" theory, theology, philosophy, morality, etc.'. But this purity was illusory, for contradictions within these areas occurred only because 'existing social relations have come into contradiction with existing productive forces'.[49] Later in the work, while still couching this social theory in general terms, Marx concluded that developments in the 'productive forces and means of intercourse' would develop destructively and would create a class in the 'sharpest contradiction' to all other classes, a class which would develop a communist consciousness, and, in emancipating itself, would free society from all class rule by abolishing the material basis of social class, private productive property.[50]

Marx and Engels periodized history by designating epochs as distinct 'forms of property' and distinguishing between tribal, ancient, and feudal forms.[51] Three stages in the development of capitalism out of feudalism were sketched: the first corresponded to the rise of a separate merchant class and the growth of manufactures outside the guild system; the second corresponded to the growth of protected commerce; the third corresponded to the growth of large-scale industry. It was then asserted that we could only begin to understand the political changes which accompanied these developments in forms of property by examining the contradiction between the 'productive forces' and the 'form of intercourse':

> The contradiction between the productive forces and the form of intercourse ... necessarily on each occasion burst out in a revolution, taking on at the same time various subsidiary forms, such as all-embracing collisions, collisions of various classes, contradictions of consciousness, battle of ideas, political struggles, etc. ...Thus all collisions in history have their origin, according to our view, in the contradiction between the productive forces and the form of intercourse.[52]

In expounding this production-orientated conception of history, it was claimed that it would be a mistake to view any of the 'subsidiary' forms of struggle as the real cause of historical change, even though the revolutionary participants were normally convinced that they were. For Marx, these 'illusions' constituted ideological thought, and in his later political writings he attempted to strip bare the ideological illusions of various political actors and parties.

Marx acknowledged the theoretical importance of *The German Ideology* in his Preface to *A Contribution to the Critique of Political Economy*, which restated the methodological 'guiding principle' which served as a theoretical framework for his studies.[53] The terminology of the central contradiction was altered, with 'relations of production' replacing the 1846 formulations 'form of intercourse' or 'social relations'. In making this alteration the emphasis was placed squarely on *production*, as opposed to the popular view, espoused at that time by Proudhon and his followers, that the chief economic problem was one of distribution.

While the relationship between the forces of production and the relations of production was held to be crucial to understanding social and political life in all private modes of production, only in capitalism could the contradiction between the forces and relations of production endanger the whole basis of private production. Marx was therefore postulating the end of thousands of years of social domination and subordination. Yet in 1846 the most advanced industrial nation, Britain, still had about half its population living in rural areas, while France and Germany were overwhelmingly agricultural. In other words, far from being in contradiction, it seemed that capitalist relations of production were ideal for the speedy development of the productive forces. At this stage, the signs that capitalism was a contradictory mode of production were the degradation of industrial workers, the starvation of land workers (particularly in Ireland), and the periodic economic crises, but Marx had yet to furnish the exposition of the *particular* contradictions inherent in the capitalist process of production. We read only that the forces–relations contradiction was produced by 'large-scale industry' at a 'highly developed' stage.[54]

The primacy given to the economic structure in *The German Ideology* meant that disputes in politics and ideas in general were to be regarded as 'subsidiary forms' of struggle, and this schema encouraged many followers of Marx to make simplistic reductions of complex phenomena to hazy notions of what was happening within the economic structure. This 'reductionism' or 'economism' has produced the frequently asserted cry from critics of Marx that his method was too 'one-sided'. Perhaps Marx and Engels set a bad example in the manuscript by their (ironic) claim that the real basis of the German opposition to Napoleon was the lack of sugar and coffee which resulted from the adoption of the economic policy known as the continental system,[55] but it was certainly not their intention to offer easy answers to the whole range of social and historical questions. On the contrary, they asserted that their approach did not 'afford a recipe or scheme ... for neatly trimming the epochs of history' and that 'the difficulties begin only when one sets about the examination and arrangement of the material – whether of a past epoch or of the present – and its actual presentation.[56]

Marx's method should be understood as an attempt to free the study of past and present social and political events from idealist assumptions, and to provide a theoretical framework which would lend direction to empirical analyses. The prescriptions for study indicated a strenuous workload for the would-be researcher, who was required to discover the material processes of production, the class relations intrinsic to those processes, and the genesis and operation of the state and the 'ruling ideas'. Furthermore, these things had to be depicted as a totality, and the reciprocal activity of the various factors involved had to be revealed.[57] This approach was hostile to both empiricism and idealism. Marx accused the empiricists of treating history as a 'collection of dead facts', and he accused the idealists of treating history as 'the imagined activity of imagined subjects'. What was demanded was the empirical investigation of the 'actual life process and the activity of the individuals of each epoch' within the framework outlined above.[58]

At one point in *The German Ideology* Marx reverted to the language of the *1844 Manuscripts* when discussing the practical premises necessary for the abolition of 'estrangement' (*'Entfremdung'*), but he put this formerly important word in inverted commas and noted in parenthesis that he was using a term 'which will be comprehensible to the philosophers'.[59]

Here he was clearly distancing himself from the philosophical discourse which he had been immersed in for over three years. This departure had been suggested a few months earlier in the eleventh of his *Theses on Feuerbach*, in which he wrote that 'the philosophers have only *interpreted* the world in various ways; the point is to *change* it'.[60] In the second part of *The German Ideology* he commented on the unsatisfactory nature of philosophy as a separate branch of knowledge by asserting that 'philosophy and the study of the actual world have the same relation to one another as masturbation and sexual love'.[61] While this remark revealed his opinion of the limitations of this particular form of intellectual discourse, in no way should it be read as a rejection of philosophical thinking *per se*. Marx was demanding commitment and relevance, and he did not see it in the practice of existing philosophy, but that did not mean that concepts such as alienation/estrangement and essence suddenly became void. In his later works the discourse shifted to political economy and political analysis and concepts such as value, labour power, surplus value, and revolution come to the fore, but his *philosophy* of method emerged from the confrontation with German philosophy, and the concepts of alienation and essential contradiction were central elements of it.

Conclusion

By 1846 Marx had developed a general theory of historical development which was to serve as a theoretical framework for his studies, and the potential contradiction between the forces and relations of production was at the heart of this theory. I referred to the forces–relations contradiction as a more sophisticated formulation than the capital–labour contradiction because it focused attention on the *development* of the system, whereas the capital–labour contradiction might have encouraged the notion that the system's future depended on the subjective power of two 'static' forces. In other words, there would be nothing to tell us why and when the relative strengths of capital and labour might change, and why the conditions in which this antagonism was being fought out were changing. It is important to note that Marx did not intend the capital–labour relationship to be defined simply by the *existence* of capitalism, but by its development, for in the *Manuscripts* he explicitly referred to the dialectical nature of the relationship, which, he claimed, broke out in a 'clash of mutual contradictions' only at a certain stage of the system's development.[62] However, most of the later formulations of the contradictory nature of the system express the inability of the existing relations of production to develop the forces of production in a rational way. Rationality, of course, is a contestable term, and whoever makes a claim for the superior rationality of one system over another necessarily operates from a consideration of what *ought* to be, even though this may not be admitted by the author. Marx wanted to reveal the ideological assumptions of the political economists, assumptions which had become enshrined in the concepts and categories commonly used in discussing economic affairs. His own assumptions, his philosophy of humanity, were set down in the writings I have analysed in this article, and they were an integral part of his science.

But is it possible to maintain the notion of 'essential contradiction' and still have a dialectical method? In making out his case for the recognition of essential contradictions, Marx claimed that the contradictory elements did not need each other, and that they lacked this facet of complementarity which was commonly found in Hegel's use of the concept of contradiction. Now as this complementarity of opposites is a denoting feature of a dialectical contradiction, it is possible to argue that Marx's defence of essential contradictions is not compatible with dialectics. Some commentators, notably Lucio Colletti, have argued that Marx returned to a Kantian framework which did not tolerate real contradictions, although Colletti accepts that Marx did come out with dialectical contradictions in his economic writings.[63] It is not possible here to engage in a detailed discussion of Colletti's dilemma, but from the analysis so far it is clear that the answer to this question rests on the distinction between essence and existence. The contradictions which Marx identified were based on different and incompatible essences, the human essence of creative activity and its outright negation in the capitalist mode of production. However, as they *existed* in capitalist society the elements of these contradictions related to each other in a dialectical way.

The essences of capital and labour *were* irreconcilable, but *pro tempore* resolutions of the contradiction could be made daily in an existential way, as, for instance, in a strike settlement or the enactment of protective legislation. The contradiction between the forces and relations of production could not be abolished within this mode of production, but the 'violent eruptions' of that contradiction in general economic crises provided 'momentary and forcible solutions'[64] within the existing system. Marx's contradictions were dialectical, but the totality in which they operated required a material *abolition*, and it is this which distinguished his dialectic from that of Hegel. While Marx's rupture with Hegel initially owed much to Feuerbach, the latter overthrew the 'old dialectic' only to replace it with an abstract materialism which failed to understand the relationships between human beings and between people and nature as historically dynamic. Feuerbach's criticisms of Hegel had a profound effect on Marx, but his own work on Hegel and political economy took him logically beyond Feuerbach's outlook even before the explicit rejection of the undialectical materialist approach in the *Theses on Feuerbach* and the first part of *The German Ideology*. The development of themes found in the 1843 and 1844 writings in later works indicate that while the Feuerbachian outlook had been superseded, what emerged was not a return to Hegel, or to Kant, but a qualitatively different social philosophy.

Notes

1. G.W.F. Hegel, *Science of Logic*, trans. A.V. Miller, (London, Allen & Unwin, 1969), pp. 824, 843.
2. G.W.F. Hegel, *Philosophy of Right*, trans. T.M. Knox, (New York, Oxford University Press, 1975), p. 162.
3. K. Marx and F. Engels, 3 *CW*, p. 8.
4. K. Marx and F. Engels, *MESW*, p. 592.
5. L. Feuerbach, *The Fiery Brook: Selected Writings*, trans. Z. Hanfi (New York, Anchor Books, 1972), p.155.
6. Marx and Engels, 3 *CW*, pp. 349–51.
7. Ibid., p. 327.
8. B. Parekh, 'Marx and the Hegelian Dialectic' in V. Roy and R. Sarikwal, eds, *Marxian Sociology* (Delhi, Ajanta Books, 1979), *passim*; and B. Parekh, *Marx's Theory of Ideology* (London, Croom Helm, 1982), pp. 88–90.
9. Marx and Engels, 3 *CW*, p. 88.
10. Ibid., pp. 88–9.
11. Ibid., p. 91.
12. Ibid., p. 75.
13. Ibid., pp. 88–9.
14. Ibid., p. 100.
15. Ibid., p. 128.
16. Ibid., p. 113.
17. Ibid., p. 186.
18. Ibid., p. 174.
19. Ibid., p. 91.
20. N. Geras, *Marx and Human Nature: Refutation of a Legend* (London, Verso, 1983), pp. 50–4.
21. Marx and Engels, 3 *CW*, p. 313.
22. H. Marcuse, *Reason and Revolution* (London, Routledge and Kegan Paul, 1973), pp. 273 ff.
23. H. Marcuse, 'The Concept of Essence' in idem, *Negations* (Harmondsworth, Penguin, 1972), pp. 43 ff.
24. Ibid., p. 74.
25. Marx and Engels, 3 *CW*, p. 186.
26. Ibid., p. 276.
27. Ibid., pp. 274–5.
28. K. Marx, 1 *Capital*, pp. 283–4.
29. Marx and Engels, 4 *CW*, p. 26.
30. Marx and Engels, 3 *CW*, p. 433–4.
31. Ibid., p. 240.
32. Marx and Engels, 6 *CW*, p. 489.
33. Marx and Engels, 3 *CW*, p. 277.
34. Marx and Engels, 5 *CW*, p. 7.
35. A detailed rebuttal of such assertions has been provided by Geras, *Marx and Human Nature*.

36. K. Marx, 2 *TSV*, pp. 117-18.
37. Ibid., p. 118.
38. Marx and Engels, 4 *CW*, pp. 117–18.
39. Ibid., p. 115.
40. Ibid., p. 120.
41. Ibid., p. 121.
42. Marx and Engels, *MESW*, p. 181.
43. Marx and Engels, 3 *CW*, pp. 293–4.
44. Marx and Engels, 9 *CW*, pp. 214, 220.
45. Marx and Engels, 3 *CW*, p. 291.
46. Ibid.
47. Ibid., p. 321.
48. Marx and Engels, 5, *CW*, pp. 43–4.
49. Ibid., p. 45.
50. Ibid., p. 52.
51. Ibid., pp. 32–5.
52. Ibid., p. 74.
53. Marx and Engels, *MESW*, pp. 182–3.
54. Marx and Engels, 5 *CW*, pp. 63–4.
55. Ibid., p. 561.
56. Ibid., p. 37.
57. Ibid., p. 53.
58. Ibid., p. 37.
59. Ibid., p. 48.
60. Ibid., p. 5.
61. Ibid., p. 236.
62. Marx and Engels, 3 *CW*, p. 289.
63. L. Colletti, 'Marxism and the Dialectic', *New Left Review,* no. 93 (1975).
64. Marx, 3 *Capital*, p. 357.

3
Marx, Engels and Dialectics

Terrell Carver

In this paper I propose to re-examine the intellectual relationship between Karl Marx and Frederick Engels, particularly their collaboration on Engels's *Anti-Dühring*, 'the best-known textbook in Marxist circles', and the basis of the even more influential work by Engels, *Socialism, Utopian and Scientific*.[1] My argument below is that two familiar 'facts' about Marx, Engels, and their views are in reality fictions.

The first fiction says that Marx and Engels speak with the same voice on all important theoretical issues; that where they have addressed themselves to different issues their works supplement each other; and that they divided their work within a perfect intellectual partnership. The second fiction is that as Marx grew older, he embraced 'the positivism then so fashionable in intellectual circles', the strongest evidence for which is the claim that he approved of Engels's *Anti-Dühring* of 1877–8 and agreed in principle with other works by Engels, such as the *Dialectics of Nature*.[2]

Though any presentation of Marxism returns inevitably to some texts by Marx himself, Marx's works have very often been subjected to interpretations of the sort encouraged by Engels. Commentators have then supported or rejected an amalgam of Marx and Engels, leaving aside the possibility that their views as individuals diverged on matters of theoretical significance.[3] While an increasing number of scholars no longer accept the first fiction, they do not then discuss in detail the issues this raises.[4] These issues are important, because Engels's works have been overwhelmingly influential in shaping Marxism and the tradition of debate about it.

By examining the most important element of the case for consistency between Marx and Engels – the claim that Marx approved of *Anti-Dühring* – and thus adding to doubts about the perfect partnership, I hope to contribute to a re-evaluation of work by Marx alone on the classic problems of philosophy and social science.

Marx, Engels and Dühring

In a letter of 7 January 1868 Engels brought a 'highly amusing' piece to Marx's attention. This was a review by Eugen von Dühring of the University of Berlin of the recently published first volume of *Capital*. The following day Marx replied that Dühring had 'obviously misunderstood various things', the 'drollest' of which was that he had confused Marx himself with Lorenz von Stein, 'because I cultivate the dialectic and Stein unthinkingly runs together the most trivial things into wooden trichotomies with a few Hegelian category-reversals'. Marx pursued Dühring's works on philosophy and political economy for a time, gleefully informing Engels of their worthlessness, but eliciting no response, other than promises from Engels to return a copy of Dühring's work on the political economist H.C. Carey.[5]

Because Dühring was a student of both Hegelian philosophy and contemporary political economy he was for Marx a particularly interesting opponent. As a theoretician he threatened Marx's ambitions within international socialism, ambitions fuelled by his passionate belief in the accuracy of his own work. In a letter to his friend Kugelmann sent on 6 March 1868, Marx mentioned both aspects of Dühring's work and commented:

> My book [*Capital*] has buried him on both counts ... He knows very well that my method of development is *not* the Hegelian one, since I [am a] materialist, and Hegel [is an] idealist. Hegel's dialectic is the basic form of all dialectic, but only *after* the stripping off of its mystical form, and it is just this that distinguishes *my* method [from others]. Concerning Ricardo, Herr Dühring has got himself so worked up, that in my presentation [in *Capital*] the weak points on which Carey and 100 others before him attack Ricardo successfully, do *not* exist [for him]. He is trying in bad faith to saddle me with Ricardian stupidities. But never mind. I must be grateful to the man, since he is the first professional who has spoken at all.[6]

Marx also said that Dühring, while seeming to defend the political economist Wilhelm Roscher, was in fact 'not unhappy that *Professor* Roscher, who blocks the way for them all [Dühring and other junior academics], is getting the boot [from me]', and that this partly explains why Dühring had taken up *Capital* in the first place.[7] Marx seems to have regarded Dühring as a serious nuisance, rather than a serious intellect.

Dühring went on to publish his *Critical History of Political Economy and Socialism* in 1871 and a *Course in Political Economy* in 1873. In 1875 a second edition of his *Critical History* appeared, as well as his *Course in Philosophy as a Strictly Scientific World Outlook and Pattern for Life*. The influence of Dühring's work among German socialists was particularly deplored by one of their leaders, Wilhelm Liebknecht, who wrote to Engels on 1 February, 21 April, and 1 November 1875, urging him to attack Dühring in the socialist newspaper *Volksstaat*. Engels does not seem to have thought the matter urgent enough to warrant this.

An article in praise of Dühring arrived for Engels's inspection on 16 May 1867 and on 24 May he wrote to Marx, expressing concern that Dühring had acquired a very vocal supporter within the socialist camp. The difficulty this caused – a genuine attack on Dühring would be taken as an attack on certain personalities within the party – was also a problem. In a 'rage' he asked Marx, 'whether it isn't about time to give our position *vis-à-vis* this gentleman careful consideration'. It appears that the impetus for *Anti-Dühring* came from Engels himself, not Marx. Unsurprisingly Marx replied to Engels in agreement: 'My view is that the "position *vis-à-vis* this gentleman" can only be taken up by criticizing Dühringwithout mercy'.[8]

On 28 May 1876 Engels wrote to Marx with news of his plan for attacking Dühring and his works. Dühring's *Course in Philosophy*, according to Engels, 'better exposes the weak aspects and foundations of the arguments introduced in the "Economy" ', the work which might have seemed of most interest to socialists. Engels's plan is logical, however; Dühring's 'banality', he comments, is revealed 'in a simpler form than in the economic book', and Engels proposes to take both together.

Thus the structure of *Anti-Dühring* was largely dictated by the subjects covered (very superficially, according to Engels) by Dühring. 'Of real philosophy', Engels complained, 'formal logic, dialectic, metaphysics etc. there is nothing, rather it is supposed to present a general theory of science' in which 'nature, history, society, state, law etc. are discussed in a supposed inner connection'.[9]

During the summer Engels reported from Ramsgate on his progress, ridiculing Dühring's ideas about nature, but not mentioning his own 'dialectic' approach:

> Corresponding to the ever-thickening seaside torpor [my] reading was naturally Herr Dühring's natural philosophy of reality. I have never before met with anything so natural as that. The whole procedure is with natural things, since everything is taken to be natural that seems natural to Herr Dühring, whereby he always proceeds from 'axiomatic propositions', for what is natural needs no proof.[10]

Apparently Marx made no comment on this, nor indeed any comment on Engels's project until 3 March 1877, when he reported someone else's (P.L. Lavrov's) reaction to the first instalments of *Anti-Dühring*, published in the newspaper *Vorwärts* (successor to the *Volksstaat*) between 3 January and 13 May 1877. According to Marx, Lavrov praised the work but said that one was not accustomed to such 'mildness' in Engels's polemical writings.[11] However, Engels had evidently asked Marx to examine Dühring's work on *political economy*, and on 5 March Marx enclosed his 'Dühringiana' in a letter to Engels, voicing an enthusiastic critique, but no real respect for Dühring or his views.

> It was impossible for me to read the wretch without hitting him over and over right on the head. Now that I have familiarized myself with him (and

the part from Ricardo on, which I have not yet read, must contain many pearls of great price), which called for great patience, I am, ever-ready with club in hand, capable in future of enjoying him peacefully. Having once worked oneself into the fellow, so that his method is weighed off, he is then, as it were, an amusing scribbler.[12]

Engels replied that Marx's 'critical history' was 'more than I need to polish off the wretch completely in this area', and that his friend Lavrov 'will have no more complaint about mildness with the final word on the "Philosophy" and still less with the "Economy" '. Engels worked on the economic section of his *Anti-Dühring*from June to August 1877, acknowledging (in a private letter) Marx's help, and on 8 August Marx sent him some notes on Quesnay's *Tableau Économique*, one of the works surveyed by Dühring.[13]

After that, comment on the substance of *Anti-Dühring* ceases in the Marx–Engels correspondence. The material prepared for Engels by Marx was *not* published in full in the first edition of *Anti-Dühring* as a complete book (Leipzig, 1878). Only in the preface to the second edition (Hottingen-Zürich, 1886) did Engels acknowledge Marx's authorship, and only in the third edition (Stuttgart, 1894) did Engels explain exactly why he had cut down the material sent him by Marx. In his preface to the second edition Engels wrote that Marx's chapter 'had to be shortened somewhat by me for purely external reasons', but in the 1894 preface he enlarged on this, saying that in certain sections of the manuscript 'the critique of Dühring's propositions was overshadowed by Marx's own developments regarding the history of economics'. Engels then explained that, 'wherever the thread of the argument makes this possible', he has now 'omitted passages which refer exclusively to Herr Dühring's writings', and published Marx's work on Petty, North, Locke, Hume, and Quesnay instead![14]

It is only in the preface to the *second* edition, dated 23 September 1885 (*after* Marx's death in 1883) that Engels claims that he 'read the whole manuscript' to Marx, 'before it was printed'. There is nothing in the Marx–Engels correspondence, in their works, or anywhere else to support this.

In the 1885 preface to *Anti-Dühring*Engels also wrote that his 'exposition' of the Marx–Engels 'world outlook' should not appear without Marx's 'knowledge'. This, Engels said, was 'understood' between them. He thus gives the reader the impression that Marx approved his work as an expression of 'their' outlook, while avoiding the statement that Marx *agreed* to any such thing. There are *no* recorded responses or revisions by Marx to the substance of Engels's work. In fact Engels does not seem to have revealed publicly duringMarx's lifetime that he had been helped on the book by Marx, and there seems to have been no move to put Marx's name on the book or to gain and publicize an *imprimatur*.

However, in the 1885 preface Engels claims much more than that Marx merely approved the manuscript. Engels argues that he had to counter Dühring's system with a positive alternative, not just negative criticism. His polemic, he says, was transformed into a more or less connected exposition of the dialectical method and of the communist world outlook fought for by Marx and myself – an exposition coveringa fairly comprehensive range of subjects... this mode of outlook [*sic*] of ours ... now finds recognition and support far beyond the boundaries of Europe, in every country which contains on the one hand proletarians and on the other undaunted scientific theoreticians.

This public, according to Engels, is keen enough 'to take into the bargain the polemic against the Dühring tenets merely for the sake of the positive conceptions'. Engels attributes the major share in developing 'the mode of outlook expounded in this book' to Marx, and then adds that it 'was self-understood [*sic*] between us that this exposition of mine should not be issued without his knowledge'.[15]

But in his surviving correspondence with Marx, Engels did not make any grand claims about countering Dühring's system with 'dialectical method' and 'communist world outlook'. The account written *before* Marx's death showed much more limited objectives:

My plan is ready. First of all I shall deal with this trash in a purely objective and apparently serious way, and then the treatment will become more trenchant as the proofs of the nonsense on the one hand and of the platitudes on the other begin to pile up, until at last a regular hailstorm comes pouring down on him.[16]

In the 1885 preface to *Anti-Dühring*, however, Engels warms to his subject. In chummy terms he announces the first premise of what we now recognize as dialectical materialism: 'Marx and I were pretty well the only people to rescue conscious dialectics from German idealist philosophy and apply it in the materialist conception of nature and history.'[17]

Engels argues that 'conscious dialectics' is manifested in *laws* of 'complete simplicity and universality' to be discovered in nature, history, and 'thought' by 'working with concepts', that is, recapitulating and rewriting natural science, history, philosophy and mathematics.[18] About the discovery of dialectical laws in history and 'thought' Engels says no more in the 1885 preface, preferring to concentrate on discoveringthe laws of dialectics in *nature*.[19]

Dialectics of Nature

Engels's 'results', other than those appearingin *Anti-Dühring*, were contained in the manuscript published after his death as the *Dialectics of Nature*. In fact he broke off work on that manuscript in order to write *Anti-Dühring*. The immediate impulse for Engels to take up a dialectical interpretation of natural science had been his highly critical reaction to the second edition of Ludwig Büchner's *Man and his Place in Nature in the Past, Present and Future. Or: Where did we come from? Who are we? Where are we going?* The plan for a critique dates from early in 1873, and in a letter to Marx of 30 May he set down his 'dialectical ideas on the natural sciences' and asked for help:

> In bed this morning the following dialectical ideas on the natural sciences came into my head:
> The subject-matter of natural science – matter in motion, bodies. Bodies cannot be separated from motion, their forms and kinds can only be known through motion; of bodies out of motion, out of relation to other bodies, nothing can be asserted. Only in motion does a body reveal what it is. Natural science therefore knows bodies by considering them in their relation to one another, in motion. The knowledge of the different forms of motion is the knowledge of bodies. The investigation of these different forms of motion is therefore the chief subject of natural science. ... Seated as you are there at the centre of the natural science you will be in the best position to judge if there is anything in it.[20]

Marx's reply to this was friendly, brief, and non-committal: 'Have just received your letter which has pleased me greatly. But I do not want to hazard an opinion before I've had time to think the matter over and to consult the "authorities".'[21] The 'authorities', so far as we know, do not seem to have been very impressed with Engels's insights, though Marx tried to break this to him gently. The chemist Carl Schorlemmer, for example, in marginal notes on Engels's letter, remarks that he agrees that the 'investigation of these different forms of motion is therefore the chief subject of natural science' and that motion of a single body must be treated relatively ('Quite right!'). But when Engels writes that dialectics, as the scientific *Weltanschauung*, cannot itself advance from chemistry to 'organic science' until chemistry *itself* does so, and then (with respect to biology), 'Organism – here I will not enter into any dialectics for the time being', Schorlemmer comments, 'Me neither'.[22] Marx's 'authority' found the science in Engels's letter more agreeable than the dialectics.

There is no more surviving correspondence between Marx and Engels concerning the *Dialectics of Nature* until Engels's letter of 21 September 1874 in which he comments that articles by Tyndall and Huxley in *Nature* have 'thrown me ... back onto the dialectical theme'.[23] Again, there is no surviving comment from Marx, though on several occasions he referred to Engels's project and even made brief inquiries for him. On 7 October 1876 he wrote to Wilhelm Liebknecht:

> Dear Library ... Engels is busy with the Dühring-work. It is a great sacrifice on his part since he has had to interrupt for this purpose a disproportionately more important work.[24]

And to Wilhelm Alexander Freund, on 21 January 1877:

> Dear Friend Freund ... If you by chance see Dr Traube remind him, if you please, that he has promised to send me the *titles* of his various

publications. This would be very important for my friend Engels who is labouring on a work of natural philosophy and, as it happens, Traube's achievements are emphasized.[25]

To Wilhelm Blos, 10 November 1877:

Generally my health forces me to forgo labour-time permitted me by the doctor for the completion of my work; and Engels, who is working on various larger writings [*Dialectics of Nature*], is still providing contributions [*Anti-Dühring et al.*] for *Vorwärts*.[26]

There is no indication here that Marx identified himself with either of Engels's works, or saw them as some aspect of their 'outlook'. In a later 'exchange' on Engels's research for the *Dialectics of Nature* Marx was very brief indeed. On 23 November 1882 Engels wrote:

Electricity has afforded me one small triumph. Perhaps you recall my discussion of the Descartes–Leibniz dispute ... *Resistance* represents in electricity the same thing as mass does in mechanical motion. Hence this shows that in electrical as [in] mechanical motion – here speed; there strength of current – the quantitatively measurable form of appearance of that motion operates, in the case of a simple transition *without* change of form, as a simple factor of the first power; but in a transition *with* change of form [it operates] as a *quadratic factor*. This is a general natural law of motion which I have formulated for the first time.[27]

Here is Marx's reply of 27 November:

The confirmation of the role of the *quadratic* in the transition of energy with a change of form of the latter is very nice, and I congratulate you.[28]

Nothing remotely substantial on Engels's project passed between the two after that. Marx died in March 1883, and Engels gave up work on his manuscript in 1886.

A Perfect Partnership?

The surviving Marx–Engels correspondence fails to support the picture painted by Engels in the 1885 preface to *Anti-Dühring*. Marx did not discuss Engels's dialectical laws, even after prodding, nor did he say anything to substantiate the contention that he and Engels were joint expositors of a universal materialism. Marx said nothing to confirm Engels's claim that he was familiar with the lengthy text of *Anti-Dühring*, much less that he endorsed it in full.

Moreover, the Marx–Engels correspondence does not corroborate the traditional account of their 'close collaboration' on all subjects, above all their theoretical work. In fact the correspondence strongly suggests that, apart from political news, family gossip and party affairs, the two worked independently for the most part, and that requests for advice on fundamental theoretical points from either side produced very little of substance.[29] If highly significant interchanges had taken place between the two when they actually met, such letters as survive would surely reflect this, or at the very least they would not be so perfunctory and non-committal. The hypothesis that the two men had important theoretical interchanges in private *does not square with the comments they actually made in their letters.* If there were evidence that would support the dialectical and materialist views propounded by Marx's literary executor (Engels), or if there were proof that their intellectual relationship was really as monolithic as Engels later claimed, who in the Marx family or among their socialist colleagues would have had an interest in destroying it? Commentators who accept or propound the traditional view that all the works of Marx and Engels are consistent and supplementary throughout their careers must now offer positive evidence, quoting both sides of a correspondence, and looking beyond Engels's uncorroborated accounts, particularly ones that were written after Marx's death.

However, if Marx found himself seriously at odds with Engels over the substance of *Anti-Dühring,* why did he not dissociate himself from it? Or had he never read it (or listened to it) in the first place?

Anti-Dühring appeared during1877–8 in instalments in *Vorwärts,* which Marx could easily have read, and it was also published as three pamphlets (1877–8) and as a book (1878). Even if Engels's story about reading the manuscript to Marx were untrue, or if Marx were not listening, it seems perverse to imagine that he ignored the content of the work altogether.

My contention is that Marx felt it easier, in view of their long friendship, their role as leading socialists, and the usefulness of Engels's financial resources, to keep quiet and not to interfere in Engels's work. After all, *Anti-Dühring* went out under Engels's name alone, and neither Engels nor Marx seems to have revealed publicly duringMarx's lifetime that Marx contributed to the chapter on political economy.

Interestingly Engels does not claim to have shown Marx the *Dialectics of Nature,* on which he worked from 1873 to 1886. In that work his views on the 'general nature of dialectics' were formulated explicitly, which was *not* the case in the *first* edition of *Anti-Dühring.* The distillation of Engels's dialectics contained in the 1885 preface put the text of *Anti-Dühring* in a different light. Engels, it seems, was canny enough to avoid creating disagreements with Marx. And Marx seems to have been similarly canny in not pressing Engels on his work.

It was possible for Marx to take the view that the *first* edition of *Anti-Dühring*would do more good than harm, since he detested Dühring's views, and Engels picks on them without mercy. Marx also recommended the book to others, referring almost gnomically to Engels's 'positive developments' and to the *political* importance of *Anti-Dühring* for 'a correct assessment of German socialism' without committing himself to every implication of the text or to the view that it could be read instead of *Capital*, a notion that Engels encouraged in private, particularly when he published a few chapters in French as the pamphlet *Socialism: Utopian and Scientific* in 1880.[30] Least of all did Marx commit himself to Engels's later glosses on *Anti-Dühring* and to what he subsequently claimed about the relationship between their separate works.

A Division of Labour?

In the 1885 preface to *Anti-Dühring* Engels makes it easy for his readers to conclude that within the Marx–Engels relationship the natural sciences were left to the latter: 'a knowledge of mathematics and natural science is essential to a conception of nature which is dialectical and at the same time materialist. Marx was well versed in mathematics'.[31] Did Marx in fact leave natural science to Engels? Or did he simply not attempt to do for the natural sciences what he had started to do for political economy and planned to do for 'law, morals, politics etc.'?[32]

It is evident from his works that Marx had a serious interest in the natural sciences, though one subordinate (like everything else) to his critique of political economy. There is no support there for the suggestion that the natural sciences were left to Engels or that they required in Marx's view a 'critique' of the sort offered by his friend in order to square them with his own conception of history and society. Moreover Marx neither endorsed nor made any claims about nature, history, and 'thought' in his surviving letters or works that remotely resemble Engels's enthusiastic speculations on the power of 'dialectics' to comprehend 'things and their representation, in their essential connection, concatenation, motion, origin, and ending'.[33]

One of the best known comments by Marx on the natural sciences occurs in *Capital*, when he writes that the molecular theory in chemistry (as expressed in a series of homologous compounds) illustrates Hegel's analysis of the transformation of quantity into quality. Here Marx cites *Hegel* and molecular theory to back up his claim that the qualitative change from master craftsman to capitalist follows from the accumulation of commodities or money beyond a critical quantity.[34] What Marx *never* did was to claim that there are dialectical laws of *matter* in motion forcing their way through these transformations, 'the great basic process', as Engels put it in the 1885 preface to *Anti-Dühring*.[35] When Marx referred in *Capital* to a correspondence between Hegel's supposedly 'pure' conceptual analysis and certain physical and social phenomena once they have been explained, he merely noted that Hegel's insight applies in such instances. When Marx termed Hegel's conclusion a 'law', he indicated that in some circumstances we can expect quantitative accumulation to produce qualitative change. In making that remark in *Capital* Marx was endorsing neither the metaphysics of Hegel nor the 'scientific' *Weltanschauung* of Engels. When Marx commented on a correspondence between Hegelian logic and the theory of chemical change the now controversial character of his words would not have been apparent, because Engels's view that one set of dialectical laws accounts for all phenomena was not explicitly published until after Marx's death. Marx admired the methods of reputable physicists and chemists, but carefully drew limits around the analogy between his methods and those of physical scientists.[36]

Though Marx asserted the existence of material reality as a presupposition for his theory, he never presented his results as in any way derived from or based on laws of *matter* in motion. Engels's 'progress' from 'conscious life-activity' to molecular motion was, so far as we know, *never* endorsed by Marx. Of course, consciousness has something to do with molecular motion, but there is no reason to suppose that Marx (if, indeed, he knew the explicit content of Engels's thesis) was any more convinced than scientists are today by Engels's 'proof' that dialectical laws of motion must underlie any satisfactory theory in psychology, history, and all other natural and social sciences. Engels *might* be right, but he has not made his case.

What Marx had to say about mathematics, physics, chemistry, biology,[37] anthropology, or logic does not disturb this picture. He pursued the natural sciences, mathematics, history and philosophy with great vigour (contrary to the fiction of the division of labour) and in so doing never endorsed the materialist dialectics pursued by Engels.

Conclusions

Neither the Marx–Engels correspondence nor the comments on the social and natural sciences in Marx's works support the 'scientific' *Weltanschauung* propounded by Engels after Marx's death and elaborated in Engels's posthumously published manuscripts. Laws of dialectics do not appear in Marx's Preface to *A Contribution to the Critique of Political Economy* of 1859, his popular work *Wages, Price and Profit*, his masterpiece *Capital* and associated manuscripts, nor in his last work of theoretical interest, the *Notes on Adolph Wagner*.

What Marx actually says about social sciences and natural science in these works does not square with Engels's grandiose claims about matter in motion and dialectical laws. And the diffidence, lacunae, and artful evasion displayed in Marx's replies to Engels do not illustrate a perfect partnership on major theoretical issues.

The exact relationship between Marx's views (as expressed, for example, in the works mentioned above) and Engels's general laws represents an area of debate interesting to anyone concerned with the nature of social science. There will be no debate, however, if the question of a divergence between Marx's and Engels's views is begged, or if the nature of such a divergence remains unexamined.

Notes

1. D. McLellan, *Karl Marx: His Life and Thought* (London, Macmillan, 1973), p. 423. For a general discussion of some of the issues raised here, see P. Thomas, 'Marx and Science', *Political Studies*, vol. 24 (1976), pp. 1–23. See also N. Levine, *The Tragic Deception: Marx contra Engels* (Oxford and Santa Barbara, CA, Clio, 1975), *passim*.
2. McLellan, *Karl Marx: His Life and Thought*, p. 423.
3. For example Karl Popper, R.N. Carew-Hunt, H.B. Acton, John Plamenatz, Bertram Wolfe, Alfred Meyer, Michael Evans and others.
4. See, for example, G. Lichtheim, *Marxism* (London, Routledge and Kegan Paul, 1967), pp. 234–43; S. Avineri, *The Social and Political Thought of Karl Marx* (Cambridge, Cambridge University Press, 1969), p. 3; A. Schmidt, *The Concept of Nature in Marx*, trans. B. Fowkes (London, New Left Books, 1971), pp. 51–61; B. Ollman, *Alienation: Marx's Concept of Man in Capitalist Society* (Cambridge, Cambridge University Press, 1971), p. xv; D.-H. Ruben, *Marxism and Materialism* (Brighton, Harvester, 1977), p. 5; and J. McMurtry, *The Structure of Marx's World-View* (Princeton, N.J., Princeton University Press, 1978), p. 7, n. 13, and p. 158, n. 7. M. Evans, *Karl Marx* (London, George Allen & Unwin, 1975), minimizes any divergences between Marx and Engels that might be shown to exist; see pp. 20–1, 78–9.
5. K. Marx, and F. Engels, *Werke*, vol. 32, pp. 8, 9, 11–12, 30, 46, 49, 722, n. 12.
6. Ibid., pp. 538–9.
7. Marx to Engels, 8 January 1868 in ibid., p. 11.
8. The vocal supporter was Johann Most. See ibid., vol. 20, p. 623, n. 1; ibid., vol. 34, pp. 12–13, 14, 541–2, nn. 18, 21, 26. See also O. Hammen, 'Alienation, Communism, and Revolution in the Marx-Engels *Briefwechsel*', *Journal of the History of Ideas*, vol. 33, (1972), Jan, pp. 81–2, where the implication that the impetus for *Anti–Dühring* came from Marx is the result of selective quotation.
9. Marx and Engels, *Werke*, vol. 34, p. 17.
10. Ibid., p. 27.
11. Ibid., p. 34.
12. Ibid., p. 36.
13. Ibid., pp. 37, 63, 68–70. A published version of Marx's manuscript appears as K. Marx, 'Randnoten zu Dührings Kritische Geschichte der Nationalökonomie, in F. Engels, *Herrn Eugen Dührings Umwalzung der Wissenschaft [und] Dialektik der Natur 1873–1882*, special edn, ed. V. Adoratskij (Moscow and Leningrad, Verlagsgenossenschaft Ausländischer Arbeiter in der UdSSR, 1935), pp. 340–71. I am grateful to the Lenin Library in Moscow for the loan of this volume.
14. F. Engels, *Anti-Dühring* (Moscow, Progress, 1969), pp. 14, 20–1; Marx, and Engels, *Werke*, vol. 20, pp. 623–6, n. 1.
15. Engels, *Anti-Dühring*, pp. 13–14.
16. Engels to Marx, 28 May 1876, in K. Marx and F. Engels, *MESC*, p. 306.
17. Engels, *Anti-Dühring*, p. 15.
18. D. McLellan, *Engels* (Glasgow, Fontana/Collins, 1977), p. 73, comments on the contrast between Engels's focus on nature and Marx's concentration on history.
19. Their discovery in mathematics he leaves aside as a project for some 'later opportunity to put together and publish the results which I have arrived at, perhaps in conjunction with the extremely important mathematical manuscripts left by Marx'. Engels, *Anti-Dühring*, pp. 16–18.
20. Marx and Engels, *Werke*, vol. 20., pp. 646–50, n. 162, and p. 666, n. 276; idem, *MESC*, pp. 281–2.
21. Marx and Engels, *Werke*, vol. 33, p. 82.
22. Ibid., pp. 80–1, 82, 84.

23. Ibid., pp. 119–20.
24. Ibid., vol. 34, p. 209.
25. Ibid., pp. 245–6.
26. Ibid., p. 311.
27. Ibid., vol. 35, pp. 118–19.
28. Ibid., p. 120.
29. The suggestion that Marx wanted Engels to be co-author of *Capital* is nonsense. In a letter of 7 July 1866 Marx asked Engels if he would like to write an 'appendix' on the armaments industry and thus appear as 'direct collaborator' in 'my main work'. Engels said that he would try, but never actually delivered anything (Marx and Engels, *Werke*, vol. 31, p. 234). The erroneous suggestion occurs in T. Sowell, 'Marx's *Capital* after One Hundred Years' in M.C. Howard and J.E. King, eds, *The Economics of Marx* (Harmondsworth, Penguin, 1976), pp. 74–5, n. 51.
30. F. Engels, *Dialectics of Nature*, trans. C. Dutt, (Moscow, Foreign Languages Publishing House, 1954), pp. 270–3 (written in 1873), pp. 29–54 (written in 1875 or 1876), pp. 83–91 (written in 1879); Marx to Wilhelm Bracke, 11 April 1877, in Marx and Engels, *Werke*, vol. 34, pp. 263–4; Marx to Moritz Kaufmann, 3 October 1878, in ibid., p. 346; Engels to Friedrich Adolph Sorge, 9–16 November 1882, in ibid., vol. 35, p. 396. Marx's rather distant preface to *Socialism: Utopian and Scientific*, was published (for reasons not yet determined) as the work of his son-in-law Paul Lafargue; see Marx and Engels, *Werke*, vol. 19, pp. 181–2, 564.
31. Engels, *Anti-Dühring*, p. 15.
32. K. Marx, *Economic and Philosophical Manuscripts* in idem, *EW*, p. 281.
33. Engels, *Anti-Dühring*, p. 33.
34. K. Marx, 1 *Capital*, pp. 423–4.
35. Engels, *Anti-Dühring*, p. 19.
36. Marx, 1 *Capital*, p. 90.
37. Marx's comments on Darwin are actually more favourable than has been argued by Shlomo Avineri. That Darwin's struggle for existence in nature resembled, according to Marx, the naturalist's own society, was rather a joke on Darwin, but Marx does not say that Darwin's portrayal of the world of plants and animals is *wrong*. Both Darwin (in the first edition of *The Origin of Species*) and Marx were unwilling to leap from conclusions about plants and animals to conclusions about human society.

Marx evidently had great admiration for Darwin's work, though very little for Darwinists. In fact Darwin's method resembled his own in a crucial respect. Darwin postulates the existence of what we now know to be genetic mechanisms *underlying* some of the apparently unrelated (or only mysteriously related) phenomena that he observes, much as Marx asserts that the 'determination of the magnitude of value by labour-time is ... a secret, hidden under the apparent fluctuations in the relative values of commodities'. This was also one of the reasons why Marx was interested in higher mathematics; underlying complex mathematical expressions there are sometimes hidden solutions, often simple formulae.

See S. Avineri, 'From Hoax to Dogma: A Footnote on Marx and Darwin', *Encounter*, vol. 38 (March 1967), pp. 30–2; for a definitive account of the Marx–Darwin affair, see also T. Ball, 'Marx and Darwin: A Reconsideration', *Political Theory*, vol. 7 (1979), pp. 469–84. For a discussion of Marx's mathematical manuscripts, see D.J. Struik, 'Marx and Mathematics', *Science and Society*, vol. 12 (1948), pp.181–96; Marx to Engels, 18 June 1862, in Marx and Engels, *MESC*, p. 128; or idem, 41 *CW*, p. 381; Marx, 1 *Capital*, pp. 167–8; Marx to Engels, 8 January 1868, in Marx and Engels, *Werke*, vol. 32, pp.11–12.

4
Recent Interpretations of Ideology

Joseph McCarney

This chapter will be concerned with two works, Jorge Larrain's *Marxism and Ideology* and Bhikhu Parekh's *Marx's Theory of Ideology*.[1] As the titles suggest, they offer accounts of the conception of ideology to be found in Marx and also, in the case of Larrain's book, in the Marxist tradition as a whole. What follows is an attempt at a critique, and expressions of agreement or approval will not loom large in it. It may therefore be well to make clear at the outset that these works are chosen for discussion as the most substantial and interesting contributions to the field to have appeared in recent years in English. Moreover, on a number of substantive issues I have no serious reservations concerning what they say. It should be unnecessary to list these points of agreement here since they will emerge, at least by implication, in the course of the argument. It may be said, however, that my misgivings over Larrain's work are concerned primarily with the treatment of Marx and Engels. On such later writers as Lenin, Lukács and Althusser, he is generally a reliable and enlightening guide. Parekh's book for its part is of unusual, if uneven, intellectual distinction, and is, at its best, on such topics as Marx's dealings with the political economists, the equal of anything to be found in the literature. There is, in addition, a major item of common ground that should be mentioned in preparation for the discussion that follows. It concerns the explicit rejection by both writers of the idea of 'false consciousness' as an adequate basis for understanding Marx on ideology.[2] The chief criticism that will be developed here is, one might say, that they fail to follow through the implications of this rejection in a sufficiently radical way.

Larrain's *Marxism and Ideology*

The thesis of Larrain's book is that Marx had a 'critical and negative' concept of

ideology, whose meaning is to be identified with 'the concealment of contradictions'. Ideology is 'a distortion which arises from and conceals contradictions'.³
In doing so it 'necessarily serves the interests of the ruling class', and 'by definition, there cannot be an *ideology* which serves the interests of dominated
classes'.⁴ Marx, we are told, 'specified the ideological distortion in terms of the
concealment of contradictions in the interests of the ruling class'.⁵

The first response to this thesis must be to point to the slightness of its textual
base. Larrain cites no passages in which there is anything resembling a direct
suggestion of a conceptual link between ideology and the concealment of contradictions. The case rests entirely on inference and conjecture in a manner that is
open to question. Thus, the fullest exposition is in terms of 'four main ideas'
which, it is claimed, 'can be drawn from' a statement quoted from Marx.⁶ But
the statement in question makes no reference to the ideological, and, moreover,
comes from a text, the third volume of *Capital*, in which there are no such references. The tendency to draw conclusions about ideology from sources which do
not mention ideology is exemplified at other points in Larrain's book.⁷ In
complaining of it, one is appealing to a rule of interpretation which he recognizes and uses polemically elsewhere. Thus, he rebukes Plekhanov for basing
claims about the 'ideological superstructure' on writings of Marx which do not
employ the expression 'ideological superstructure'.⁸ Larrain's point is well
taken. The rule being invoked may, like any other, be abused through excessive
literalness. But it seems important not to lose sight of it altogether, if commentary is not to enter the windy spaces where 'anything goes'.

Larrain does, of course, make use of passages in which Marx is unquestion-
ably dealing by name with ideological forms whose function is to conceal
contradictions. Indeed, there can be no doubt that Marx regards such concealment as a typical strategy of bourgeois ideology, at least in its period of decline.
But it cannot on that account be assumed to be definitive of ideology in general.
To assume that it can is to commit an error, which, strangely enough, Larrain
has clearly identified in another connection. He does so in the course of pointing
out that Martin Seliger's view of Lukács is 'based upon a misunderstanding'.
Seliger 'mistakes the critical appraisal of bourgeois ideology for the negative
character of the concept of ideology'.⁹ Larrain should, perhaps, have applied the
distinction which Seliger confuses to his own case. He would then have been
bound to admit that while the passages he cites serve very well to flesh out
Marx's critical appraisal of bourgeois ideology, they have no tendency to establish the negative character of his concept of ideology. The flaw in Larrain's
procedure, it may be suggested, is that he falls victim to 'Seliger's fallacy' on a
large scale and in relation to Marx and Engels rather than Lukács.

There is another aspect of Larrain's position which should be considered: the
insistence that, in Marx's conception, ideology necessarily serves the ruling class
alone. In support of it, he writes: '*not once* is the term "ideologist" or "ideological" used by Marx or Engels to refer to the working class or to its intellectual
representatives'.¹⁰ The subsequent discussion, however, provides all the grounds
one needs for doubting this assertion. Misgivings start with the sentence that
immediately follows, in which Larrain speaks of the use by Marx and Engels of

these terms 'to refer to all the other classes'. Strictly speaking, he should not have made this admission, for, on his official view, only the ruling class should be allowed an ideology and ideological representatives. More significant, however, is his citation of a reference in *The German Ideology* to the 'ideological superstructure of the proletariat'.[11] Elsewhere, he comments that Marx 'consistently applied his negative concept of ideology to all distortions which concealed contradictions, even those which appeared from within the working class'.[12] Moreover, in the course of explicating Marx, he refers to the Luddite movement as 'a clear-cut example of early working-class ideology'.[13] These references have the effect of demolishing the claim that not once do Marx and Engels speak of ideology in connection with the working class. The inconsistency here is not of much importance in itself, but it does suggest something of the difficulty facing a social theorist who seeks to confine ideology to a single class. In the interests of having a serviceable category one can hardly avoid slipping back from the impossible standard that this sets.

At this point we may move from considering Larrain's treatment of the evidence for his view to considering how he treats apparent counter-evidence. The chief barrier he has to surmount is the famous 'Preface' of 1859 to *A Contribution to the Critique of Political Economy*. There Marx refers to the conflict between the 'material, productive forces' and the 'relations of production', and goes on to speak of the 'legal, political, religious, artistic or philosophic – in short, ideological forms in which men become conscious of this conflict and fight it out'.[14] The suggestion that it is in the ideological forms that men become conscious of the fundamental social conflict, which Marx explicitly refers to as a contradiction, seems hard to square with the view that the defining function of ideology is to conceal contradictions. Moreover, the suggestion that all parties to the conflict fight it out in the ideological forms seems hard to square with the view that, by definition, ideology serves the ruling class alone.

Larrain recognizes the difficulty presented by this text and offers a number of responses to it. The most radical of them may be considered first. It consists, in effect, in reworking the text so as to eliminate the offending elements. Thus, he acknowledges that the opposition of forces and relations of production is, for Marx, a contradiction. But he suggests that when Marx uses the notion of contradiction to refer to it, he does so 'improperly'. What we have is better understood as a 'non-correspondence'.[15] It follows that even if one admits that ideology yields awareness of the forces–relations conflict, this does not affect the definition of ideology as contradiction-concealing, for what is revealed in this case is not really a contradiction. A second linguistic shift disposes of another conclusion which the 'Preface' might naturally be taken to imply. In speaking of men 'fighting out the conflict' Marx is presumably referring to class struggle. Hence, it seems one may infer that the class struggle in the realm of ideas is fought through the ideological forms, that it is, in short, an ideological struggle. Larrain wishes to block any such inference. For, 'what, within Marxism, has been traditionally called "ideological struggle"', he 'would prefer' to call 'class struggle on the terrain of ideas'.[16] This would substitute for a convenient and established usage an awkward circumlocution. But it is a move deeply grounded in the logic of Larrain's position. It ensures that not only is the achievement of consciousness referred to in the 'Preface' not the achievement of a consciousness of *contradictions*, but also that the conflict through which it is achieved is not, in so far as it involves classes, a conflict of *ideological* forms. The nature of Larrain's thesis is such that in the end the concepts of contradiction and ideology have to be written out of the 'Preface' altogether. It requires what he recognizes as a rejection of the unequivocal practice of Marx and traditional Marxism in these matters. This is surely a substantial revision for what purports to be a work of exegesis.

There is a supplementary line of response to the 1859 'Preface' to be found in Larrain's account. Its starting point is a tacit acceptance of the fact that such later writers as Lenin, Lukács and Gramsci read the text in the most natural way as presenting an epistemologically neutral conception of ideology, as, simply, the intellectual medium of class struggle. Their readiness to be over-impressed by this particular source is then given a special explanation. It was due to ignorance of *The German Ideology* which had not been published in full when they wrote. Larrain's case at this point depends on stressing the significance of *The German Ideology*, and, by comparison, playing down that of the 'Preface'. It seems on general grounds a doubtful preference. But the assumption that there is a substantive choice to be made between the two on the subject of ideology should itself be questioned. There is an obvious contrast in terms of scale of treatment. *The German Ideology* is a lengthy work given over entirely to an onslaught on a particular ideological form, the 'German ideology' of the title. As one might expect, the tone of its dealings with the ideological is generally – though, as we have seen, by no means uniformly – pejorative. But however frequent the references to ideological defect, this has no power of itself to establish that ideology is, as such, defective. To suppose otherwise is 'Seliger's fallacy'. This observation is enough to dispose of almost all of the alleged support for a negative conception that the work provides. There is, however, a well-known passage that needs some further discussion. Its key sentence is standardly rendered in English as follows:

> If in all ideology men and their circumstances appear upside-down as in a *camera obscura*, this phenomenon arises just as much from their historical life-process as the inversion of objects on the retina does from their physical life-process.[17]

It is difficult at this point to avoid referring to the treatment of the issue in my book *The Real World of Ideology*.[18] For Larrain conducts his own discussion in relation to that work. It may be best to recapitulate briefly the two main points that were made there. Although Larrain touches on both, it is quite unclear what his verdict on them is and they still seem to me to be decisive.[19]

The first is that the discussion suffers from a suspect translation. The original of the key phrase 'in all ideology' is '*in der ganzen Ideologie*' and this seems more naturally rendered by some such locution as 'in the whole ideology'. Taken in this way, it is clearly a reference not to ideology as such, but to a specific ideology; that is, to the 'German ideology'. Such a reading is power-fully supported by contextual consideration in ways detailed in my book. To accept it is to be relieved of any temptation to suppose that a theoretical state-ment about ideology is being made here. In the second place, for most commentators, including Larrain, it should be impossible to suppose this, even if the usual translation is retained. For they are generally unwilling to allow that ideology is necessarily committed to the idealist ontology, that it is by definition idealist. Yet the error of upside-downness picked out in the remainder of the statement is clearly the specifically idealist reversal of the true order of priority of consciousness and reality. Such commentators will have to read the statement as a hypothetical in which the antecedent is assumed to be false. Its purpose then can only be to demonstrate counter-factually the explanatory power of materi-alism: 'even if, as is not the case, all ideology were idealist, still this too could be explained on materialist premises'. Taken together, the effect of these points is to suggest that, on any viable reading, no definition of ideology is being canvassed here, still less one in terms of cognitive negativity or defect.

Larrain's book is concerned not just with Marx, but with Marxism, and some-thing should be said about his treatment of the other major figures in the tradition. So far as Engels is concerned, he is inclined to stress the congruence of view with Marx. This must be accepted as formally correct; though if the objec-tions raised here are sound, it will involve the same misconception of Engels's position as of Marx's. There is, however, a complication to be noted. It is that Larrain detects the 'seeds' of the 'positive' conception of ideology in the work of Engels, especially after Marx's death.[20] This is surprising, for the best-known contribution of the later Engels to the debate is the introduction of the notion of 'false consciousness' in the famous letter to Mehring. Hence, commentators have generally been led to locate his distinctive influence as being on the side of a negative interpretation, regardless of whether this is also taken to be the authentic doctrine of Marx. Larrain, as mentioned earlier, attaches little signifi-cance to the 'false consciousness' suggestion. But if it is set aside, there is the puzzle posed by his claim that the 'weight of the majority of Engels's statements … are remarkably consistent in supporting a negative concept of ideology', and that, like Marx's, they 'massively support a critical concept'.[21] All one can say is that if this is the situation, Larrain has signally failed to document it. For, apart from the 'false consciousness' case, he cites not a single reference which supports a negative concept of ideology as distinct from ones which refer pejora-tively to particular ideological items. Moreover, he overlooks such usages as Engels's reference to the 'ideological Left',[22] and he cites only in part the restatement of the 1859 'Preface' doctrine in the 1885 'Preface' to *The Eight-eenth Brumaire*.[23] There Engels speaks of Marx's discovery of 'the law according to which all historical struggles whether they proceed in the political, religious, philosophical or some other ideological domain, are in fact only the more or less clear expression of struggles of social classes'.[24] Thus, the ideologi-cal domains constitute a medium for the expression of class struggles: this seems close to the heart of the original Marxist theory of ideology.

It was made clear at the outset that no objections will be raised to the details

of Larrain's account of such figures as Lenin and Lukács. What is open to question, however, is his understanding of their relationship to Marx, and hence, of
the shape of the Marxist tradition as a whole. In his view, Marx's negative
concept of ideology was 'totally transformed' by Lenin into a positive or neutral
one,[25] and Lukács's position on this was a 'basic endorsement' of Lenin's.[26] On
this reading, the Marxist tradition of ideology emerges just as broken-backed as
it does from the work of such a systematically hostile commentator as Seliger,
and for the same basic reason – an alleged dislocation between the original negative or pejorative view and a later Lenin- and Lukács-inspired positive or non-
pejorative one. It is a reading which presents Larrain at least with a problem:
'how it is possible that, with few exceptions, the most important Marxist theoreticians have held a positive and neutral conception which conceives various
ideologies existing in terms of the interests of opposed classes'.[27] The beginning
of wisdom here is to see that this question is wholly misconceived. The theoreticians Larrain has in mind were in truth engaged in the organic development of
Marx's original insight, and so in constructing the classic Marxist conception of
ideology. The real puzzle is not why did Lenin and Lukács get Marx wrong, but
why do so many contemporary commentators conspicuously fail to get him
right. But this is an issue which cannot be pursued here.[28]

The idea of the concealment of contradictions provides, according to Larrain,
'a very precise and specific meaning for ideology'.[29] It would be worrying if this
were indeed so, for one might wonder how so constricted a view could cope
with all the fantastic shapes, of say, bourgeois ideology. On a closer look,
however, the idea of concealment opens up considerably. It turns out that there
are at least four different ways in which 'the ideological concealment is
achieved'. These are the 'denial' of contradictions, their 'misunderstanding',
their 'displacement' and their 'dilution'.[30] This seems to cast the net very widely
and over areas having little to do with 'concealment' in any conventional sense.
Indeed, the suspicion that now arises is that the ideological approach to contradictions must turn out to embrace everything short of their full scientific
treatment as provided by Marx. Hence, the entire tradition of anarchist thought
and of pre-Marxist and non-Marxist socialism will have to be assigned to
'ideology', that is, on Larrain's conception, to the service of ruling-class interests. It is at least doubtful whether such ruthlessness would accord with the spirit
of Marx's practice of ideological analysis. But Larrain's account seems out of
tune with that spirit in a number of respects.

It is true that Marx associates contradiction-concealing, in all the ways Larrain
understands it, with what he calls 'the ideology of the political economists'. But
these are devices he tends to discuss in connection with 'vulgar economy' rather
than the 'classical' version. To the major figures of classical political economy
he is prepared to attribute both a grasp of the contradictions of bourgeois society
and a willingness to display them. Thus, to cite a well-known instance, Ricardo,
we are told, consciously 'made the antagonism of class interests' the 'starting
point of his investigations'.[31] Throughout the discussion of the political economists the chief emphasis is not on the ways they deny, misunderstand, displace
or dilute the contradictions, and where they are acknowledged as committing

these offences it is not by virtue of doing so that they qualify as bourgeois ideologists. That status inheres in the very foundations of their outlook on society. The vital clue is given by what Marx immediately goes on to say about Ricardo after the praise just quoted; the trouble is that he naively takes 'this antagonism for a social law of nature'. The secret of the ideology of the political economists, as depicted by Marx, is not that it necessarily conceals contradictions, but that it regards arrangements characteristic of bourgeois society, including its contradictions, as natural and eternally valid features of all human society. Larrain's approach cannot do justice to the centrality of this aspect. Parekh, on the other hand, is well placed to do so, and to the consideration of his views we may now turn.

Parekh's *Marx's Theory of Ideology*

Parekh's account of Marx's concept of 'ideology' is somewhat complex. In its 'most common and important' usages the term is said to mean 'idealism', on the one hand, and 'apologia', on the other. Both usages, we are told, occur throughout Marx's life, but the second gradually became dominant and in any case represents the wider concept. Hence, the main body of Parekh's book is concerned with the understanding of ideology as apologia. In this aspect it is 'a body of thought systematically biased towards a specific social group'[32] which 'necessarily *distorts* its subject matter.[33] The distinctive feature of ideological bias and distortion is its universalizing the forms of thought and conditions of existence of such a group. Thus, 'Marx gives the name "ideology" to a body of thought resulting from the universalisation of a partial and narrow social point of view'.[34]

At the core of this thesis is a certain understanding of what is involved in Marx's critique of Hegel and of the political economists. The one is said by Parekh to be the model for the other. It is perhaps fortunate that in his own discussion the two topics are not so closely integrated as this would suggest. For the treatment of Hegel and of idealism in general is the least satisfactory part of the book.[35] What he has to say about Marx on the political economists, both 'classical' and 'vulgar', is, however, as suggested earlier, an exemplary piece of commentary. In this he is aided by the overall logic of his approach. For here his distinctive way of conceptualizing the ideological has its natural home. The drive to universalize is indeed the central strategy of the ideology of the political economists, as depicted by Marx. Its point is precisely captured by Parekh:

> On the basis of their ahistorical and biased definitions, they had no difficulty showing that the proposal to abolish commodity production, wage labour or capitalism itself flouted the human condition and was Utopian and irresponsible.[36]

Thus, the political economists served the bourgeoisie because their theories worked to subvert the legitimacy of any form of practice that aspired to over-throw the bourgeois order. Fundamental to this ideological project is what Parekh calls 'the logic of legitimisation'. In terms of it the tactic of concealing the contradictions can be allowed, as he shows, its derivative but still significant role.[37] As he also shows, however, universalizing the social arrangements, including their contradictions, serves that logic at a still deeper level.

Yet even here we do not reach rock-bottom. For it would be premature to take the naturalizing, dehistoricizing tendency as a defining feature of bourgeois ideology, still less of ideology in general. This may be all the more obvious if one is concerned to have a concept of ideology suited to the needs of contemporary social theory. We live in a relatively self-conscious and historically conscious age in which intellectuals generally have assimilated something of the lessons of Marx and of the shocks which the bourgeois order has suffered since his time. It would be a simple matter to find defenders of that order who, far from supposing that it is eternal because grounded in human nature, are well aware that it is a historical product to be sustained by deliberate and strenuous effort.[38] The moral is surely that all attempts to capture bourgeois ideology in terms of some distinctive strategic content are likely to fail before the ever-fresh revelation of its actual variety and versatility. What is needed, one might suggest, is a definition in 'formal' rather than 'material' terms, that can display the inner principle of unity of the phenomena without arbitrarily restricting their scope. Marx's conception, as characterized at one point by Parekh, seems to supply just what is needed:

> For Marx the dominant ideology consists of different kinds and levels of ideas drawn from different historical sources and contributed by such diverse groups as the vulgar writers, the philosophers, the journalists and the ordinary members of the dominant class .... Its main unifying principle is the justification of the existing social order, and such a practical consideration is too nebulous and weak to achieve theoretical unity.[39]

Here we approach the crux of the matter, and in a sense all that is needed in explicating Marx on ideology is to hold fast to this 'unifying principle' and work out its implications. It is suggestive of the uneven character of Parekh's discussion that he would not himself be an entirely suitable guide for that project. To insist, as he does, that the social order can only be ideologically justified by being universalized and dehistoricized is to do less than justice to the actual complexity of social life and the ingenuity of its interpreters, a trap into which Marx's dealings with these matters do not fall. It remains to be seen why Parekh fails to live up to the promise of his own best formulations.

In the meantime, the question of the value of his account of ideology for contemporary social inquiry should be taken a little further. An important factor is the claim that the

> group towards which an ideology may be biased need not ... be a class in the narrow sense, and may include a professional group, a nation, a social order, a race or a subgroup within a class.[40]

As an illustration, Parekh remarks that

> a philosopher who proposes to structure society on the model of the univer-
> sity, the political discussion on the model of the academic seminar, and
> assigns a leading role to the academics, generalises the conditions of exis-
> tence and the characteristic forms of thought of the academic, and is an
> ideologist.[41]

The first point to note about this is that it significantly extends Marx's usage. If
there is anything clear and consistent in that usage, it is that ideologists are
inseparably bound to classes in Parekh's 'narrow' sense as their 'spokesmen'
and 'representatives'. Marx gives no reason to suppose that one might qualify
as an ideologist through supporting a group such as academics, unless that
support were part of some larger tendency affecting the class situation. It is the
possibility of giving a class analysis that must ultimately license talk of
ideology. Nevertheless, at least if one agrees to suspend ontological doubts
about such 'groups' as races and nations, it may be thought that what Parekh
proposes is a natural extension of Marx's usage in the direction most useful for
sociological inquiry. For it may well be convenient to have a concept which
collects forms of consciousness just in virtue of their systematic bias towards
groups of all kinds, encompassing all such tendentiousness in the social world.
It sheds some light on Parekh's position, however, if one notes how ill-placed
he is to reap the benefits of this development. The chief obstacle is the
continued insistence on the universalizing of local conditions as the hallmark of
ideological bias. Thus, for instance, British universities have in recent years
fought vigorous intellectual battles on their own behalf without necessarily
being committed to proposals for structuring society as a giant university. If one
is willing to allow the academic community its own ideology, it seems a pity
not to be able to recognize that it has been deployed in such battles. The point
is that Parekh seems to fall between two stools here. His account departs from
the strict letter of Marx, while remaining too refined and schematic for purposes
of general social theory.

Looked at from another standpoint, the difficulty is that there is a tension
between Parekh's definition of the concept of ideology and the scope he claims
for it, between, to use old-fashioned terms, what it connotes and what it denotes.
This tension shows itself in other ways. Thus, he very properly insists that Marx
did not confine ideology to the ruling ideas, but recognized that society contains
both dominant and subordinate ideologies.[42] The requirements of universalizing
and dehistoricizing are, however, difficult to fit with this insistence. For they are
modelled on, and only truly appropriate to, the situation of the dominant
ideology. A view that takes existing arrangements out of history may suit a
ruling group by blocking off visions of alternatives. But it can scarcely meet the
needs of radical elements who must surely benefit from the freedom of historical
awareness. The universalizing condition runs into similar difficulties. It may be
acceptable for Parekh to illustrate it by claiming that the bourgeoisie wish all
people to define themselves as bourgeois and pursue appropriate objectives, at

least if the idea is not that they should think of themselves as, literally, owners of capital, but that they should be thoroughly 'bourgeois' in spirit.[43] It is less plausible to support that, to take a group which he accepts as a fully-fledged class, landowners wish everyone to define themselves as landowners either in the spirit or the flesh. The point involved here is a variation on a theme familiar in Marxist writings, that not all classes possess a totalizing vision which aspires to make society over entirely in their own image. Yet one must surely allow, as Parekh wishes to, that they may pursue their particular visions in and through ideology. Once again he has difficulty reconciling his various objectives. It is entirely commendable that he should wish to secure for the concept of ideology a wide field of application. Yet the substantive conditions he builds into it impede this aim. If one asks why he should erect such barriers to the working out of his own deepest insights, the answer is not far to seek. It lies in the systematic pressure of his epistemological preoccupations.

At the beginning of his book Parekh asserts a position from which he never departs – that, for Marx, ideology was 'an epistemological category designed to conceptualise a specific form of thought'.[44] In constructing his category, Marx was, we are told, drawing on certain themes in the Western philosophical tradition. Philosophers in that tradition have, according to Parekh, 'almost all' been agreed that 'the assumptions underlying a form of inquiry limit and distort the knowledge offered by it', and, furthermore, that 'non-philosophical forms of inquiry have a tendency to advance illegitimate universalist claims'.[45] Marx's contribution was to add a social dimension to this traditional picture. He suggested that the assumptions that mediate knowledge are partly social, derived from the conditions of existence of the inquirer's social group. So what is universalized are forms of thought characteristic of that group and the distortions that result are distortions in its favour. What Marx did was to borrow 'some of the basic epistemological doctrines of the Western philosophical tradition', integrating them with 'his socially grounded epistemology', and 'the result was his theory of ideology'.[46]

It has to be said that Parekh provides no textual evidence of a link between Marx's concept of ideology and the doctrines in question. This is, of course, not at all surprising, and the explanation that there is no such evidence to provide hardly needs to be laboured by now. It may be more interesting to trace the consequences which follow in this case from the epistemological approach to ideology. It leads Parekh to criticisms of Marx which, when looked at closely, dissolve in a way that reveals serious tensions in his own position.

What is contrasted in Parekh's account to the adoption of a 'narrow social point of view' is the adoption of 'the standpoint of the whole'. On the basis of this contrast, he concludes that, contrary to the traditional interpretation of Marxists from Lenin and Lukács to Colletti and Adam Schaff, Marx could not possibly have thought of himself as adopting in his theoretical work the standpoint of the proletariat. For he aspires to objective science and, hence, finds the proletarian point of view 'partial, inadequate and somewhat partisan'.[47] Instead, he 'aims to stand on the shoulders of *both* the bourgeoisie and the proletariat',[48] as a 'free agent of thought', developing his theories 'as a scientist thinking freely, and not from within a class point of view.'[49] Indeed, he went so far as to imagine that 'complete social self-consciousness can be attained, and that it is possible to rise above not only one's class but also society'.[50] These aspirations are, in Parekh's view, naive and mistaken, and his criticism is driven home unsparingly: 'In conferring upon self-consciousness the power to transcend the deepest influences of class and society', Marx 'remained an "idealist"'.[51] Moreover, his naiveté in this matter infects his concept of criticism:

> Marx argues that the genuine criticism of a social order must transcend its fundamental assumptions or horizon of thought. Since ... no individual can fully transcend the prevailing horizon of thought, Marx's concept of criticism is incoherent.[52]

These are grave charges. On further examination, however, it turns out that Parekh has himself assembled all the materials needed to show that they are wholly unfounded. An important factor here is the attention he gives to Marx's insistence, as against idealism, that 'an individual is socially constituted and social in the innermost depths of his being'.[53] For Marx, as Parekh makes clear, a society is 'not a collection of individuals, but a system of positions', and of these 'class is the most important'.[54] It is plainly correct to stress the fundamental role of these insights in Marx's thinking, but quite unwarranted to support that he ever betrayed them for a fantasy of intellectuals as free spirits soaring in a vacuum above their class and society. Marx was able to combine the necessity of social roots with the aspiration to the whole for a reason which Parekh does not consider, but which was obvious to the Marxists whose traditional interpretation he rejects. This is the conviction that the standpoint of the whole and that of the proletariat were identical in the historical circumstances of the time. Once again, all the vital ingredients in the theoretical background are supplied by Parekh. A central element is the theme of the proletariat as the 'universal class' which, as he puts it, 'represented the true interests of mankind and a higher level of humanity'.[55] He then proceeds to collapse his own dichotomy of particular and universal standpoints. For Marx, he argues, 'mankind realises itself in and through the classes'. It 'does not exist independently of the classes', and it 'becomes an abstraction if detached from the classes'.[56] The epistemological implications of this theme are explicitly drawn:

> The scientific importance of the proletariat in Marx's thought is broadly the same as the political, and is similarly grounded. Even as Marx stresses the political role of the negative class, he stresses its epistemological role ... it is a national and organized class, and hence capable of viewing society as a totality.[57]

The moral of this careful and accurate exposition is surely plain. It is that, for Marx, to adopt the standpoint of the proletariat is precisely what it means to adopt the standpoint of the whole. It supplies the only content that proposal could have. This identification is at the heart of his thinking on the matter. It is, of course, by no means free from difficulties, but it is at least not vulnerable to those raised by Parekh. It is not idealist because of aspiring to rise above all social determinants, nor is it incoherent because of the hopelessness of that aspiration.

Critical Social Inquiry and the Dialectic

The reference to Marx's concept of criticism should be taken further. For it touches on a controlling assumption in the work of both Larrain and Parekh, the assumption that Marx's view of ideology has to be set in the context of the project of critical social inquiry. This assumption supplies much of the pressure behind Larrain's insistence on the negative concept. That concept is held to be important as 'a valuable analytic tool for a contemporary critical social science'.[58] The popularity of positive and neutral conceptions, on the other hand, had 'undercut the centrality of the concept of ideology in the social sciences'.[59] Parekh, too, is anxious not 'to emasculate the critical force and explanatory power of the concept of ideology'.[60] But his chief concern is to distinguish sharply between the ideological-apologetic and the scientific-critical approaches to society. Critical knowledge 'not only explains but also judges, accuses and points a way out'.[61] Moreover, for Marx, 'the truth about society is only revealed to the critical eye'.[62] Hence it is that he was 'first and foremost a humanist' who 'in all his works, including *Capital* ... evaluated the social institutions and practices on the basis of how they affected the human well-being'.[63]

For Larrain, the crucial point is that ideology is a concept which refers to 'undesirable situations' in a way that 'cannot but imply ... a critique of a distorted state of affairs'.[64] It is clearly a specifically epistemological mode of criticism that is involved here. Ideology refers to what is undesirable because distorted, and the distortions in question are cognitive distortions. Thus, in the key formula that 'ideology conceals contradictions', the critical weight is borne by the notion of concealment. The fact that it is contradictions that are the victims of distorted cognition is, of course, important for some purposes of the argument, but irrelevant for constituting the critical status of social inquiry. What now emerges is a fairly commonplace notion of criticism owing nothing in particular to Marx. The trouble with ideological beliefs is, to put it crudely, that they are false. It is entirely reasonable to suppose that such falsity is a defect and that pointing it out is therefore a criticism. But it seems a pity to appropriate so rich and resonant a concept as ideology for this activity. Parekh's conception of Marxist criticism is a good deal more plausible. At least it fits in with an overall view of Marx's system which allows for an intelligible link with socialist practice. On this view, critical force derives from a conception of human well-being which enables one to assess the present in the light of its emancipatory potential. This is a familiar and, in many ways, attractive view of the significance of Marx's work. It may well be that the assumption that this work is, essentially, critical social theory can only be given substance by falling back in the end on some version of Parekh's proposal. But that assumption, in spite of its current popularity, should itself be questioned. To do so is indirectly to challenge the epistemological obsession of Western Marxism that has made of ideology something negative, the disreputable 'other' of science.

The suggestion that will be outlined here is that the project of critical social inquiry is inherently suspect because it cannot do justice to the most distinctive theme in Marx's methodological reflections, the theme of the 'dialectical' character of his science.[65] He always acknowledges Hegel to be the 'inventor' of dialectic and the quickest way forward at this point may be to see what its inventor had to say about it. In the *Philosophy of Right* we are told that:

> dialectic is not an activity of subjective thinking applied to some matter externally, but is rather the matter's very soul putting forth its branches and fruit organically. This development of the Idea is the proper activity of its rationality ... To consider a thing rationally means not to bring reason to bear on the object from the outside and so to tamper with it, but to find that the object is rational on its own account.[66]

It is difficult to see how Larrain's or Parekh's view of criticism could qualify as dialectical on these terms. For it is difficult to see how such activities as referring to 'undesirable situations' or 'judging, accusing and pointing a way out' could be conceived of other than as activities of 'subjective thinking applied to some matter externally'. The point is perhaps best made in terms of the notion of rationality, a central category of the dialectical tradition. It is also, of course, of vital concern for the project of critical inquiry. As that project is usually understood, however, what is necessary to constitute the inquiry as rational is that the critic be rational: any rationality on the part of the object of criticism is redundant for the purpose. In its essential meaning the critique of society is precisely a bringing of reason to bear on the object from the side of the subject. The sense that the object is rational 'on its own account' need have no part in it, as the versions offered by Larrain and Parekh testify. Yet this sense is indispensable if we are to be entitled to speak of dialectic. And unless we can do that, we shall be unable to grasp Marx's conception of science and, hence, in turn, of the other categories of social consciousness, including ideology. We know, roughly at any rate, how to account for the rationality of the object for the purposes of Hegelian dialectic: it has in one way or another to be referred ultimately to the workings of the Idea. A century of debate has not left a similar consensus on how to achieve this for a materialist dialectic, and it remains the major item on the agenda of Marxist philosophy.

Notes

1. J. Larrain, *Marxism and Ideology* (London, Macmillan, 1983); B. Parekh, *Marx's Theory of Ideology* (London, Croom Helm, 1982).
2. Larrain, *Marxism and Ideology*, pp. 103–04; Parekh, *Marx's Theory of Ideology*, p. 217.

3. Larrain, *Marxism and Ideology*, p. 231.
4. Ibid., p. 25.
5. Ibid., p. 109.
6. Ibid., p. 33.
7. Ibid., pp. 35, 127.
8. Ibid., p. 60.
9. Ibid., p. 71.
10. Ibid., p. 48.
11. Ibid., p. 170.
12. Ibid., p. 225.
13. Ibid., p. 40.
14. K. Marx and F. Engels, *MESW*, p. 182.
15. Larrain, *Marxism and Ideology*, p. 152.
16. Ibid., p. 161.
17. K. Marx and F. Engels, 5 *CW*, p. 36.
18. J. McCarney, *The Real World of Ideology* (Brighton, Harvester Press, 1980), pp. 85–92.
19. In addition to being non-committal on key points, Larrain's discussion of my views is unsatisfactory in other ways. In part this is due to its reliance on suspect claims which are dealt with elsewhere above; for instance, that Engels 'kept referring to ideology in a negative sense' and that 'neither Marx nor Engels ever talked about a proletarian ideology in a positive sense' (Larrain, *Marxism and Ideology*, p. 117). In part it is due to the disappointing level of argument and the tendency to paint a coat of rhetoric over all knotty points. This should be illustrated briefly: the list could be greatly extended if need be. First, Larrain attempts to rebut my suggestion that expressions such as 'ideological distortion' may—within a negative view of ideology – simply add verbiage by invoking the contrast with non-ideological distortion (ibid., p. 115). This has the air of being a contribution to the debate, but it merely reiterates what I explicitly admit. My point is simply that having to rely on a contrast that is so lifeless in terms of Marx's work is a large price to pay (McCarney, *Real World of Ideology*, pp. 84–5). Second, Larrain asserts that, unable to find 'any substantial positive support' for my version of *The German Ideology*, I try to win by default 'as if casting doubts on the opposite interpretation' would make mine 'the necessary one' (Larrain, *Marxism and Ideology*, p. 115). This sidesteps rather than confronts my claims to have found such positive support, but in any case, the procedure being derided is by no means silly where, as here, the alternatives are soon exhausted. The issue is, after all, whether *The German Ideology* supports a neutral or a negative view of ideology. The impression that Larrain has not always thought through what he wishes to say is strengthened by his reliance on the blank assertion that: 'In order for the proletariat to be able to destroy ideology in general, its own thought must be free from ideology' (Larrain, *Marxism and Ideology*, p. 117). In a general way, this hardly strikes one as intuitively obvious, arousing as it does echoes of text-book speculations about the qualities needed for driving fat oxen. In any case, compare: 'In order for the proletariat to be able to destroy class society in general, it must not itself be a class.'
20. Larrain, *Marxism and Ideology*, pp. 53–4.
21. Ibid.
22. Marx and Engels, 7 CW, p. 378. This reference is noted in Parekh, *Marx's Theory of Ideology*, p. 48.
23. Larrain, *Marxism and Ideology*, p. 53.
24. Marx and Engels, *MESW*, p. 95.
25. Larrain, *Marxism and Ideology*, p. 69.

26. Ibid., p. 70.
27. Ibid., p. 43.
28. For further discussion see McCarney, *The Real World of Ideology*, Ch. 4.
29. Larrain, *Marxism and Ideology*, p. 208.
30. Ibid., p. 39.
31. K. Marx, 1 *Capital*, p. 96.
32. Parekh, *Marx's Theory of Ideology*, p. 214.
33. Ibid., p. 32.
34. Ibid., p. 29.
35. This should be amplified. In part the trouble is that Parekh's account is not altogether coherent. Thus, idealism is introduced as a form of philosophical dualism; Hegel is taken to be the archetypal idealist; yet Hegel is explicitly said to have rejected 'a dualistic system' (ibid., pp. 2, 76). In part the trouble is that the detailed interpretation of Hegelian idealism is highly idiosyncratic and yet is attributed to Marx without any discussion. Thus, idealism is said to dehistoricize and desocialize 'the knowing subject' and 'the activity of knowing' (ibid., p. 187). Moreover, it attempts 'to lay down the timeless and universally valid moral principles, without realizing that men are not pure spirits, and moral human needs and social relationships' (ibid., p. 5). It seems that Hegel is being taken to task here for the lack of insights whose possession we owe to him more than to any other figure in intellectual history. There is no reason to hold that Marx's view of him is defective in this way.
36. Ibid., p. 106.
37. Ibid., p. 58.
38. To cite an instance at random, see Peregrine Worsthorne's explanation of what Marxism means to him in his 'Marxism', *Marxism Today*, vol. 27 (March 1983), p. 28.
39. Parekh, *Marx's Theory of Ideology*, p. 61.
40. Ibid., p. 31.
41. Ibid.
42. Ibid., pp. 33, 48.
43. Ibid., pp. 28, 29.
44. Ibid., Introduction.
45. Ibid., p. 17.
46. Ibid., p. 214.
47. Ibid., p. 183.
48. Ibid., p. 180.
49. Ibid., pp. 184–5.
50. Ibid., p. 148.
51. Ibid., p. 222.
52. Ibid., p. 224.
53. Ibid., p. 223.
54. Ibid., pp. 18, 20.
55. Ibid., p. 178.
56. Ibid., p. 180.
57. Ibid., p. 181.
58. Larrain, *Marxism and Ideology*, p. 3.
59. Ibid., p. 43.
60. Parekh, *Marx's Theory of Ideology*, p. 32.
61. Ibid., p. 192.
62. Ibid., p. 151.
63. Ibid., pp.175–6
64. Larrain, *Marxism and Ideology*, p. 89.

65. See, for instance, Marx, 1 *Capital*, pp. 102–3.
66. G.W.F. Hegel, *Philosophy of Right*, translated with notes by T.M. Knox (Oxford, Oxford University Press, 1952), pp. 34–5.

5
Defending Theoretical Openness: Deconstruction and Post-Marxism

Peter Jowers

Throughout its history Marxism has displayed an openness to theoretical innovations occurring outside its own parameters. It has also sought to demarcate between those which can supplement it positively and those which are unacceptable because they are fundamentally at odds with its deepest assumptions. The debate between defenders of 'orthodoxy' and 'Post-Marxism' is about the acceptability or otherwise of insights drawn from post-structuralism.[1] In this paper the impact of Jacques Derrida's deconstructive project upon the work of Laclau and Mouffe is examined. I argue that their Post-Marxism does challenge orthodoxy but that the power of their critique is such that it is orthodoxy which has to be abandoned. Many of the criticisms which have been made of their work are well founded. In particular, there are two general aspects of their argument which are unacceptable. First, there are elements in Derrida's work which are logically contradictory and find their way into Post-Marxism. Second, there are inconsistencies in their adaptation of deconstructive insights. Their break with orthodoxy is not complete enough.

Post-structuralism has been dominated by the work of Derrida, Lacan and Foucault. Disagreements between them cannot be given the treatment they deserve.[2] Neither can Derrida's enormous output be covered, including recent shifts in the emphasis of his work.[3]

Marxism stresses the unity of theory and practice in praxis. This gives rise to three elements. Core conceptual frameworks – 'epistemes', paradigms; substantive theory; and strategy. Debate between orthodoxy and Post-Marxism has been conducted at the level of core framework and strategy, bypassing substantive empirical theory. I shall contend that there is nothing inherent in Post-Marxism as a conceptual framework which vitiates coherent substantive work upon which emancipatory strategies could be founded. Conceptual frameworks are organized sets of assumptions from which are derived logically interrelated concepts which are hierarchically organized. Orthodoxy allows considerable variation at lower levels, or at the edges of such sets, but holds central assumptions to be inviolable if the relevant theories are to be characterized as Marxist. Post-Marxists challenge these core assumptions in several ways. First, the burden of the Post-Marxist case is that orthodoxy attempts an impossible 'closure' which has resulted in 'totalitarianism' when historically successful. Second, it has added innumerable *ad hoc* assumptions. There is an implicit Lakatosian theme here. Orthodoxy is a declining 'research field' which, to preserve its core, adds an ever-growing number of *ad hoc* assumptions. Nowhere are these more evident than in the conception of 'hegemony' within twentieth-century Marxism. Third, this results in strategic immobilism. Fourth, the key role assigned by orthodox theory to the revolutionary potential of the working classes must be abandoned.[4] These are extraordinary claims. They apply to orthodoxy, not Marxism as a whole.

The response has been fivefold. First, the reaffirmation of the centrality of the working class.[5] Second, the accusation that Post-Marxism is incoherent *in toto*, that it has no logical structure and no conception of agency. It is 'subjectivism without a subject'.[6] Third, that without any fundamental normative values the notion of emancipation is incoherent.[7] Fourth, that Post-Marxism is reductionist. It is a form of 'ideologism' which completely overemphasizes superstructural components because of its reliance upon models of society derived from language. This results from the 'exorbitization' of linguistic models inherent in the structuralist/post-structuralist paradigm. A sub-argument of this claim is that Post-Marxism is agent-centred and consequently offers no coherent institutional analysis of stable historical processes.[8] Fifth, that its characterization of a particular tradition constituting 'orthodoxy' rests upon fundamental misunderstandings and misreadings of Marxist classic texts.[9]

Not all the turns of accusation and counter-accusation, in what has been a very vituperative debate, can be pursued here. I shall divide my arguments into three parts. First, I briefly examine Derrida's arguments. Second, I shall try to show how they have been analogically adapted by the Post-Marxists and seek to trace their impact upon the discussion of the hegemony presented by Laclau and Mouffe while simultaneously providing an immanent critique of the areas of weakness in their argument. I close with some remarks upon the implications of the Post-Marxist project.

Derrida and Deconstruction

A splinter in the eye is the best magnifying glass.

T. Adorno.

Post-structuralism attacks the concept of structure. If Saussure's key insights were that language is a system of difference and rules of combination such that meanings could be generated, the key is that such differences (phonetic, syntactic and semantic) be stable. They must have an iterable identity even if it is a relationally derived one. Structure, to be generative, was conceived of as having deep rules of combination and difference as well as surface expression derived from them. It was acknowledged the rules were arbitrary. The generative model was then extended from 'natural language' to a range of semiosis such as written texts, film and so on, and by Lévi-Strauss to mythic and social structure. Post-structuralism takes up Saussure's insight that 'in linguistic systems there are only differences without positive terms'.[10]

The Limits of Structure

Derrida's best-known attack upon the foundations of structuralist pretensions is the essay 'Structure, Sign and Play in the Human Sciences'.[11] This attack on Lévi-Strauss and structuralism in general hinges on the idea that any concept of structure entails an implicit notion of a centre or fixed origin to all aspects of the structure which lies outside the structure itself but guarantees it. All ideas of structures as generative systems can be traced to something exterior to them which as an unexamined foundational assumption gives them their orientation, balance and meaning. Such foundations guarantee the coherence of the system. But, like Gödel's theorems, two consequences stem from such assumptions: first, all logical systems which are non-simple can generate internal contradictions; and second, such undecidables, if 'plugged' or eradicated by extension of the founding axiomatics, give rise to further contradictions which in turn need covering, and so on *ad infinitum*. The consequence of this, as noted by Tarski, is that there cannot be any axiomatic, deductive, formal and unambiguous system which is complete.[12] As Ryan notes, for any formal system to be complete:

> it must assume a transcendental position that is not one item of [its] formal logic; it must assume an outside to the series that acts as a paradigm. Otherwise, the axiomatic system or the master principle will simply be part of the world being described formally.[13]

Thus such founding assumptions 'escape structurality'. It is a centre which determines the structure as a whole but itself escapes determination. Aristotle's unmoved mover comes to mind, as does the famous 'last instance of the economy'. This problem, specific in this instance to structuralism as exemplified by Lévi-Strauss, is but one instance of a long tradition in the West of searching for such guarantees in what Derrida will call 'the transcendental signifier'. All constituted appeals to some originating presence or guarantor of truth whereby varied paradigms were taken as leading to truth, order and an intelligible world. That which conditions but is unconditioned is 'contradictorily coherent':

> The concept of centred structure is in fact the concept of a play based upon a fundamental ground, a play constituted on the basis of a fundamental immobility and a reassuring certitude, which is itself beyond the reach of play.[14]

A key to understanding the deconstructive project and Post-Marxism lies here. Derrida argues that such founding centres or transcendental signifiers have been irredeemably called into question:

> at the moment when European culture ... had been *dislocated*, driven from its locus, and was forced to stop considering itself the culture of reference. This moment is not first and foremost a moment of philosophical or scientific discourse. It is also a moment which is political, economic, technical and so forth.[15]

Note that in this argument Derrida has appealed to logic, history and the psyche. 'Reassuring certitude', 'political', and so on, are appeals to a ground which is extra-discursive and which guarantees his argument. This, as will become evident, contradicts many of his deconstructive arguments and if left would prove fatal not only to his enterprise but to that of Post-Marxism.

Derrida argues that once the exterior guarantee is abandoned 'the domain of the play of signification is extended infinitely ... everything becomes discourse'. Search for such centres 'expresses the force of a desire'.[16]

'Play' as used by Derrida can be understood either in the sense of pleasurable activity or in the sense of movement within two articulated elements. This latter is exemplified in the ambiguity or 'play' of the word itself. This seemingly trivial point indicates the extension of the notion of the undecidability inherent in all signs. Signs are meaningful only as part of a system of differences. Their meaning is relationally determined. When cited they carry concealed within them as traces the economy of difference which gave them temporary stability. As citation this absence affects the meanings determined in the new context.

Textuality and Presence

If the notion of an externally determined 'transcendental signifier' is abandoned, the decisive move of all deconstruction, then all that is left are a series of discourses occurring on the same plane. Post-Marxism applies this argument to orthodox Marxism. In contrast, orthodox Marxists' claims that Post-Marxism is a form of 'perspectivism' and that there is an absence of normative standards can only be made from a meta-discursive vantage point.

Derrida sustains an onslaught against foundationalism on a number of fronts. The most often cited quotation with which he is beaten is that 'there is nothing outside the text'.[17] There is little that is remarkable in Derrida's contention. All he is arguing is that any claim about the structure of reality has to be expressed within a system of meaning if it is to be communicated. Such statements enter the conditions of textuality. Appeals to sensation or intuition as somehow primary will not do. Appeals to literality are fictive. Derrida is not offering an idealism but a prolonged meditation on the complex issue of the relation between textuality and that which lies outside it but which cannot be discussed except by way of the former.

What is at stake with deconstruction in the current disruption is the re-evaluation of the relation between the general text and that which might have been thought of as simply outside language, discourse or writing, as realities of a different order.[18]

To question this relationship is hardly unique to deconstruction. It is at the core of analytical philosophy and contemporary philosophy of science derived from Wittgenstein's later writings. Quine has argued:

The totality of our so–called knowledge or beliefs, from the most casual matters of geography and history to the profoundest laws of atomic physics or even of pure mathematics and logic is a man-made fabric which impinges on our experience only along the edges.[19]

Quine also argues that the abstract entities of mathematics are on an equal footing with physical objects and Gods, neither better nor worse except for differences in the degree to which they expedite our dealings with sense experience.[20] Even Quine's experiential edge should be called into question as it does not really lie outside the order of signification. Feyerabend argues that 'facts' are constituted by 'whole sets of partially overlapping, factually adequate, but mutually inconsistent theories'.[21] Roy Bhaskar argues a realist case which assumes a structured reality independent of our structured knowledge of it. He contends that 'both knowledge and the world are structured and changing; the latter exists independently of the former ... . On this view science is not an epiphenomenon of nature, nor is nature a product of man.'[22]

Realists accept the existence of a world external to thought. But there is a crucial difference between arguing that there is an irreducible residue called *matter* and the argument that it has form. To argue that things *exist* is different from claiming that they are beings with form. Form as a concept is linked to the concept of entity. Of matter we know nothing independently of concepts such as 'indivisible', 'small', and so on. Our theories are built upon such universals but these are terms within textuality. Reflection on beings becomes reflection upon language and semiosis. Derrida's deconstruction of language opens up the possibility for reflection upon not only the relation between it and reality but also the untheorized link between identities established discursively and philosophical traditions which have discussed 'beings'.

Once a referential theory of meaning, or, as Laclau and Mouffe put it, 'the idea that language is a nomenclature which is in a one-to-one relationship to objects', is abandoned then meditation on reality becomes a meditation on language. It is the sense of language as a series of stable meanings coupled with referentiality which has given rise to conceptions of reality as a series of stable objects or entities. If our understanding of language alters, so too will that of reality. If language is conceived relationally this opens up the possibility of conceiving of reality in the same terms.[23]

Thus far Derrida can be understood as having made three moves. First, an attack on foundationalism such that no discourse can do other than make truth-claims and has no logical priority over any other. Disputation is either *intra*-discursive or, more interestingly, *inter*-discursive. Either the judgement of a truth-claim is intrinsic to the discourse concerned or is 'conversationally' disputed. In the former there will be agreement as to what constitutes substantive evidence. In the latter this is subject to dispute. Second, Derrida breaks with referential theories of meaning. The radical and unique quality of deconstruction which differentiates it from analytical philosophy is the third move, to argue that linguistically determined identities contain, as part of their inherent condition, a fundamental instability.

Such foundationalism has been attacked repeatedly by Derrida in relation to two terms: *presence* and *supplement*. I discuss this by way of his revealing discussion of why writing has always been regarded in the philosophical tradition as a supplement to speech. The challenge to any referential theory of meaning has been the danger posed by unstable meaning. If a link is to be established between stable linguistic identity and a world of entities then language must be a 'transparent' medium. Transparency is challenged by the instability of meaning which writing exposes and calls for interpretation.[24] Interpretation is an indication of the impossibility of the desire to arrest the play of meaning. Hence the traditional hostility to the figurative use of language.

In speech, however, the same mental structure, capacity for experience, externally stable objects and the shared language are assumed unconsciously and 'guarantee' linguistic exchanges. Subjects are assumed to be capable of commanding the linguistic structure as a whole. Speech assumes a 'natural bond of sense to the senses'.[25] Speech has been privileged because the effects of the pull of differences and the inherent instability at the heart of language are systematically effaced. These facets become 'the unperceived, the non-present, the non-conscious'.[26] Speech has been preferred as a medium of truth because its signifiers, as sound, disappear as soon as they are uttered. They do not obtrude or remain for interpretation. If misunderstanding occurs speakers can explain themselves.[27]

This set of assumptions, which includes an appeal to unmediated experience, underlies both foundationalism and the hierarchy between speech and writing. Derrida merely argues that both share the necessity of structure and can be subsumed under the term 'inscription' or generalized writing. Any term would do. The attack upon presence simultaneously reveals the manner in which any foundationalism generates the notion of supplementarity and a hierarchy in which presence guarantees the superiority of 'origin' over the 'supplement'.

Three Neologisms: Trace, Supplement and Differance

The appeal to unmediated direct experience is a form of what Derrida calls 'auto-affection'. Its possibility is rejected. There can be no direct sensation or intuition. As Ryan puts it: 'The semblance of "being as presence" – a perceptible plenitude in the present moment – is thus simply the effect of complex chains of relations whose texture is never "present" as such.' Nothing, either as subject or substance, can be apprehended as a unique being apart from the web of relations and forces within which it is situated.[28]

Derrida's work is replete with neologisms. Often these are developed from the text which is subject to deconstruction. The practice aims at unsettling the possibility of any easy hermeneutic 'translation' founded upon a series of stable concepts. The signs chosen to illustrate the multiple meanings which can be derived from any reading drive home the wider argument that most discourse rests upon logocentric appeals to presence. Presented as clusters of interlinked terms, they are used in a quasi-conceptual manner, but are chosen such that a series of possible meanings is generated. As Derrida's supplementary text unfolds, these multiple possibilities are explored. Univocal meanings for such terms are undermined and this in turn forces reflection upon their use in the 'pre-text' such that they are thrown into doubt.

An early series of neologisms was drawn from Derrida's exploration of Freud. In these writings Derrida counterposed Freud's conception of the psyche with that of the model of the Cartesian ego. His target was the notion of the possibility of unified subjectivity reproducing itself in time. This encounter with Freud cannot be pursued in any detail; here I note merely some of the angles Derrida takes on the term 'trace' as used by Freud. Traces are connected with Freud's theory of the relation of memory to the unconscious and the link between repression, the possibility of perception and a subject's access to unmediated presence. Traces represent a past which monitors the present. They signify the split or mobile quality of subjectivity and how 'past time' as memory intersects with the present. Thus the non-identity of the subject is displayed. More interestingly, another series of arguments is woven into this exposition. Freud himself repeatedly used the figures of writing and inscription to discuss traces and their part in dreams and the unconscious. His repeated appeals to the hieroglyphic and other forms of writing to explain traces are stressed. Freud never settled upon a satisfactory model for the interplay of traces and consciousness, and all his attempts were themselves intensely figurative. He attempted a series of definitions, each a metaphorical construction, each containing traces of his previous formulation. Further, the very term 'trace' indicates, because linked to memory, something it is not. One of its French senses which Derrida plays on is that of 'spoor', as in the trail of an animal in snow which a hunter might track. Derrida tracks a series of signifiers in Freud which contain their own traces of a sense of trace which itself is always a sign of something absent. It is an absence which determines the subject's access to presence which is itself always merely a sign, or absence. Thus Derrida signals endless semiosis. Freud's text is itself a hieroglyph, a dream text. Derrida mimics Freud's own 'interpretations' to reveal them as mere supplements, as mere possibilities. Space precludes following the trail of the trace any further.[29]

The term 'supplement' extends the attack on presence and referentiality. It also introduces several key developments in Derrida's argument. The system which grounds knowledge in the primacy of unmediated presence, which occludes the priority of the trace and the non-transparency of all signs, is called 'logocentrism'. Discourses which appeal to 'transcendental signifiers' appeal to logocentrism to ground their truth. Thus they aim at 'closure'. That is, they generate truth-claims on the basis of a structure of difference and combination which is not recognized as arbitrary or unstable. The 'truths' of the system rest upon stable differences where the signifiers are referentially guaranteed by an unacknowledged appeal to a referential theory of meaning. Thus they always appeal to an origin which lies outside the structure but which guarantees the coherence of the whole. A supplement is something added to such a system. It has two meanings. It can be an 'addition' which merely fills out the system or a 'substitute' which insinuates itself or intervenes. It implies a compensation for something which should be in the system but which is not. It is in this second sense that supplements are 'dangerous' in that they fill something which is lacking in that which they are added to. As such they threaten the logocentric certainty of the discourse in question.

Derrida shows over and over again how the logocentrism of such discourses is incoherent and how as a consequence they are consistently supplemented in attempts to stabilize them. But in the process their self-sufficiency is threatened. Consequently, supplements are placed on the exterior of such discourses as marginal additions, in the form of hierarchical displacement. They are deemed parasitical. Hence in deconstructive practice a common move is to take the supplement(s) to show both how the discourse cannot do without it (them) and yet simultaneously downgrades it (them). Writing, for example, is seen throughout philosophy as a derivation of a derivation. Presence guarantees truth. Speech is the nearest to unmediated truth so, although derivative, is allowed as a guarantor of communicating about truth. Writing is conceived of as a derivative form of speech. His argument is that all three are underpinned by the 'absent' economy of traces, fully occluded in appeals to presence, partially so in the case of speech and less so in writing. If the system of traces is acknowledged, then all three are on a par and are just different forms of 'inscription'. The supplement, because it is acknowledged as a substitute for the naturalness of presence, threatens the argument. Yet writing is the medium through which philosophy works. It contains an appeal to speech as productive of truth in a system of signification it simultaneously decries. It is thus incoherent, undermined on its own terms.

Differance (note the *a*) is a neologism which connects such arguments to the instability of any economy of traces or system of differences. It seeks to challenge the structuralist notion of a stable system of linguistic (social) differences and combinatory rules which defines the event or generated outcome of that structure. Structures are perceived only *post festum*. They are deductions from a series of events. Derrida argues that new 'events' (acts of textuality) may alter the structure of the whole. This is a possibility, not a necessity. The argument concerning iterability and alterity will show how this can occur. Differance also refers to the rejection of presence as guarantor of truth. It contains the sense of deferral. Deferral implies being carried away. Signs always defer the access to presence because, given the argument about traces, signification constantly carries subjects away from presence. Supplement always indicates such deferral.

Iterability and Alterity

At the core of the deconstructive enterprise is a challenge to closure, using either claims about reality or claims about the possibility of definitive interpretation. More technically, it is an affirmation of the endless play of semiosis which cannot be arrested by appeal to foundations in the form of presence or any other 'transcendental signifier'. All discourse has an exterior in the form of other discourses. All signs are capable of being repeated and altered. This is their condition. If a sign is incorporated in a closed discourse it can be reiterated. Stable communication occurs. Large areas of life are governed by this process. But the possibility of using signs in other contexts, in other discursive economies, means their significance can be altered.

As is well known, we often appeal to context to stabilize a meaning which is opaque. When we interpret texts we 'frame' them.[30] With a multiplicity of possible discursive economies, no context can be appealed to definitively. Any such appeal is an attempted closure. Hence such appeals take on the form of supplementarity. They both attempt to supply a deficiency, in this case the 'clarity' of the text or practice under consideration. In this case they are mere addition. But as extra writing (taken in the general sense) they threaten the original text by being substitutions for it. The most common move in all interpretative framing is to appeal to an origin whereby the possibility of multiple interpretation is denied. This commonly takes the form of an appeal to 'authorial intention' or to some reconstructed historical context. In the former, intention is supposed to guarantee a univocal interpretation. But because it entails appeals to letters, diaries and so on, it needs these as supplements to the core text and must, to be consistent, imply the non-problematic nature of authorial intent within them. Such interpretative strategies also appeal to individual subjectivity as an original source of intention. This cannot be done in the case of unknown authors such as Homer and folk tales. Some other context is then found, such as social structure. All appeals to origins and a unified subject are anathema to the deconstructive enterprise.

Interpretation is often referred to by Derrida as the 'respectful doubling' of a text in which this framing process as supplementarity which alters meaning is denied. Deconstruction acknowledges it and locates it in the general possibility of endless semiosis or 'dissemination'. It concentrates on the possibility of alterity as the traditional view over-stressed iterability. Nevertheless it must be stressed that signs are used within closed discourses; they can be very stable and iterable. They contain this other possibility of instability as a condition of their use. Post-Marxism has been led astray because it overemphasizes this one side at the expense of the possibility of iterability. Substantive research would tease out this interplay. Neither moment can be given hierarchical prominence.

The arguments concerning iterability and alterity are most fully developed in Derrida's exchange with John Searle, detailed examination of which would take me too far afield.[31] It must be stressed that Derrida does not deny intention, merely that it governs the entire scene. The debate was triggered by Derrida's discovery that, despite Austin's attempt to provide a theory of speech acts which did not rely on intention but attempted to formalize those contexts which determined the force of an utterance, Austin was forced to appeal to intention. Searle, in his defence of Austin, explicitly acknowledged the role of intention in determining meaning. He argued that 'there is no getting away from intentionality.... In serious literal speech the sentences are precisely the realisation of intentions'. He reintroduces Austin's original distinction between serious and non-serious speech acts.[32] Derrida discovers the old hierarchy between original serious speech and parasitic non-serious forms. Searle then excludes the latter from consideration. Derrida attempts to displace the axiomatics of this opposition in a manner similar to that which altered the relation between speech and writing. There is a need for 'an analysis which can account for structural possibilities'.[33] His argument is that something can be part of a signifying sequence only if it can be repeated (reiterated) but that iteration contains as part of its condition of possibility both identity and alterity. Identity alone is not enough because signs carry hidden within them traces from other contexts. They are only identical in a relational sense to other elements within a discourse. They are internally divided or not identical with themselves. It is around citation that the non-identity is revealed. A sign (or complex of signs) receives its first meaning relationally. In another context, these relations are altered by those established in the second use. Though the sign remains, its force is altered.

Attempts to distinguish between serious and non-serious speech have to have recourse to intentionality. But we are never sure of this. Think of a sentence and then frame it with the intention of irony, seriousness, sarcasm, jest, and so on. Each frame alters which sense of intentionality is being appealed to. The frame, while faithful to the words of the text, ceaselessly alters its force. Add unconscious motive, desire, parody, and so on, and the problem is compounded. Also, intentionality is individualist in its focus. Derrida's play on the copyright sign and acknowledgements in Searle's article focuses upon the intersubjectivity of much textuality. The possibility of reframing derives from the undecidability inherent in any sign. The outcome is that, although meanings are context bound, contexts are boundless. As Culler notes, any assumed context is open to further description and can be altered. Second, any attempt to codify context can always be grafted onto the context it sought to describe and thus escape the previous formulation.[34] If Derrida's argument has force it means that both stability and instability are conditions of all iterable identities. The actual practice of deconstruction often seeks to show how previous interpretative frames which issue in a history of commentary on texts can be displaced, thus altering the force of the text under scrutiny, while simultaneously arguing that their reading is but one of multiple possible readings. Appeals to intention seek definitive and univocal interpretation under the sign of truth.

Deconstructive Textual Practice

Deconstruction is not only a form of textual commentary though this has been its commonest form. The Post-Marxists widen the notion of textuality to mean discourse in Foucault's sense. This is explored below; suffice to say here that it includes as practices social relationships and institutions. Deconstruction focuses upon the necessities which govern texts, on the relation between what authors command and the traces they do not. Deconstructors seek to produce critical readings which reveal the interplay between what is attempted, and how this is not achieved because of the systematic play of a system of traces which cannot be commanded.[35] They seek to show the types of hierarchy closure induces. This might take the form of fixing upon the appeal to sight and all its cognates as part of the appeal to presence. It might mean using the tropes and metaphors with which a text is studded to show how philosophical arguments fixated with clarity and stable meaning are undermined by their recourse to a form of language which is inherently unstable. By definition, metaphor contains an instability of meaning.[36] Deconstruction teases out the implicit rather than explicit assumptions that appear but are not acknowledged within texts. It asks 'where is this statement being made from?' rather than 'what does it mean?'[37] Repeatedly it deconstructs the logocentric matrix. Deconstruction is also aware of its own provisionality in avoiding attempted closure in the form of definitive readings. Often, and this has aroused much hostility, it uses the subordinate pole of an implicit hierarchy present in the text under scrutiny as its organizational frame. It often disavows clear beginnings, uses numerous effects to displace recuperative readings, and employs foregrounding in order to emphasize the non-transparency of language. Neologisms with unstable meaning are spawned in order to stress this facet of language.

The multiple sources of textuality are emphasized. Texts are read against a series of prior texts to show how they participate in a general intertextuality rather than being controlled by a single author.[38] Intertextuality derives from the alterity inherent in signs once the notion of intention and closure guaranteed by appeals to origin and presence have been abandoned. As Derrida argues:

> Every sign, linguistic or non-linguistic, spoken or written..., in a small or a large unit, can be cited, put between quotation marks; in so doing it can break with any given context in a manner that is absolutely illimitable. This does not imply that the mark is valid outside of a context, but that on the contrary there are only contexts without any centre or anchor.[39]

Deconstruction and Politics

Derrida has argued that deconstruction 'should not be separable from [any] politico-institutional problematic ... this means that, too political for some, it will seem paralysing to those who recognise politics by the most familiar roadsigns'.[40] Earlier I noted the link between the relational identity of signs and the altered conception of 'beings' this gives rise to. This applies also to politics. All theoretical discourse on politics will identify conceptually those entities it seeks to explain. If the link between such concepts and their relational instability is stressed, then it is not surprising that deconstruction alters the roadsigns as to what is political.

Eagleton has recognized after early hostility that

> Derrida is out to do more than develop new techniques of reading: deconstruction is for him *ultimately* political *practice*, an attempt to dismantle the logic by which a particular system of thought, and behind that a whole system of political strategies and social institutions, maintains its force.[41]

There has been unremitting hostility to deconstruction in its American form by Eagleton, as if French deconstruction were original and the other parasitic.[42] To try and divide such chaff from the wheat in American versions of deconstruction would take me too far afield. To argue that deconstruction is apolitical is an inadequate response. Post-Marxism attempts to take seriously the idea that to be politically effective we might have to alter the roadsigns in order to understand contemporary developments and to develop effective strategies.

Derrida has argued that the axiomatics governing discourses are not 'the peaceful coexistence of facing terms but a violent hierarchy. One of the terms dominates the other (axiologically, logically etc.), occupies the commanding position.'[43] What is made explicit is that in writing of textuality Derrida has a conception of the link between language, practice, truth and power.

Negative critique has long played a part within Marxism. Deconstruction both is and is not such a critique. The term carries its own traces. Traditionally critique has meant the exploration of the assumptions and internal logical consistency of an argument motivated by a desire to question them in the name of superior 'truth'. Deconstruction is not so naive. If critique means mere '*Aufhebung*', a going beyond on the journey to a fuller truth, then deconstruction is not of this form. Deconstruction is a dialectics of displacement without preconceived destination. Its metaphors have been those of the 'tear', the 'violent opening' and the fold.[44] What is torn open, a pre-existing axiomatics, remains so only before being recuperated and folded within another closure, another series, another system. Indeed, all of the unstable neologisms developed by Derrida in relation to specific texts have already hardened into an axiomatics of deconstruction. This paper is not exempt. Post-Marxism is such a tearing but such is its fluidity that perhaps it needs a temporary stability in order to compete with the 'certainties' of orthodoxy.

Weaknesses in Derrida's Arguments

There are several glaring deficiencies in Derrida's version of deconstruction. First, appeals within an argument to politics have to be conceived discursively. Such is the power of inherited discourse that this is exceedingly difficult to sustain at all times. If a particular context is being appealed to, such as the eighteenth-century background to Rousseau's writings in the discussion of the supplement, or the decline of Eurocentric certainty in the argument about the challenge to foundationalism as noted above, Derrida cannot appeal to history or conceptual categories without asserting their textual quality. This he does repeatedly. So too do the Post-Marxists. This can be avoided, but extreme care must be taken not to be governed by the systems one is deconstructing or the argument that they are appealing to a 'transcendental signifier' can be turned back on deconstructors.

Second, appeals to desire smack of a foundationalism. The failure to account for individual 'style' in the sense of 'identity' has resulted in a gradual decline in interest in Derrida's work in France. The debate between Lacan and Derrida cannot be pursued here but it is of vital importance to clarify the relationship between assertion of a desire for closure and a non-foundational theory of the operations of desire.

Third, although the link between power and textuality is repeatedly asserted, nowhere is it ever specified in anything other than the vaguest terms. It is Marxism's ability to specify such linkage that makes it such a powerful social theory. As we shall see, this is also the area of greatest weakness in Post-Marxism. Tentative observations as to how this might be overcome will be indicated below.

Finally, if, as Rorty has noted, philosophy has oscillated between grand theory and critical deconstructive forms, it is wellnigh impossible to conceive how collective action can operate on the basis of a consistent fluidity of identity and theoretical activity which gives no stability to the actors or the objects of their action. Some intermediate point for political practice is necessary between the closure of an orthodoxy and the fluidity of deconstruction.[45] I now turn to inquire whether Post-Marxism can achieve this end and answer some of these criticisms.

Post-Marxism

Post-Marxism focuses on the undemocratic consequences of an orthodox Marxist tradition. Post-Marxism, using the insights of post-structuralism, has as its *topos* attempts to 'redefine socialism as a sectorial specification of democracy, or local instantiation of a higher order concept'.[46] Laclau and Mouffe present their argument in three parts. First, they define and deconstruct an 'orthodox' tradition. Second, they present the consequences of this move in a reconstructed version of the concept of hegemony. Finally, they indicate what the possible strategic consequences of this reformulation are. My remarks here will centre upon their characterization of orthodoxy and their reconstructed version of the concept of hegemony.

Laclau and Mouffe offer a 'critique and deconstruction of the various discursive surfaces of classical Marxism'. They present a polarity and hierarchy in which Post-Marxism subsumes classical Marxism, the components of which are diluted within 'that infinite intertextuality of emancipatory discourses in which the plurality of the social takes place'. Based upon their sense of the new social movements, a contrast is drawn between a closed and essentialist discourse and a social surplus of alternative discourses which exceeds classical Marxism and thus constitutes an exterior to it which challenges its internal closure and its claim to be a meta-narrative. Logically, the stakes are quite simple and derived from Derridean arguments as outlined above. Either a theory claims as an a priori principle to be capable of explaining social and historical processes in total, or it does not. If not, then any non-totalizing theory has to accept both that it is only one possible discourse among many and that additional social non-theoretical discursivity will always exceed attempts to explain it and thus constitutes a discursive exterior or surplus. Specific discursive claims have to be located in a general field of discursivity which will threaten the 'moments' or 'identities' it establishes. The instability of these entities has to be accepted as they are always capable of being reinscribed within another discourse. In their reinscription they alter. A non-foundational discourse has to reject attempts to 'determine a priori agents of change, levels of effectiveness in the field of the social, and privileged points and moments of rupture'. Any discourse rejecting closure must recognize itself as one of many emancipatory processes. 'Socialism is *one* of the components of radical democracy, not vice versa.'[47]

Classical Marxism, or orthodoxy, is investigated genealogically, taken in Foucault's sense. A particular tradition is chosen which is determined by the development of the concept of hegemony. The core argument is that the concept of hegemony developed as a necessary supplement to fill insufficiencies in the closed paradigm of orthodoxy necessitated by the actual 'surplus' of events. Like all supplements, it was pushed to the margins, treated as an *ad hoc* addition. But as with 'differance' it was outside the closure and its logic 'carried orthodoxy away'. If acknowledged properly, hegemony alters all the differences in the original. It challenges the very closure which prompted its emergence. As supplement it exposes the limits of that closure.

One problem of genealogies is that they are selective. There are notable gaps in the tradition Laclau and Mouffe discuss. Critical theory which bears strong affinity in its concerns with post-structuralism is never mentioned. One cannot resist the suspicion that there is selectivity at the heart of their genealogy in order to make their binary reversal more violent. A more subtle and judicious treatment of the tradition would only strengthen their case.[48] Laclau and Mouffe concentrate upon Kautsky, Bernstein, Luxemburg, Lenin, Trotsky and Gramsci.

Orthodoxy is repeatedly castigated as a closed discourse, a meta-narrative which appeals to an unproblematical identity of theory and actuality via a naive recourse to 'presence', which asserts the transparency of its concepts through a theory of meaning based on reference to the real. Theoretical identities correspond to actual social forces and processes. Orthodoxy is variously characterized as: essentialist, economist because of its economic reductionism, classist, stagist because of its assertion of laws of development, rationalist because of its belief that social totality can be rationally apprehended and explained as an organically unified whole. These specific critiques can be subsumed under the terms 'closure' and 'transparency', which are also used repeatedly.[49] There are complex discussions of these various treatments of hegemony which cannot be covered here.

A foundationally guaranteed Marxism is necessarily authoritarian. Laclau and Mouffe contend that this derives from the claim to have apprehended the laws of motion of the infrastructure. Existing tendencies are deemed transitory, the future is guaranteed. Until then the Party becomes the guarantor of 'science' and becomes the sole depository of wisdom from whence it makes its strategic decisions in the name of the working class. Strategic judgements are justifiable by translating them back to the infrastructure where 'objective' historical interests are forged. It is on the basis of this characterization that a fundamental dualism appears, that between *necessity* and a supplementary *contingency*. The infrastructure supplies the necessity. The key to comprehending it has been found. Predictions and strategy are based upon an unproblematic science. When a gap opened between it and necessary practice in the form of forging alliances or class unity this was explained on the basis of contingency.

Contingency must, by definition, be unlimited. Orthodoxy introduces a spurious form of contingency. Whenever orthodoxy is adhered to, contingency appears under the name of hegemony. The component parts of social existence are deemed to be determined in their specificity. Thus the contingent is constrained, limited in its free play because it intersects with necessity. It appears as a supplement, as a dualism which is not a dualism. Hence the form of the supplement which is necessary but which is not allowed to disturb the core of orthodoxy. The contingent is not allowed to be the full negation of necessity. Its range being limited, it can still be enclosed within the totalizing model but, because it threatens it, it is consigned to the margins.

As the trajectory of historical actuality diverged from orthodox expectations, the range of the contingent had to be expanded but was always subsumed within the totalization of the stagist model. Laclau and Mouffe argue that this can be detected in the arguments of Lenin and Trotsky. On the orthodox account the necessary stages for proletarian revolution had not occurred in Russia. To enable the proletariat to act, a division between the necessary 'interior' of the stagist model and a contingent 'exterior' developed to sustain the former. The result was a double narrative. In the first or 'grand' narrative, the stagist paradigm was retained. The stages of history are the plot, the 'fundamental' classes the characters. But because the bourgeoisie is incapable of fulfilling its historical mission its role is taken over by another character. This transfer to another 'character' is the second narrative. Contingent features are thus reassimilated into the grand narrative. That the actual course of the revolutionary period could have been genuinely contingent is a suppressed possibility. Hegemony, which stressed the leadership of the working classes within a class alliance, could never allow that the relations of class forces and the forging of identities could have been radically contingent. A genuine discussion of contingency never occurred. Under the sign of hegemony conceived in the narrow form 'there is a subtle sleight of hand making it disappear'.[50]

Within their exposition of orthodoxy another conception of hegemony is elaborated. Hegemony in its Leninist version is derived from the grand narrative. There is a chain of deduction from infrastructure, to objective interests, to classes, to interests, to parties, to alliances. Hegemony is always a superstructural phenomenon, the superstructure always has its contingent surface constrained. Hegemony is always a linkage between externally forged parties. Their identities are predetermined prior to the linkage which takes the form of leaders and led, is thus always undemocratic and issues in authoritarian political practice. Such conceptions are founded on closure in which the identities and relationships specified by the model are *reiterated*: they are repetitions of a predetermined identity guaranteed by the interior chain of differences established by the closed model. If iterability is challenged and *alterity* becomes possible, several consequences follow. First, the chain traced above which established identity on the basis of 'interests', and so on, is broken. If this is rejected then core aspects of orthodoxy have to be rejected. Hegemonic articulation on this model becomes the meeting ground of several discourses which through interdiscursive and democratic negotiation establish a temporary 'collective will'. In the process new identities and the relationships between them are forged, opening up the possibility of new theory and strategies. This is a model of genuine contingency. 'Hegemony supposes the construction of the very identity of social agents.'[51] Laclau and Mouffe's analysis of Gramsci cannot be dealt with in detail. They find an awareness of the fluidity of social identities in his conception of 'collective wills' but argue that at root his appeal to fundamental classes around which hegemony is constructed returns to the essentialism of an orthodoxy which must be broken with.

The response of critics to such arguments has been that in the breaking of the chain leading from infrastructure to alliance, the explanatory power of Marxism is abandoned to a perspectival pluralism incapable of genuine social analysis. I would merely note here that alterity, in the Derridean argument, intersects with iterability. What this would imply for Laclau and Mouffe is that the social contains both. There is, as Mouzelis has pointed out, no contradiction between accepting the ultimate discursivity of the social and the actuality of areas of social stability and institutional continuity:

> insofar as Laclau and Mouffe do not identify discourse with language, then I agree with their view that *all* institutional arrangements, whether durable or not, are discursively constructed. *But there is no reason why one should link discursive construction with fragility and precariousness* – labelling any reference to institution durability as essentialist.[52]

Over one argument, the centrality or otherwise of the working class as the key collective agent of historical emancipation, one move is to argue, as Geras has done, that this is merely a realistic heuristic rather than an a priori assumption. Such an argument only has validity as a critique of Laclau and Mouffe's arguments if the whole structure of orthodox assumptions becomes heuristic. There is little sign of this in Geras's work so that that particular claim seems more a sleight of hand to avoid the charge of essentialism. In Laclau and Mouffe's version the working classes become one possible but not necessary collective actor. Whether or not they so act in any context is contingent. It will depend upon their political, that is, 'discursive' construction as a collective agent. Their role cannot be read off from some predetermined assertion of objective interests. Laclau and Mouffe overemphasize the fluidity of the social by taking only one moment of the Derridean argument. Their cogent case is weakened by this. It might be asked what a non-essentialist analysis of the institutional and persistent quality of discourses, conceived in the Foucauldian sense as a complex interrelationship of textuality, practices and social relationships, might look like. Here I would only point to the path-breaking work of Edward Said's *Orientalism* [53] as a model.

Alterity depends upon the idea of citation, of a discursive possibility of relational 'identities' being reframed. This is a key conception for Laclau and Mouffe. The plurality of discourses exemplified by the new social movements means both that society is more than any attempt at discursive mastery of it and that subjects are constituted within discourses as subject positions. Laclau and Mouffe insist upon the incomplete, open and negotiable quality of every identity. All discourses display 'regularity in dispersion'. It is only when challenged from a context of exteriority that a particular discourse can be 'signified as a totality'. Meta-narratives have no exterior and hence are unchallengeable. No discourse, if conceived as part of a general field of discursivity, can ensure a given and delineated positivity. All discursively derived identities are both fixed and unfixed because of their possible reinscription within another exterior discourse. Fixity comes from the system of dispersal internally employed within a specific discourse. There can, however, be no instability without stability. Discourses attempt to dominate the field of discursivity by attempting to arrest the flow of signifiers. This they do around privileged discursive points, the centring assumptions of any discourse. These privileged signifiers Laclau and Mouffe, following Lacan, call 'nodal points'. They stabilize the discursive chain. In orthodoxy they would be key concepts such as modes of production, the fettering thesis, and so on.

On these rather abstract statements Laclau and Mouffe's conception of both subjects and hegemonic articulation can be understood. They reject the dispersed subject of structuralism. Nodal points in discourses give stability to subjects. Key terms such as 'rights', 'man', and so on, have been historically developed and give substance to iterable identities and relationships. Not all are positive, as their extended forays into women's location in discourses and racism indicate. If discourses are both stable iterable series and open to alterity because of the action of other discursive dispersals, then the germs of sophisticated analysis of hegemonic struggle are at hand. It becomes a matter of substantive theory to determine whether or not stability or alterity is predominant in any specific context. What these notions do not sustain is the type of challenge mounted by Meiksins Wood and Anderson:

> The post-structuralist evacuation of both subject and structure is not a promising foundation for constructing a political programme. With no subject interior to history, no human purpose or agency and with no intrinsic order or direction, no logic of process, no social identities nor structural constraints, what would be the impulse, the objective and modalities of political action? [54]

For Anderson this results in 'subjectivism without subject'.[55] The notion of discourse contains regularity and iteration. Without it the concept is incoherent. With the notion of dispersal from nodal points a structure which can be identified and relationships which can be explained occur. Stability also allows for the identity of subjects to be theorized while simultaneously avoiding foundationalism built upon some 'transcendental signifier'. Simultaneously the exteriority of other discourses can help explain alteration in subjectivity in the same discursive manner. Appeals to historical subjects constitute the standard orthodox claim to be able to identify essential collective actors. Laclau and Mouffe do over-stress fluidity but in principle the challenge of Meiksins Wood and Anderson is a mere caricature of their arguments.

Hegemonic articulation results from the possibility of alterity. Laclau and Mouffe's extended discussion of how it works in practice cannot be explored here. Suffice to say that 'moments' occurring within a discourse are part of a system of dispersal which give them iterable stability. These are contrasted to 'elements', which are any differences not securely articulated in the interior of a discourse. Given exterior discourses and the logic of alterity, moments can be transformed into elements. They become free-floating, their meaning can be altered, though as signifiers they may remain unaltered. Because they are always relational, when integrated in another economy their force alters. The detaching and migration of such moments occurs because the field of identities never manages to be fully fixed. All discourses aspire to closure, to a fixing of a system of dispersal such that a univocal version of social reality can be determined.

The crux of Laclau and Mouffe's case is that, given the plurality of discourses in the modern age, this is an impossibility. Hence the possible alterity of any moment. The surplus potential in the general field of discursivity threatens stable identities. Such 'floating signifiers' are incapable of being wholly articulated in a discursive chain. Hence the inherent potentiality for instability, of detaching them and reincorporating them anew. Such arguments can be understood in relation to the 'tear' and 'fold' metaphors noted earlier. A moment may be torn from a chain. For example, the signifier 'growth' and the related notion of 'consumption', when reinscribed within the Green discourse, take on a range of negative connotations in its economy of dispersal. In the general field of interdiscursivity, growth can no longer be linked to nodal points such as unending expansion of consumption, or of the condition of overcoming scarcity such that emancipation occurs. Interestingly, adjacent signifiers alter. Consumption in such a discourse returns to an earlier sense – 'to consume' as destruction. Torn from one system, folded into another, relationally determined moments are destabilized. Polysemia disarticulates a discursive structure.[56] It re-emphasizes the impossibility of closure.

'Antagonism' is a key term in Laclau and Mouffe's argument. It reveals the limit of the social. Discourse establishes the social as a regulated economy of differences. Antagonism reveals the artifice of the system of positivities thus established. If challenged, such systems call subjects' identities into question. A peasant expelled from her land loses identity as a peasant. A new identity as outworker, wage-labourer, rural bandit or guerilla fighter may occur. But there is a space, between the tear and the fold, where no positivity occurs. Not all torn identities are folded or reinscribed in a new system of oppositions which can then be described positively. Reinscription may not fully occur. I have in mind the fate of aboriginal peoples when their world is destroyed or the Peace Convoy in Britain. In that failure they appear as the non-social within the social, as non-persons without identity. They become floating signifiers to which innumerable contradictory meanings are attached.[57]

The Implications of Post-Marxism

The constitution of identities is at the heart of hegemonic practice. Laclau and Mouffe's general thesis is that Post-Marxism points towards an emancipatory politics of genuine interdiscursivity which is founded upon a generalized move towards radical democracy. Its opposite is also a possibility in the form of an increasingly authoritarian practice imposing through force a closure around stable identities. In this final section I outline how they arrive at this thesis. My argument will be that they can be defended against foundationally derived criticism but that their argument is weak in two senses. The first is that they overemphasize fluidity by drawing upon only one side of deconstruction. Charges that, in the form their argument has been presented, their theory cannot deal with systematic social regularity, processes and institutions must be accepted. The second general charge is that they do not adhere to the full implications of deconstruction. In consequence their thesis oscillates between an innovatory theory with massive potential and older non-discursive and foundationally-derived arguments. The result is an incoherence which in principle can be overcome.

The redefinition of socialism as a sector of radical democracy derives from three interrelated arguments. One concerns the discursive fluidity of modern society. The second concerns the impact of democratic claims as the key nodal point of contemporary political life derived from the impact of the French Revolution which have been gradually extended from a narrowly political sphere to the economy, gender relations, and so on, by being reinscribed in diverse discourses. Neither can be accepted in the form Laclau and Mouffe present it. The third component is derived from them. They contend that once foundationalism is abandoned, with it must go a political imaginary derived from pre-modern modes of political struggle. These were bipolar, based upon popular subject positions. Struggles for political rights in this form entailed paratactical divisions where relations between dominant and subordinate social agents were characterized by extreme exteriority. Subject identities were sharply divided between two competing series which did not intersect. Their challenge to the centrality of the working class derives from these arguments. Laclau and Mouffe contend that:

> In societies with a low technological level of development where the reproduction of material life is carried out by means of fundamentally

repetitive practices, the 'language games' or discursive sequences which organise life are *predominantly* stable. This gives rise to the illusion that the being of objects, which is a purely social construction, belongs to the things themselves. [58]

Hence philosophies of identity and essentialism. With modernity 'all that is solid melts into air' and the historicity of being becomes 'fully visible'. On this dichotomy, which is extended by social fluidity which takes the expressive form of varied social movements, closure becomes more and more an impossibility. Polysemia derives from these disruptive processes inherent in modernity. Such an argument cannot be taken at face value. It becomes a foundational binary divide. Substantive work to sustain the argument is called for. Even Laclau and Mouffe have to admit qualification, hence the word 'predominantly'. On the other side of the equation 'fully visible' is contradictory; for if the discursive quality of being was fully visible why would they have to rail against closure so vehemently? A much more nuanced, archeologically grounded version of this argument is needed, even if the general point is conceded. Presented merely as the outcome of technology and the rhythm of capitalist transformation, it becomes another foundationalism, less nuanced than even the traditional Marxist explanations it attempts to supersede.

The second aspect of their thesis, that of the spread of radical democracy, is even more poorly presented. They claim that 'the more democratic principle of liberty and equality first had to impose itself as the new matrix of the social imaginary or to use our terminology, to constitute a *fundamental* nodal point in the construction of the political'.[59] Surely anything 'fundamental' is at least quasi-foundational? The fluidity of the modern, and the specific form of radical democracy they argue for are in grave danger of being undermined by these types of assertion which violate the deconstructive grounds of their overall argument. Debates as to the regularity of practice and identity and the emergence of democracy belong to the domains of substantive research conducted in a non-foundational archeological manner which simultaneously acknowledges the discursive quality of these processes. To be fair, Laclau and Mouffe do indicate that the term 'radical democracy' is underdeveloped and needs supplementing with the insights of political philosophy. There is no doubt that this move is afoot within socialist theory. It is ironic that this argument is cited as elitist by Meiksins Wood at the time when her mentor, Perry Anderson, is quite obviously moving in the direction of exploring the articulation of various democratic forms.

The consequence of modern discursive fluidity and the nodal role of radical democracy, when coupled with a deconstruction of orthodoxy, results in the reconstruction of the notion of hegemony. The polar model of hegemony as alliance constituted around fundamental classes is abandoned. Hegemonic articulation then becomes multi-centred. There can be no ontologically privileged explanation of hegemony. 'Once we reject the ontological plane, which would inscribe hegemony as the *centre* of the social and hence its essence, it is evidently not possible to maintain the idea of the singleness of the nodal hegemonic point.'[60] Subjects within a discourse may aspire to impose their sense of the world as such a centre. There may be all sorts of embedded reasons why certain discourses are more hegemonic and can articulate more elements than others, but if they were successful they would end hegemony, for closure would be the result. The continuation of the potential instability of all differences founded upon democratic practices is the precondition of hegemonic practice.

Numerous well-known consequences flow from the idea of a multiplicity of hegemonic attempts. First, with ontological grounding abandoned, no collective agent can be granted or denied either theoretical or strategic primacy. Second, since hegemony concerns articulation, at its core is the construction of new discursive economies. For example if orthodoxy wishes to become Greener, there is a world of difference between incorporating such discourse within the standard core assumptions of the model as merely a difference within a pre-existing dispersal and the displacing of certain key assumptions which disrupt the economy of the model as a whole. The debate about the role of the working class is similar. Post-Marxism is not about the rejection of the possibility of its central role, it merely argues that this cannot be taken as an a priori fact and that other sites of struggle will have, in different contexts, other collective agents as the emancipatory motor around which hegemonic aspirations will temporarily coalesce. A further consequence is that if Laclau and Mouffe are more or less correct in their assumptions, then we in the West should not look to ruptures in the form of Revolution of the pre-modern Jacobin type constituted around polar forces.

Derrida, though we have noted his linking of textual hierarchies to violence, is not the only citation in Laclau and Mouffe's work. There is no desire for democracy without its absence. Throughout the work Foucault's (much criticized) Nietzschean linking of truth claims and power is implied. Discourses determine innumerable sites of power and resistance.[61] Nevertheless there is one issue with which I choose to end. This is the argument that Post-Marxism gives no grounds as to why agents might desire emancipation in the form of radical democracy.

Geras seeks to defend classical Marxism by claiming that it has a foundational conception of 'human nature' without which no emancipatory drive can be understood. The deeper claim is that normative criteria can only be transcendentally grounded. Geras argues that Laclau and Mouffe 'do not trouble to explain how one ... concept of "Man" can be adjudged better than another once *human nature* has been excluded, just what in that case are the reasons for preferring it'.[62] He contends 'we need reasons for preferring this discourse to others'. One can only concur with this latter statement. But there is a world of difference between basing strategy on norms and necessarily accepting the uncontested certainty of these norms. They cannot be grounded transcendentally. We are constituted within inherited discourses, many of which claim such grounding. This means they are and will be contested. There is no Archimedean point to adjudicate between such claims.

Habermas, who accepts this fact, attempts a transcendental grounding in procedural norms rather than substantive ones. When he writes that even 'collective identities bob up and down on the flow of interpretations and are better pictured as a fragile network than as a stable centre of self-control', this is remarkably similar in form to the arguments of Laclau and Mouffe.[63] Habermas's well-known route out of this dilemma is to argue that norms concerning discursive communication replace discourse about substance. The 'ideal speech' situation is derived from the argument that all discourse implies truth-claims the procedural implications of which can be formalized. But, as Dews points out, Wellmer has shown that even the rationality of consensus does not guarantee truth as 'the fact of consensus cannot be taken as an additional ground for the truth which is agreed upon, since the cogency of arguments can never be immune from revision'. It is argumentative openness which constitutes us as human beings, not specific norms. Even if 'truth' is arrived at within the unlikely framework of unconstrained dialogue, it will contain substantive elements which might need altering under different conditions. Laclau and Mouffe, in the light of such arguments, do not need any appeals to 'human nature'. Procedural commitment to democratic openness supplies the necessary norm. Even under conditions of unconstrained discourse there would be a need for contestation of truth-claims.

In conclusion, understanding Derrida and post-structuralism helps our comprehension of Post-Marxism. Post-Marxism's many flaws derive not from its abandonment of Marxism but from its failure fully to develop the nuances of Derrida's subtle arguments and from its inability to make a full break with the closure it so correctly diagnoses in one strand of Marxist theory. The core assumptions of 'orthodoxy' have been challenged; the debate is serious; and the possibilities of Post-Marxism have yet to be realized in the substantive work and multi-dimensional struggles ahead.

Notes

1. The key texts in this debate are: E. Laclau and C. Mouffe, *Hegemony and Socialist Strategy: Towards A Radical Democratic Politics* (London, Verso, 1985); P. Anderson, *In the Tracks of Historical Materialism* (London, Verso, 1983); E. Meiksins Wood, *The Retreat From Class* (London, Verso, 1986); N. Geras, 'Post-Marxism', *New Left Review*, no. 163 (May–June 1987), pp. 40–82; E. Laclau and C. Mouffe, 'Post-Marxism without Apologies', *New Left Review*, no. 166 (November–December 1987), pp. 79–106; N. Mouzelis, 'Marxism or Post-Marxism', *New Left Review*, no. 167 (January–February 1988), pp. 107–23 and N. Geras, 'Ex Marxism without Substance: Being A Real Reply to Laclau and Mouffe', *New Left Review*, no. 169 (May–June 1988), pp. 34–62.
2. For an outstanding examination of the genealogy of post-structuralism from an orthodox stance, see P. Dews, *Logics of Disintegration* (London, Verso, 1987).
3. For the best general discussion of Derrida's work, see J. Culler, *On Deconstruction* (London, Routledge and Kegan Paul, 1983). See also C. Norris, *Deconstruction and Deconstructionism* (London, Methuen, 1982). For an excellent summary of the differences between Foucault and Derrida, see E. Said, 'The Problem of Textuality', *Critical Inquiry*, vol. 4 (1978), pp. 673–714. For the only full attempt to articulate Marx and Derrida, see M. Ryan, *Marxism and*

Deconstruction: A Critical Articulation (Baltimore, MD, and London, Johns Hopkins University Press, 1982), esp. pp. 9–42.

4. Laclau and Mouffe, *Hegemony*, pp. 178–9.
5. For one typical orthodox response, see Meiksins Wood, *The Retreat From Class*, pp. 188–9.
6. Ibid., pp. 78ff.; and Anderson, *Tracks*, pp. 51–4.
7. Geras, 'Ex Marxism', pp. 50–2.
8. For the original exorbitization argument see Anderson, *Tracks*, pp. 51–4. For the agent-institutional dichotomy, see Mouzelis, 'Marxism or Post-Marxism', pp. 113–14, 119–20.
9. Geras, 'Post-Marxism', pp. 58-62; idem, 'Ex Marxism', pp. 43–50. I cannot examine the details of this debate. Suffice to observe that it exemplifies the Derridean possibility of 'misreading' and the endless supplementarity texts give rise to.
10. F. de Saussure, *A Course in General Linguistics* (London, Peter Owen, 1960), p. 120.
11. J. Derrida, 'Structure, Sign and Play in the Discourse of the Human Sciences' in idem, *Writing and Difference* (London, Routledge and Kegan Paul, 1978), pp. 278–94.
12. J. Bronovski, cited in Ryan, *Marxism and Deconstruction*, pp. 17–18.
13. Ryan, *Marxism and Deconstruction*, p. 16.
14. Derrida, *Writing and Difference*, p. 279.
15. Ibid., p. 282.
16. Ibid., pp. 279–80.
17. For a typical attack, see Anderson, *Tracks*, p. 42. For Derrida's original statements see J. Derrida, *Of Grammatology* (London and Baltimore, MD, Johns Hopkins University Press, 1976), p. 158; idem, *Positions* (London, Athlone Press, 1981), p. 32.
18. Derrida, *Positions*, p. 91.
19. W.V. Quine, 'Two Dogmas of Empiricism', reprinted in Morick, H., ed., *Challenges to Empiricism* (London, Methuen, 1980), p. 50.
20. Quine, 'Two Dogmas', cited in Laclau and Mouffe, 'Post-Marxism', p. 90.
21. P. Feyerabend, in Morick, *Challenges*, p. 178.
22. R. Bhaskar, *The Possibility of Naturalism* (Brighton, Harvester, 1979), p. 25.
23. Laclau, and Mouffe, 'Post-Marxism', pp. 89–90. For a similar case, see also the general argument, ibid., pp. 86–92, and Ryan, *Marxism and Deconstruction*.
24. Culler, On *Deconstruction*, p. 22.
25. Derrida, *Of Grammatology*, p. 35.
26. Ibid., p. 68.
27. Ibid., pp. 164–7.
28. Ryan, *Marxism and Deconstruction*, p. 22.
29. For the texts of this encounter see Derrida, *Of Grammatology*, pp. 27–73; idem, 'Freud and the Scene of Writing' in idem, *Writing and Difference*, pp. 196–230. For an excellent discussion of these issues and an overview of Derrida, see A. Megill, *Prophets of Extremity* (London, University of California Press, 1985) pp. 257–338.
30. Context is often designated by Derrida as 'frame', a usage derived from a passage in Kant's *Critique of Judgement* in which Kant discusses the difference between paintings (*ergon*) or works and their surrounds (*parergon*). For Kant all meaning derives from a work, the frame being an incidental surrounding, frame or 'margin'. For Derrida, such marginality is a sign of the usual hierarchy. Contexts as frames affect meaning, hence the usage. See J. Derrida, 'The Parergon', *October*, vol. 9 (1979), pp. 3–40. For the fullest treatment see idem, *The Truth in*

Painting (Chicago, University of Chicago Press, 1987), pp. 1–14.

31. The basic texts in this confrontation are J. Austin, *How To Do Things With Words* (Oxford, Oxford University Press, 1975); J. Searle, 'Reiterating the Differences: A Reply to Derrida', *Glyph*, no. 1 (1977), pp. 198–208; J. Derrida, 'Signature, Event, Context', *Glyph*, no. 1 (1977) pp. 172–97; and idem, 'Limited Inc.', *Glyph*, no. 2 (1977), pp. 162–254.
32. Searle, 'Reiterating the Differences', p. 202.
33. Derrida, 'Limited Inc.', p. 195.
34. For extensive examples of how this process occurs, see Culler, *Deconstruction*, pp. 125–7.
35. See Derrida, *Of Grammatology*, p. 158; B. Johnson, 'Introduction' in J. Derrida, *Dissemination* (London, Athlone Press, 1981), esp. p. xv.
36. For an outstanding example of how even philosophical discussion of metaphor cannot itself escape using metaphors, see J. Derrida, 'The Retrait of Metaphor', *Enclitic*, vol. 2, no. 2 (1978), pp. 5–34.
37. Johnson, 'Introduction', p. xv.
38. R. Barthes, *Image, Music, Text* (London, Fontana, 1977), p. 146.
39. Derrida, 'Limited Inc.', p. 185.
40. J. Derrida, cited in Culler, *Deconstruction*, p. 156.
41. To follow Eagleton's path to such recognition see T. Eagleton, *Walter Benjamin* (London, Verso, 1981), p. 144 ff.; idem, *The Rape of Clarissa* (Oxford, Oxford University Press, 1982). This citation comes from idem, *Literary Theory: An Introduction* (Oxford, Oxford University Press, 1983), p. 148.
42. Eagleton, *Walter Benjamin*, p. 142.
43. Derrida, *Positions*, p. 41.
44. These are drawn from J. Derrida, *Éperons/Spurs* (Chicago, Chicago University Press, 1979).
45. Homi K. Bhabha raises this issue succinctly when he writes: 'Can such split subjects and differentiated social movements, which display ambivalent and divided forms of identification, be represented in a collective will?...How do we construct a politics ... [requiring] ... repeated passages across the differential boundaries between one symbolic bloc and another, and the positions available to each?' H.K. Bhabha, 'The Commitment to Theory', *Social Formations*, vol. 5 (1988), pp. 14–15.
46. P. Anderson, 'The Affinities of Norberto Bobbio', *New Left Review*, no. 170 (1988), p. 30.
47. Laclau and Mouffe, *Hegemony*, pp. 2–5, 178–9.
48. For example, M. Jay, *Adorno* (London, Fontana, 1984); Dews, *Logics of Disintegration*, pp. 220–42.
49. Geras, 'Post-Marxism', pp. 44–5.
50. Laclau and Mouffe, *Hegemony*, p. 51.
51. Ibid., p. 58.
52. Mouzelis, 'Marxism or Post-Marxism', p. 114.
53. E. Said, *Orientalism* (London, Penguin, 1985).
54. Meiksins Wood, *The Retreat From Class*, p. 78.
55. Anderson, *Tracks*, pp. 51–4.
56. For details I cannot deal with here, see Laclau and Mouffe, *Hegemony*, pp. 112–14, 122–30.
57. For a brilliant analysis of such processes see E. Stallybrass and A. White, *The Politics and Poetics of Transgression* (London, Methuen, 1986).
58. Laclau, and Mouffe, *Hegemony*, p. 97 (emphasis added).
59. Ibid., p. 155.
60. Ibid., p. 139.

61. For a clear statement of his position see M. Foucault, *Power/Knowledge* (Brighton, Harvester, 1980), p. 131.
62. Geras, 'Ex-Marxism', p. 51.
63. Cited in Dews, *Logics of Disintegration*, p. 229.

6
Marx's Politics – The Tensions in the *Communist Manifesto* [1]

John Cunliffe

> The bourgeois revolution in Germany will be but the prelude to an immediately following proletarian one.[2]

In this paper I assess the recent controversy over the claimed inconsistency between the general theory presented in Part I of the *Communist Manifesto* and the strategy for Germany advanced in Part IV of that work. The main justification for such an assessment is that this claimed inconsistency raises 'crucial questions concerning not just the coherence of the *Communist Manifesto* itself but also of Marxist theory as a whole'.[3] In the controversy, three positions have been presented:

(a) that there is an inconsistency, because the general theory restricts the possibility of a successful proletarian revolution to advanced capitalist countries, whereas the strategy for Germany allows for such a revolution in a backward country;

(b) that there is no inconsistency, because the particular strategy did not actually call for an *immediate* proletarian revolution in backward Germany, despite appearances to the contrary;

(c) that there is no inconsistency, because the general theory is sufficiently flexible to accommodate the particular strategy even at face value.[4]

My concern will be to defend an interpretation of the general theory which is more flexible than position (a), in that it can accommodate the possibility of an immediate proletarian revolution even in backward Germany; contrasts with position (b), in that accommodation is not based on a presumed contrast between the ostensible and the actual strategy; but is against position (c), in that this flexibility cannot accommodate the possibility of that revolution being an isolated event confined to Germany alone. The key to this interpretation lies in Marx's consistent emphasis on the international dimension of capitalism, involving a complex interaction between countries at different stages of economic and political development. In other words, this interpretation rests on the theory of combined and uneven development, which has been aptly described as one of those 'Marxist notions whose suggestiveness is equalled only by their elusiveness'.[5]

The inconsistency identified in position (a) is derived from an 'economic determinist' account of the general theory, in which the overall requirement that communism is a condition of material abundance, which only mature industrial capitalism can provide, is held to entail the specific requirement that communism could be introduced only in a country where there is mature industrial capitalism. That account, however, is completely at odds with the very first formulation of the general theory, in *The German Ideology*. Here, the overall requirement is presented and indeed emphasized, but the specific 'entailment' is rejected – and, moreover, the explicit reference is to Germany itself.

> To lead to collisions in a country, this contradiction (between productive forces and forms of intercourse) need not necessarily come to a head in this particular country. The competition with industrially more advanced countries, brought about by the expansion of international intercourse, is sufficient to produce a similar contradiction in countries with a backward industry, e.g., the latent proletariat in Germany brought into view by the competition of English industry.[6]

Communism, then, is considered a prospect in backward Germany because that country had already become part of an interconnected international economic system. By the same token, however, this interconnection ruled out the realization of that prospect in Germany alone, or for that matter within any other single country in isolation from others. There could be no 'local communism'. On the contrary, communism could be introduced only 'as the act of the dominant peoples all at once and simultaneously' precisely because capitalism had rendered each nation dependent on the revolutions of the others.[7] All this seems quite clear: communism was a condition of abundance; it could nevertheless be realized in backward Germany, but not in Germany alone.

In itself, of course, this demonstrates nothing with respect to the *Manifesto*, which is the next statement of the general theory and the central concern of this paper. All the same, it would be surprising if there had been any radical alteration in the theory, even allowing for the tentative nature of Marx's views at the time. On the other hand, the estimate of Germany's prospects might well have changed, a change reflecting not any modification in the theory, but an assessment of developments within that country in the period between 1845 and 1847.

Part I of the *Manifesto* presents an analysis of the general tendencies of capitalism as an international economic system over a historical epoch, with few explicit references to specific countries or definite time-scales. Hence, the vital issue arises as to how these general statements are to be applied to particular settings in time and place. A familiar interpretation, and indeed one which is often taken to represent *the* view advanced in that work, is some version of position (a), presented above. Each individual country must directly experience the full development of mature industrial capitalism before becoming eligible for the introduction of communism construed as material abundance. This suggests a 'normal' course of economic and political development, based on some combination of the experiences of the more advanced capitalist countries. In their turn, less advanced ones are fated to rehearse this experience step by step (or stage by stage). If Germany is admitted as an exception to this rule, its anomalous status can only be some form of special pleading. The rule remains intact.[8]

In this form, however, any such view can be sustained only at the expense of ignoring another most significant theme in the *Manifesto*, namely that of 'combined and uneven development'. As Part I of the *Manifesto* indicates, at any given time capitalism as an international system will embrace countries at different stages of economic (and political) development, with some form of interconnection between them:

> The bourgeoisie has through its exploitation of the world market given a cosmopolitan character to production and consumption in every country. To the great chagrin of Reactionists, it has drawn from under the feet of industry the national ground on which it stands.... In place of the old local and national seclusion and self-sufficiency, we have intercourse in every direction, universal interdependence of nations...[9]

In turn, this interconnection leads to the related emphasis on the need for some type of international action to realize communism, a realization conditional on the 'united action of the leading civilised countries at least'.[10]

These related emphases can be variously construed, according to the form of interconnection envisaged between a set of capitalist economies at various stages of development. Some of these construals confirm, and indeed reinforce the 'determinist' account, whereas others deny it. Running from the strongest to the weakest, these construals might be:

(i)   that a necessary and sufficient condition for a successful proletarian revolution is the presence of mature industrial capitalism in all of those interconnected countries, and the sufficient condition that this revolution is simultaneous and successful in all of them;

(ii) that a necessary condition for a successful proletarian revolution in any one of those countries is the presence of mature industrial capitalism in that country, and the sufficient condition that there is a simultaneous and successful revolution in all other such countries;

(iii) that a necessary condition for a successful proletarian revolution in any one of those countries is the presence of mature industrial capitalism in that country;

(iv) that the sufficient condition for a successful proletarian revolution in a country in which industrial capitalism is immature is a simultaneous and successful one in all countries in which industrial capitalism is mature; and

(v) that a successful proletarian revolution can occur in a country in which industrial capitalism is immature, without any simultaneous and successful revolution occurring in countries in which industrial capitalism is mature.[11]

Of these construals, (iii) represents the unrefined 'determinist' account outlined previously, an account which ignores rather than accommodates the theme of 'combined and uneven development'. On this view, 'uneven' development merely implies that as each country matures industrially so it will become eligible for communism, with different countries reaching the required level at differing times. This process, moreover, is considered peculiar to each country, with no allowance being made for the effects of 'combined' development. If construal (iii) in isolation seems implausible, perhaps it could be retained as one element in a formulation which specifies an additional requirement in order to accommodate the relevant theme. The alternatives here are construals (i) and (ii). Of them (i) is too stringent because the degree of interdependence assumed is so great that it cannot incorporate any unevenness in development; all must wait until all are ready, with any revolution being more or less indefinitely postponed. In contrast, (ii) is more plausible, so plausible that it must be incorporated in any subsequent formulation. Here, the degree of interdependence between advanced capitalist countries is considered such that a successful revolution could occur only simultaneously in all of them. The problem with (ii), nevertheless, is that it denies the interconnection of the advanced and non-advanced capitalist countries. Only the former are thought jointly eligible for communism and it is immaterial for the latter whether it is introduced or not. In any case, they, too, would still have to endure the full development of capitalism before becoming eligible in their turn. This is difficult to reconcile either with the repeated assertion of interdependence between all capitalist countries or with the frequent stress on the dependence of non-advanced on advanced ones. What is needed is a formulation which can accommodate these points while retaining the emphasis in (ii).

In relation to construal (iv) we must distinguish between two versions; it is after all one thing to assert that non-advanced capitalist countries might be decisively influenced by a successful revolution in advanced ones, and quite another to argue that they might take the lead in establishing communism by acting as a catalyst for its introduction in those countries. The first version asserts that with respect to countries in which capitalism is mature the conditions stipulated in construal (ii) hold, but these conditions are now restricted to those countries. The position of less advanced ones is interpreted in a markedly different manner; and it is so because their dependence on advanced countries is now taken to be very close. Consequently, any successful revolution in advanced countries could have a decisive impact on less advanced ones, so decisive that they could avoid (at least in some respects) merely rehearsing the experience of those countries. The second version, in contrast, allows not just a revolutionary response in a backward country (or countries) but a revolutionary initiative issuing from it. The argument here is that some type of anti-capitalist revolution might well occur in a country in which that economic system is weak and immature. In isolation, however, such a revolution could not achieve communism in the relevant sense, and a necessary condition of its success would be a simultaneous and successful revolution in advanced capitalist countries.

There remains the most implausible construal (v), which quite simply ignores the emphasis on both communism as a condition of abundance and on capitalism as an international system leading to national interdependence.

It is difficult to choose between all of these construals exegetically, if only because neither Marx nor Engels consistently subscribed to any single one of them.[12] At the time of the *Manifesto* they were mainly concerned with revolutionary prospects in three Western European countries, whose interconnected capitalist economies were taken to be at the following (very approximate) levels of development: Britain advanced; France less advanced; and Germany backward. The strategy for Germany, understood as calling for an *immediate* proletarian revolution in an admittedly backward country, cannot be reconciled with construals (i), (ii) or (iii), which all restrict the introduction of communism to an advanced country or countries; both versions of construal (iv) allow an immediate proletarian revolution in Germany, but not in Germany alone; and construal (v) allows precisely that possibility.

Unfortunately, perhaps, in the *Manifesto* there just is no clear and unambiguous statement equivalent to construal (iv), in which the general theory allows for a proletarian revolution in a backward capitalist country, provided that it takes place in the setting of a wider revolution embracing advanced countries as well. Neither, for that matter, is the particular strategy for Germany explicitly related to any general strategy, with revolutionary prospects there being related to those in Britain and/or France. There is merely a laconic statement to the effect that the impending bourgeois revolution in Germany would occur in the setting of European capitalism at the time, and nothing at all is said about the prospect of a proletarian revolution in either of the more advanced capitalist countries of the day.[13] When taken as a whole, nevertheless, the *Manifesto* does seem to imply if not state construal (iv) rather than construal (v), and arguably that version of (iv) in which a revolution in a backward country could succeed only by acting as a precursor of successful revolutions in advanced ones.

Moreover, if construal (iv) is the view advanced in the *Manifesto*, it seems quite consistent with the general theory (and if construal (v) were the view advanced I would concede happily and readily that it is inconsistent with that theory). Indeed, all of the other construals fail to reconcile some of the apparently conflicting requirements imposed by, first, the strategy for Germany;

second, the emphasis on communism as a condition of abundance; and third, the stress on the 'combined and uneven' development of capitalism. The familiar and unrefined 'determinist' account, construal (iii), attaches such overriding significance to the second requirement that both the first and the third are discounted. Similarly, construal (v) can meet only the first requirement, to the exclusion of the other two. The more refined 'determinist' views, construals (i) and (ii), fare better in that they reconcile the second and third requirements, but at the expense of the first. Only the still more refined 'determinist' view, construal (iv), satisfies all three requirements.

This, I hope, is not to rescue consistency by denying 'the actuality of ambiguity and contradiction', a denial which has been properly condemned.[14]

Notes

1. This is a revised version of an article which appeared originally in *Political Studies*, vol. 30, no. 4 (1982), pp. 569–74.
2. From K. Marx, and F. Engels, *Manifesto of the Communist Party*, Part IV, in idem, 6 *CW*, p. 519.
3. M. Levin, 'Deutschmarx: Marx, Engels, and the German Question', *Political Studies*, vol. 29, no. 4 (1981), p. 537.
4. Position (a) is presented in ibid., pp. 537–54; (b) is presented in R. Hunt, *The Political Ideas of Marx and Engels*, vol. I (London, Macmillan, 1975), esp. pp. 185–91; and (c) is presented in A. Gilbert, *Marx's Politics* (New Brunswick, NJ, Rutgers University Press, 1981), esp. pp. 5–13 and pp. 256–71.
5. J. Elster, 'The Theory of Combined and Uneven Development: A Critique' in J. Roemer, *Analytical Marxism* (Cambridge, Cambridge University Press, 1986), p. 56.
6. Marx and Engels, 5 *CW*, p. 74–5.
7. Ibid., p. 49.
8. Some of the problems here are indicated in M. Evans, *Karl Marx* (London, George Allen & Unwin, 1975), pp. 166–8.
9. K. Marx, and F. Engels, 6 *CW*, p. 488.
10. Ibid., p. 503.
11. Some of the construals are presented in S. Moore, 'A Consistency Proof for Historical Materialism' in M. Cohen, T. Nagel and T. Scanlon, *Marx, Justice and History* (Princeton, NJ, Princeton University Press, 1980), pp. 256–67.
12. This is shown conclusively in H. Draper, *Karl Marx's Theory of Revolution*, vol. 2 (New York, Monthly Review Press, 1978), pp. 169–200.
13. Marx and Engels, 6 *CW*, p. 519.
14. Levin, 'Deutschmarx: Marx, Engels, and the German Question', p. 553.

7
The *Grundrisse*, the Individual and Freedom

Paul Smart

Introduction

It is the *Grundrisse*[1] which, more than any other single work by Marx, reveals the breadth of his analysis of capitalist political economy, elaborating the economic scope of the critique already evident in a nascent form in writings such as the opening chapters of *The German Ideology* and the *Economic and Philosophic Manuscripts*, while at the same time developing the theory of alienation as an expression of the antagonistic relation between labour and capital, thus predating and informing the examination of this crucial relation in *Capital*. In other words the *Grundrisse* is pivotal for anyone interested in both the antecedents to his 'mature' materialist interpretation of history, the essential continuity of his thought, and, perhaps most importantly, the importance his critical observations have for revolutionary action understood as self-determination by social individuals. It is this last aspect which will be the focus of attention of my discussion. As a negative corollary of the positive pivotal status of this key text, the *Grundrisse* also serves to expose the insupportable nature of the claims made by those who wish to promote the idea that there is a radical disjuncture between the young/early Marx and the mature/late Marx; it also challenges those who would have us believe that Marx solved the riddle of the sands by discovering invariable laws of history which, given time, would bring about of their own accord the eventual demise of capitalism and herald the new order. This is not to say that the 'authentic' Marx continued to be the Hegelian humanist of the early works, or that his thought developed without interruption along the lines mapped out at the beginning of his intellectual career, but that the textual evidence alone shows that Marx was consciously and constantly modifying and reworking his analysis to perform new tasks in the face of new problems. It is also worth noting at this point that the contemporary functionalist approach (especially that of Cohen[2]) to Marx, which I believe adheres to a version of the 'disjuncture' thesis, makes reference to the *Grundrisse* only as a methodological adjunct to the seminal *Capital* and a preparatory exercise for the definitive 1859 *Preface*.[3] In other words, it contains, in a nascent form, the functional determinism of the later works. In fact it can be maintained that the latter should be regarded only as parts of the general project outlined in the former, and further, that *Capital* and the *Preface* can be more fully understood only if we have a working knowledge of the method employed by Marx in the *Grundrisse*. It was a method which he believed exposed the contradictory nature of capitalist concepts and categories; revealed the antagonistic character of capitalist social relations, based as they are on the appropriation of surplus value; and which convinced him that only the labouring classes through revolutionary activity could achieve their own liberation, and that the impersonal laws of history only define *general* tendencies and not *inevitable* consequences.

This is not to devalue the contribution of *Capital*, rather to suggest that it should not be regarded as the definitive Marxian statement on all aspects of bourgeois relations of production and their historical contingency. Reading *Grundrisse*, on the other hand, offers tantalizing insights into areas of Marx's critique undeveloped or entirely absent from other examples of his later work, but which are still situated in the same methodological framework. One such insight is his analysis of individual freedom in the context of bourgeois, 'formal' individuality, and the consequent exposure of this freedom and individuality as the formally proclaimed but concretely unsubstantiated content of capitalist social relations, which are themselves the presupposition for revolutionary human emancipation.

However, on first inspection the *Grundrisse* may appear simply to repeat Marx's previous observations on alienation and to restate the methodological and ontological presuppositions of earlier works (especially if we rely upon the extracts supplied by those who wish to promote the cause of the uninterrupted continuity thesis, e.g. Kamenka, Avineri, McLellan, and so on[4]). For example, with regard to the apparent ontological primacy of individuals, there appears to be little difference between such comments as 'Individuals producing in society – hence socially determined individual production – is, of course, the point of departure',[5] and 'As individuals express their life, so they are. What they are, therefore, coincides with their production, both with *what* they produce and *how* they produce'.[6]

The same goes for the incidence of similar passages concerning alienation. But it is in the notebooks of 1857–8 that, for the first time, Marx combined a materialist dialectic with a systematic critique of political economy. Essentially, Marx's exposition of alienation (along with its revolutionary consequences) was to be fully integrated within a detailed examination of the forces and relations of the bourgeois mode of production. This enabled him to identify what he now believed to be both the positive and negative aspects of the contradiction within capital; the contradiction between constantly developing forces of production and the relations of production. For example, this revealed not only the nature of capitalism's negation of past economic formations and social relations, but also its positive tendency to posit the presuppositions for communal production. But this was no 'invisible hand' at work here, this was not the workings out of 'world spirit', or the necessary precondition for the eventual triumph of the *idea* of freedom. For Marx these processes were the result of living labour expended by past and present generations, creating and recreating the conditions of class antagonism in pre-revolutionary society, an antagonism which would accompany and assist the eventual demise of capitalism.

It is also in the *Grundrisse* that Marx evaluates the revolutionary implications of capitalism's constant restructuring of the forces of production in its perpetual pursuit of extracting greater surplus value. In particular it is the increase in the productivity of living labour, that is, surplus labour time (and the related decrease in necessary labour time) under capital, that as free time in post-revolutionary society will be a major precondition for the liberation of individuals, enabling them to pursue their own consciously determined ends. However, under the guise of capitalism the increasing productivity of labour serves only to heighten the level of exploitation and the intensity of estrangement experienced by individual workers. The very conditions which are a product of expended labour power, come to oppose the wage labourer as determinants which appropriate labour one-sidedly, so that products are produced not by conscious objectification nor for collective consumption, but for the realization of their exchange value as commodities for the benefit of the capitalist. Therefore, the forces of production, the materials transformed by these forces, the product which is the result of this process of transformation, and the labour power consumed by commodity production, are all estranged from the individual worker employed by capital. Indeed, within capitalism, knowledge, in the form of science and art incorporated within the forces of production, is perceived by the worker not as a conscious product of collective individuality, but as the property of those forces of production which immediately confront the worker as constant capital in the form of machinery.

So, by incorporating the newly discerned factor of the tendency for the productivity of labour to increase, Marx not only exposes the reason for capitalism's drive for concentration and centralization – the pursuit of maximizing the amount of surplus labour time extracted from living labour – but also posits the autonomy of the value of free time, that is, 'releases labour time from its function as the primary condition of wealth, and creates the material conditions for the formation of mass individualities'.[7] The examination of this new factor in the *Grundrisse* was to underpin Marx's analysis of bourgeois economics in *Capital*:

He [the capitalist as 'capital personified'] is fanatically bent on the valorisation of value; consequently he ruthlessly forces the human race to produce for production's sake. In this way he spurs on the development of society's productive forces, and the creation of those material conditions of production which alone can form the real basis of a higher form of society, a society in which the full and free development of every individual forms the ruling principle.[8]

In the following an attempt will be made to follow through some of the introductory observations made above, especially those concerned with Marx's critique of 'bourgeois' notions of freedom and his discussion of individual self-determination that emerges from that critique. This will be done with the understanding that Marx's application of Hegel's dialectic extends to its employment as a technique enabling him to highlight both the positive and negative aspects of contradictions underlying the form of production based on capital; not merely exposing the conflictual nature of prevailing material conditions of production, but also revealing the disjuncture between the form and the content of legitimatory codes of justice and moral principles coexistent with bourgeois social relations. It was therefore the rational core of Hegel's method which was of interest to Marx[9] and not its mystical or metaphysical shell with its accompanying teleological necessity.[10] It was this objective, materially based and demystified application of the method which would lay bare the dynamic laws of bourgeois economy, thus revealing not its universality, but its contingency. Therefore, Marx believed that this would show how contemporary conditions of production are 'engaged in *suspending themselves* and [by the same token were] positing the *historic presuppositions* for a new state of society',[11] giving signs both of its past and what may supersede it, 'foreshadowings of the future'.[12] For Marx it would hopefully be a future of 'universally developed individuals, whose social relations, as their own communal relations, are hence also subordinated to their own communal control'.[13] This was no Utopian vision, the evidence of such a future lay within existing social relations which, after all, were the product of past and present generations. It would be the responsibility of future generations to transform the potentiality into reality.

In order to construct a picture of what a self-determining social individual might look like, I shall turn first to Marx's critical analysis of the relationship between 'isolated' individuals in bourgeois social and economic relations, focusing particularly on the categories of circulation and money. This will be done with the understanding that such relations are a transitory manifestation of the historical development of the social individual, and that they reveal the possibility of an emancipated existence. So, once the historical nature of relations of production based on capital, and the contingency of the whole network of laws and norms which are supportive of them, had been ascertained, Marx believed that the universality claimed by prevailing theories about the individual, either as a rights-bearing moral agent or as a want-maximizing, self-interested rational actor, could be effectively debunked. This leads on to the second part of my discussion which is an elaboration of what I understand to be Marx's tentative and unsystematic appraisal of the post-capitalist society of emancipated social individuals. I believe that Marx meant it to be an equivocal description and that he believed he had a good reason for its being so; to expect anything more substantial is to misjudge the task he set himself and to underestimate the ability of social individuals consciously to change themselves. I therefore subscribe to the view that there is no teleology in Marx's system, nor is there an a priori construction of a 'communist society', because neither is possible or desirable in an analysis which is committed to the view that it is only free, self-determining individuals in social relations who can transform their own society.

The Individual, Circulation and Money

For Marx one of the starkest examples of alienation in capitalist production lay in the process of circulation. This process had not only become a social power viewed by individuals as either a natural or a spontaneous relation, but also had been provided with sets of accompanying laws some of which claimed universality for the process itself, while others sought to enforce its consequences through juridical codes and legal 'rights'. Marx wished to expose the relations of circulation for what they really were: a moment of the contingent exploitative expropriation of surplus value by capital.

Circulation in capitalism, Marx insists in the *Grundrisse*, is exchange, that is, the mediation of products from particular forms of production in general exchange in the form of exchange value (money). In this way products become commodities produced to realize exchange value. Such a form of circulation has as its fundamental condition a form of production which appropriates the products of labour 'through and by means of divestiture and alienation' for another.[14] Marx goes on to say that

> circulation as the realization of exchange value implies: (1) that my product is a product only in so far as it is for others, hence suspended singularity, generality; (2) that it is a product for me only in so far as it has been alienated, become for others; (3) that it is for the other only so far as he himself alienated his product, which already implies (4) that production is not an end in itself for me, but a means.[15]

Under capital such a set of relations constitutes an alien social power which appears to the individuals participating in production as an objective, spontaneously arising interrelation, *not* as a transitory facet of a system of production based on the exchange of exchange values which itself is a historical 'moment' of production in general. But this is the very system which, as Marx points out, is the one which 'bourgeois economists' uphold as the basis for individual freedom, who see the

> collision of unfettered individuals who are determined only by their own interests – as the mutual repulsion and attraction of free individuals, and hence as the absolute mode of existence of free individuality in the sphere of consumption and exchange.[16]

Meanwhile bourgeois politicians and lawyers construct constitutional and juridical systems which uphold this 'freedom', viewing it as an expression of universal laws of human nature and human society. Nothing, for Marx could be so absurd and mistaken. Capital may well have established itself as the dominant mode of production, having successfully overcome the barriers of earlier systems of production, but it was incapable of suspending all limits to its complete triumph, or of freeing the majority of individuals, because of the eventually insurmountable barriers which were the product of its own contradictory nature. So, in its 'negation of the guild system etc.',[17] capital did not set free individuals but only itself through free competition; indeed, Marx says of competition that it is 'nothing more than the way in which the many capitals force the inherent determinants of capital (i.e. the constant pursuit of increased surplus value) upon one another and upon themselves',[18] thereby reproducing forms of production which expropriate labour in the shape of commodities embodying exchange value; as the predominance of capital is the presupposition of free competition, so is the free competition between capitals the denial of the free development of individuality. For Marx then, the freedom claimed for the individual in a society of free competition is

therefore at the same time the most complete suspension of all individual freedom, and the most complete subjugation of individuality under social conditions which assume the form of objective powers, even of overpowering objects – of things independent of the relations of individuals themselves.[19]

According to Marx the process of circulation in capital expressed as the 'free' and 'equal' exchange of equivalents is, therefore, merely the formal epiphenomenon of the form of production founded in the creation of exchange value, which relies upon the exploitative relation of 'exchange of *objectified labour* as exchange value for living labour as use value'.[20] Marx views this as essential to an understanding of the alienation of labour within relations of production based on capital, in which labour relates to its objective conditions, which, after all, are a creation of labour itself, as alien property. Such a form of exchange has as its presupposition the

separation of labour from its original intertwinement with its objective conditions, which is why it appears as mere labour on one side, while on the other side its product, as objectified labour, has an entirely independent existence as value opposite it.[21]

The labour of the individual is therefore posited not as an end in itself, or recognized as an expression of creative human consciousness, but in capital is total alienation, sacrificing the human end-in-itself to an entirely external end.[22] Under such conditions objectification becomes the process of dispossession, erecting an objective power opposite labour which does not belong to the worker but to the 'personified conditions of production, i.e. to capital'.[23] For Marx the labour performed by individuals in social relations is that uniquely human capacity which should be the basis for conscious, creative self-determination, that is to say, freedom. However, under capital, the alienated labourer perceives such productive activity in purely instrumental terms, surrendering living labour to capital in exchange for 'objectified labour'[24] in the form of exchange value in its purest form, money. This relationship is part of the elementary precondition of bourgeois society: 'that labour should directly produce exchange value, i.e. money; and, similarly, that money should directly purchase labour, and therefore the labourer'.[25]

In Marx's view, money, as the purest form of exchange value, is the clearest embodiment of the contradiction of that social mode of production corresponding to it, capital. That is, it is both a fact and a relation – a fact as the mode of exchange *par excellence*, and a relation as an expression of exploitation. And yet, as Marx points out, for the bourgeois, money is the epitome of equality, it appears to transcend inequality, particularly in the market where each individual is engaged, apparently on an equal footing, in the exchange of exchange values:

> it is in the character of the money relation ... that all inherent contradictions
> of bourgeois society appear extinguished ... and bourgeois democracy even
> more than the bourgeois economists takes refuge in this aspect ... in order
> to construct apologetics for the existing economic relations.[26]

This arrangement is only reinforced by those laws which guarantee the fulfilment of contracts based on the exchange of equivalents made by 'equal' and 'free' parties.

Marx's analysis of money in capitalist relations of production therefore provides him with a further opportunity to expose the merely *formal* freedom and equality of individuals expounded by those who posit capitalism as the absolute form of production. Individuals are merely conceived of as exchangers of exchange value in the form of both commodities and labour. Labour power itself becomes a commodity possessing exchange value for both the worker as the 'owner' of living labour capacity, and for the owner of capital in the form of potential surplus value. Once in possession of the 'mediator' of exchange values, money, the individual regards others in the market as mere exchangers of exchange value. Such a relationship becomes, under capital, a formalized social relation: 'i.e. each has the same social relation towards the other that the other has towards him. As subjects of exchange, their relation is therefore that of *equality*'.[27] But this formal equality coexists with a concrete inequality between the possessors of labour power and the owners of the means of production, which, after all, is the necessary presupposition of relations of production founded on capital. The *formal* freedom of capitalist circulation and the *formal* equality of the exchange value, Marx reminds us, are both historically conditioned by capitalist relations of production. Under such a situation the individual is dependent on a social relation (of capital) which reduces individual activity, individual acts of production, to exchange values. The social bond between individuals is expressed in exchange value, that is, the individual's own activity has a meaning only in so far as it realizes exchange value. The product as a product of objectification is viewed merely as the instrument for engaging in exchange – an attitude further enforced through the development of the division of labour. Each individual's 'private' end is, in such conditions, the production of a general product (exchange value). Each, therefore, possesses in the form of exchange values (money) the 'power' over the activity of others as expressed in the production of exchange value embodied in commodities. In such circumstances

> activity, regardless of its individual manifestation, and the product of activity, regardless of its particular make-up, are always *exchange value*, and exchange value is a generality, in which all individuality and peculiarity are negated and extinguished.[28]

Such a situation will prevail as long as the presupposition of the predominant mode of production remains the creation of surplus value via the appropriation of labour by the owners of capital. Under these conditions the individual is alienated from both the social character of production and the social form of the product. The relationship between individuals under capital is one of 'indifference' even though the form of production in which they participate is one of social reciprocity and mutual interconnection which exist to a degree hitherto unknown. And yet, 'in exchange value, the social connection between persons is transformed into a social relation between things'.[29] It is only when these relations are understood in terms of the antagonistic contradiction on which they are based, that the absence of genuine freedom and equality becomes all too apparent.

Marx perceived bourgeois production as the era of personal independence which is founded on objective dependence. It is the era where for the first time 'a system of general social metabolism, of universal relations, of all-round needs and universal capacities is formed', but in which there is the total isolation of individual private interests from those of others.[30] This contradiction will remain as long as the prevailing conditions of capitalist production are perceived by the majority as natural, spontaneous and absolute and the accompanying legal and political structures are viewed as legitimate. However, if we understand these relations as an expression of exploitation based on the one-sided expropriation of surplus value by and for capital, and understand that this condition is itself a contradictory one resting on the antagonistic division between capital and labour, Marx believes that we can identify these relations as the presupposition for a classless society; production based on exchange value is the prior condition of a society of universally developed individuals. Or as Marx himself puts it in his characteristically blunt manner: 'universal prostitution appears as a necessary phase in the development of the social character of personal talents, capacities, abilities, activities'.[31] Capital, in pursuing surplus value, continues to develop and revolutionize the means of production in ways which it hopes will more effectively extract surplus labour. However, the potential of such developments will never be fully realized within capitalist relations of production because, by their very nature, they are concerned not with the satisfaction of the multifarious needs of social individuals, but with the realizing of profits for the owners of the means of production. These bourgeois relations, based as they are on private property and the exchange of exchange values, deny the mass of individuals conscious control over those forces of production which are the estranged product of their collective consciousness. Indeed the conditions of production appear as determining the character of labour performed and as consuming the activity of the worker in the process of producing the product which is capital's. But the growing productivity of the forces of production (and its growing discordance with the increasingly conflictual social relations) is the key to the emancipation of individuals, so when investigating the nature of production under capitalism, Marx adopts the technique which exposes the essential disharmony between its ideal form (bourgeois political economy) and its appearance (concrete forces and relations) and reveals the negative and the positive attributes of the contradictions working themselves out in the bourgeois mode of production.

> Forces of production and social relations – two different sides of the development of the social individual – appear to capital as mere means, and are merely means for it to produce on its limited foundation. In fact, however, they are the material conditions to blow this foundation sky-high. [32]

For Marx the source of surplus value for capital is surplus labour time, which is that productive activity carried out by workers after they have produced sufficient exchange value in the form of commodities necessary for the reproduction of their living labour capacity, hence 'necessary labour time'. Capitalism, in this pursuit of surplus value, employs and constantly redevelops the instruments of production (that is, the technology of machinery) in ways that will extract the greatest amounts of surplus labour time at the same time as reducing necessary labour time. As less 'immediate labour' (perceived by the capitalist as a component of circulating capital) is required to produce greater quantities of products, so the sum of labour objectified in fixed capital expands. More efficient machinery serves this very purpose under capital in that it allows the worker to work a longer part of his or her time for the benefit of capital, 'to work longer for another' than he or she would have done under earlier forms of production.[33] The instruments of production therefore appear to reproduce the relations of production based on capital, that is, the appropriation of living labour by objectified labour in order to transform the materials of production for the creation of surplus value. So machinery, as both objectified labour and fixed capital, in determining the conditions of living labour, confronts the individual as a 'ruling power', as an 'alien attribute' of capital, and not as the 'accumulation of knowledge and skill, of the general productive forces of the social brain',[34] consciously controlled[35]: 'In machinery, objectified labour itself appears not only in the form of product or of the product employed as means of labour, but in the form of the force of production itself'.[36]

In such circumstances living labour, the 'life expression' of the individual, is to living labour capacity, that is, the individual worker, an alien activity. But Marx reminds us that although such wage labour appears repulsive and forced,[37] it is a transitory aspect of an historical form of production which has inverted the relationship between social labour and its product, the objective conditions of production. Moreover, such an inversion – the private organization of social production – is an historical and a contingent necessity, 'a necessity for the development of the forces of production solely from a specific historic point of departure, or basis, but in no way an *absolute* necessity of production'.[38] In other words, it is the historical expression of a moment in the development of the forces of production accompanied by a tendential set of social relations which reflect and reinforce, through various means, the expropriation of surplus labour from living labour. Therefore, under capital the worker's activity appears as nothing more than the directing of the machine's work onto the raw materials; the role of supervision and the guarding against interruptions become the worker's lot, while the machine exercises the skill, strength and virtuosity. 'The workers' activity, reduced to a mere abstraction of activity, is determined and regulated on all sides by the movement of the machinery, and not the opposite';[39] dead labour controls the living. It is through such an inversion that capital increases the productivity of labour, while at the same time striving for the greatest possible reduction of necessary labour. However, these two necessary tendencies of capital are also the presuppositions for the future free development of individualities, but they will remain unrealized presuppositions as long as machinery remains the most appropriate form of the value of fixed capital, subsumed under capital's relations of production.[40]

Within Marx's analysis of the nature of bourgeois 'freedom', and his exposure of the disjuncture between its formal articulation and its concrete expression, rests a picture of what genuine freedom might look like. In other words what is implicit in his critique of capitalist relations of production and what emerges out of his assessment of the contradictions that characterize the development of this mode of production, is the existence of a practicable alternative to the 'spontaneous order' and the 'invisible hand' of the 'disinterested' market. But, in the following section I want to maintain that such an alternative was not an a priori construct around which Marx built an elaborate social theory; I will also dispute the claim that the Marxism of Marx was based on a number of teleological assumptions, which provided him with a set of superior, end-dependent principles that he subsequently applied to his damning judgement of capitalism. If he had adopted either strategy then we would expect to find an extensive and elaborate defence of one or the other at some stage during his intellectual development. The fact that his own position evolved out of a direct attack on universalist and teleological systems (see especially his condemnation of the idealism of the likes of Proudhon, and his critique on the theory of justice implicit in the Gotha Programme[41]) appears to suggest that Marx sought a novel and radical alternative that he hoped would place the role of system-building, in theory and practice, in the hands of the subjects of the system itself – conscious, self-determining, social individuals.

Self-determination, Social Freedom and Revolution

Marx's concept of disposable time (free time) is derived from his examination of machinery as fixed capital, particularly in so far as it increases the proportion of surplus labour time to necessary labour time, thus 'enabling labour, through an increase of its productive power, to create a greater mass of the products required for the maintenance of living labour in a shorter time'.[42] This tendency becomes for Marx the condition for the emancipation of labour.[43] As capital strives towards universality and pursues the objective already inherent in its earliest stages of development – the world market and the real subsumption of all society – it encounters barriers in its own nature, which eventually reveal that capital is the greatest barrier to the continued development of the forces of production.[44] Nowhere does this realization become more apparent than among the wage labourers themselves, who hitherto have regarded disposable time as antithetical, in that it is the time in which they produce surplus value for capital.[45] Such disposable time has led to labour's sustained degradation, so that its activity in the process of production appears as 'a complete emptying-out, this universal objectification as total alienation, and the tearing-down of all limited, one-sided aims as a sacrifice of the human end-in-itself to an entirely external end'.[46] However, with the worsening of the endemic crisis of capitalism, and the increasing inability of capital to control the consequences of such a crisis within existing relations of production (that is, the decreasing ability of capital to ride the storm through: the concentration and centralization of the mode of production; the concomitant drive to reduce necessary labour time to a bare minimum; and the reduction of the cost to surplus value of circulation through time and space), workers come to recognize singly and as a class that their separation from the products of their own labour has hitherto been forcibly imposed, and that such a condition had rested on the consistent denial of their own realization.[47] Subsequently, once this condition of exploitative divestiture and expropriation is understood by those who sell their labour power as being the consequence of the production of surplus value for the owners of capital, and once the relations of production commensurate with commodity exchange are perceived as historical and transient, the overthrow of these relations by the labouring classes becomes for them the immanent and necessary presupposition for the emancipation of the mass of individualities.

With the 'violent overthrow' of capitalism[48] and the concomitant appropriation by the workers of their own surplus labour, disposable time ceases to have an antithetical existence in that its inverted character under capital is suspended and transformed in the conditions of 'communal production' to free time. Under such conditions the individual's act of production both confirms his or her individuality as a conscious objectifying agent and is recognized as such by others engaged in productive activity, thus confirming the social nature of production. The labour of social individuals is a liberating activity which 'obtains its measure from the outside, through the aim to be attained and the obstacles to be overcome in attaining it'.[49] In communal production the individual, in consciously positing the aim, engages in labour which is self-realization, 'objectification of the subject, hence real freedom'.[50] This state of affairs is in direct contrast to that described by Adam Smith, who for Marx epitomizes the bourgeois economists' (and for that matter bourgeois society's) attitude to labour. Such a view saw all labour as an imposition, 'a curse', which in the time it takes to perform demands a corresponding sacrifice of freedom and happiness, both of which are only fully expressed in the state of 'tranquility'. Marx admits that this situation may well be true for labour under capital which is, after all, external, forced drudgery,[51] but it is a historical inversion of the actual relationship between the life activity of the individual and its objective conditions. Necessary labour will still be an essential component of communal production (as it is of all previous modes of production), but it will not only be performed for the sake of genuine social need rather than for the owners of the means of production, it will also occupy less of the individual's time as 'social production will grow so rapidly that ... *disposable time* will grow for all'.[52] And it is in the disposable time released by the forces of production that the free development of individuals takes place, employing the means created by those forces for their own ends,[53] which are immediately perceived by the community as contributions to the general, social product.[54] Social worth would therefore be recognized within the activity of production itself and not in the exchange value produced. In the latter, labour is posited as 'general only through exchange', but on the foundation of communal production the 'exchange of products would in no way be the *medium* by which the participation of the individual in general production is mediated'.[55] Under capital the interrelationship between different individual producers is estranged from its immediate, communal, social relation and is transferred to the market where their products as commodities represent exchange value, which is realized by capital. However, in communal production, 'communality is presupposed as the basis of production. The labour of the individual is posited from the outset as social labour'[56] and whatever he or she produces is viewed as a particular contribution to the general social product. Marx believes that in such circumstances individuals will reproduce themselves as social individuals,[57] and that the wealth of the community will be measured in terms of the 'universality of individual needs, capacities, pleasures, productive forces ... the full development of human mastery over the forces of nature ... the absolute working out of [the individual's] creative potentialities'.[58] The development of all human powers will be regarded as an end in itself, in which the individual will participate, reproducing himself or herself *not* in 'one specificity' or through one particular function, but realizing his or her 'totality' as a social individual through the all round development of his or her own capacities.

For Marx the future society of emancipated individuals would require as its precondition the development of the forces of production by relations of production based on capital. In particular it would be the increasing productivity of labour – and the concomitant increase of surplus labour time, disposable time, free time – under capital that would serve as the necessary presupposition for communal relations of production. Marx's investigation of capital was therefore concerned with the character of those relations of production which generate and develop the productive forces, but which by their very nature are relations which prevent the utilization of these forces for the benefit of society as a whole. He wished to show how the capitalist mode of production is not a natural, absolute form of production, but one which incorporates within it, in an inverted form, a relationship between labour and its increasing productivity which reveals the necessity for capital's destruction. It is in the *Grundrisse* that Marx's discussion goes beyond its previous concentration on alienation as the negative condition of a mode of production based on competition, and establishes the positive condition of the new levels of productivity as the basis for human freedom. As such the *Grundrisse* was a watershed for Marx, for it signalled the incorporation of his earlier criticisms of ideology and his analysis of the 'driving forces of history' within a systematic critique of political economy, while at the same time preserving and strengthening his belief in the necessary triumph of a community of emancipated individuals, whose free social development is the precondition for a free society.

Notes

1. K. Marx, *Grundrisse*.
2. G. Cohen, *Karl Marx's Theory of History: A Defence* (Oxford, Oxford University Press, 1978).
3. K. Marx, *Preface to 'A Contribution to the Critique of Political Economy'* in K. Marx, and F. Engels, *MESW*.
4. S. Avineri, *The Social and Political Thought of Karl Marx* (Cambridge, Cambridge University Press, 1968); E. Kamenka, *The Ethical Foundations of Marxism* (London, Routledge and Kegan Paul, 1972); D. McLellan, *The Thought of Karl Marx* (London, Macmillan, 1971); idem, *Marx's Grundrisse* (London, Macmillan, 1971); idem, *Karl Marx: His Life and Thought* (London, Macmillan, 1973); B. Ollman, *Alienation: Marx's Critique of Man in Capitalist Society* (Cambridge, Cambridge University Press, 1971).
5. Marx, *Grundrisse*, p. 83.
6. K. Marx, and F. Engels, 5 *CW*, pp. 31–32.
7. B. Badaloni, 'Marx and the Quest for Communist Liberty' in E.J. Hobsbawm, ed., *The History of Marxism*, vol. I (Brighton, Harvester, 1982).
8. K. Marx, 1 *Capital*, p. 739.
9. Marx to Engels, 14 January 1858, and Marx to Kugelman, 6 March 1868, in K. Marx, and F. Engels, *MESC*, pp. 93, 187.
10. Marx, 1 *Capital*, pp. 102–3. See also T. Carver, 'Marx and Hegel's *Logic*', *Political Studies*, vol. 24, no. 1 (March 1976), pp. 57–68.
11. Marx, *Grundrisse*, p. 461.
12. Ibid.
13. Ibid., p. 162.
14. Ibid., p. 196.
15. Ibid.
16. Ibid., p. 649.
17. Ibid.
18. Ibid., p. 651.
19. Ibid., p. 652.
20. Ibid., p. 515.
21. Ibid.
22. Ibid., p. 488.

23. Ibid., p. 831.
24. Ibid., p. 462.
25. Ibid., p. 225.
26. Ibid., pp. 240–1.
27. Ibid., p. 241.
28. Ibid., p. 157.
29. Ibid.
30. Ibid., p. 158.
31. Ibid., p. 163.
32. Ibid., p. 706.
33. Ibid., p. 701.
34. Ibid., pp. 693–4.
35. I am well aware that the distinction between circulating and fixed capital, and variable and constant capital, is one that is not developed by Marx in *Grundrisse* to the level of sophistication present in 2 *Capital* (see especially pp. 290–305), but I do not think that this affects my discussion detrimentally.
36. Marx, *Grundrisse*, p. 694.
37. Ibid., p. 611.
38. Ibid., pp. 831–2.
39. Ibid., pp. 692–3.
40. Ibid., p. 701.
41. See K. Marx, *The Poverty of Philosophy*, in Marx and Engels, 6 *CW*; and Marx, *Critique of the Gotha Programme* in Marx, *The First International and After* (Harmondsworth, Penguin, 1974).
42. Marx, *Grundrisse*, p. 701.
43. Ibid.
44. Ibid., p. 410.
45. Ibid., p. 708.
46. Ibid., p. 488.
47. Ibid., p. 463.
48. Ibid., p. 750.
49. Ibid., p. 611.
50. Ibid.
51. Ibid., p. 463.
52. Ibid., p. 708.
53. Ibid., p. 706.
54. Ibid., p. 171.
55. Ibid.
56. Ibid., p. 172.
57. Ibid., p. 832.
58. Ibid., p. 488.

8
Need and Egoism in Marx's Early Writings

Christopher J. Berry

Uncontroversially a prominent concern in Marx's writings of 1843–4 was the relationship between civil society and the state. This concern manifested itself in a criticism of Hegel's account of this relationship. As Marx himself was fond of pointing out, negative criticism is still dependent on its target, and, looked at in this light, his own early writings are dependent on Hegel's analysis. Though this dependence is widely accepted its extent has not been fully appreciated. My modest aim is to draw attention to some hitherto unappreciated aspects of this dependence to the end of uncovering *some* conceptual assumptions and 'moves' that Marx makes in his pre-1845 writings. I am not claiming that Marx is somehow more of a Hegelian than previously thought, merely that he uses implicitly a number of Hegel's arguments for his own ends. And, of course, from the fact that Marx does use these arguments nothing follows that commits me to denying either the significance of Marx's dependence on Feuerbach and others or Marx's own originality in this work.

The Context of Marx's Argument

In this opening section I establish the context and assumptions of Marx's argument.

As Joachim Ritter and Manfred Riedel, in particular, have argued, Hegel's separation of civil society from the state effected a conceptual revolution.[1] On Riedel's reading, traditional political thought had regarded the terms 'state' and 'civil society' as synonyms (as equally constituting the *societas civilis*) in explicit contrast to the family or household (the *societas domestica*). Hegel's tripartite division of ethical life into family, civil society and state shatters this dichotomy. The family (*oikos*), from being charged with the economic task of production, became a sentimental institution based on love.[2] The household's previous economic function was now the responsibility of civil society, which was conceived of as a system of needs and particular socio-legal relationships. On the basis of this interpretation, Riedel, here echoing Marx, declares that civil society has become, in Hegel's hands, a depoliticized arena. Civil society is identified conceptually as standing apart from the distinctively universal and political sphere of the state as the sphere that occupies itself with particular and economic activity.

That Marx did adopt this non-political characterization of civil society can be clearly seen in his discussion of the 'rights of man' in *On the Jewish Question* (1843).[3] In this essay Marx declares that these rights of man (*Menschenrechte*) are those of 'egoistic man, of man separated from other men and from the community'.[4] This egoistic man occupied by his 'private desires' (*Privatwillkür*) is drawn into himself, is an isolated and self-sufficient monad. The meaning of these statements derives not so much from a conception of 'rights' as from a particular notion of 'man'. This is evident from the full context of these remarks, namely, the distinction between the rights of man (*droits de l'homme*) and the rights of the citizen (*droits du citoyen*). The latter are political rights which are exercised in community with others so that their content is constituted by participation in the 'political community or state' (*politische Gemeinwesen, am Staatswesen*).[5] Marx takes it that the former (the rights of man) cannot pertain to the state. Given Marx's acceptance of Hegel's characterization of civil society, it follows *by definition* that these (non-political) rights must therefore pertain to that sphere.

That 'man' belongs to civil society and that he is egoistic are points both made by Hegel.[6] He had declared that it was in civil society that it was possible (and, moreover, only there appropriate) to speak simply of 'man' because it is only from the perspective of needs that 'man' as opposed to legal person, moral subject, family member or political citizen can be appositely discerned. Man as a creature of needs aims at their satisfaction and (initially) this is the selfish or egoistic satisfaction of 'subjective particularity'.[7] It is this identification of man *simpliciter* with selfish need satisfaction that Marx has taken over.

For Marx it is because 'man' belongs to civil society that the rights that pertain there are those of egoism. In civil society the only bonds between individuals are those of 'natural necessity, need and private interest'.[8] Hence it is that the right which most accurately reflects this circumstance is the right to private property or the 'right to enjoy and dispose of one's resources as one wills (*willkürlich*) without regard for other men and independently of society'.[9] This right of self-interest (*das Recht des Eigennutzes*) thus constitutes the foundation of civil society. Since this right is held asocially other individuals (themselves bearers of the right of self-interest) will be perceived as threats or hindrances. The spirit of civil society is thus one of mutual antagonism, it is the Hobbesian *bellum omnium contra omnes*.[10] Similarly for Hegel the spirit of civil society is one of atomistic particularity which affords, because of its dependence on selfish need satisfaction, accidental caprice (*Willkür*) and subjective desires, a 'spectacle of extravagance and misery' as well as 'physical and ethical degeneration'.[11]

Hegel's depiction of civil society – or more accurately of its first moment, the system of needs – was explicitly derived from the new science of political economy. Marx also explicitly made this connection in the *Economic and Philosophic Manuscripts*[12] when he wrote 'society as it appears to the political economist is civil society'.[13] However, Hegel and Marx diverged in the significance that they attached to this point. Hegel was impressed by the ability of this science to discern order within the apparent disorder of its subject-matter. This order he then interpreted as the first glimmerings of the process whereby the egoism of the burgher was educated into an increasingly social (political) awareness. Marx rejected this interpretation and he poured scorn on Hegel's attempts to reconcile civil society and the state by means of the bureaucracy, a hereditary monarchy and a corporately elected (from the 'estates' of civil society) legislative assembly.[14] Marx's own attempts at reconciliation initially took the form of repoliticizing civil society, thereby in effect ending its conceptual separation from the state.[15] Later this 'radical democratic' solution was replaced by the reverse process, so to speak, namely, the universal expansion of the economic foundation of civil society to encompass the state, that is, communism. This latter universalization required the replacement of the egoistic particularism posited by the political economists and the concomitant reconstruction of the notion of 'need'. It is upon that replacement and reconstruction that I wish to focus.

Marx and Hegel on Exchange

The initial point of this focus is Marx's account of the process of barter or exchange supplied in his *Excerpts from James Mill* (1844).[16] In this account we will see that Marx for his own purposes uses Hegel's analysis of civil society and the more general framework of the *Philosophy of Right*.

According to Marx, Mill's premise is that shared by all political economists, namely, he conceives of the relationship between men in terms of the relationship between the owners of private property.[17] The consequence of adopting the ownership of private property as his premise leads the economist to conceive of an individual producing 'only in order to have'.[18] Such production has a selfish aim because the individual produces only in order to have something for himself; each individual producer's aim is the realization or 'objectification (*Vergegenständlichung*) of his own immediate selfish needs'. Marx proceeds to unfold an inner logic from the premise of private property. This logic is that outlined by Hegel under the heading of 'Abstract Right' in the *Philosophy of Right*.

The three phases of Abstract Right are property–contract–wrong. Since Abstract Right constitutes the first moment of the actualization of the Idea of Right it means that Hegel's initial premise, like that of the political economists, is private property. This similarity does not mean that Hegel has the same concept of property as found in the economists – he clearly does not.[19] Indeed it is significant that Hegel's discussion, while establishing *in his own terms* the necessity of private property, is critical in this section of the alternative utilitarian (economistic) accounts. Indicative of this is his explicit statement that property is not a means to the end of needs satisfaction but is a substantive end or end-in-itself.[20] Marx takes over Hegel's criticism without subscribing to his positive argument.

The first logical step unfolded by Marx mirrors Hegel's move from property to contract. From the premise of private property it follows that two property owners interact because of some mutual need or necessity (here Marx says the economists provide the correct answer,[21] a point we will come back to). Their interaction takes the form of exchange or barter and it is determined by the 'specific nature of the object which constitutes their private property'.[22] Hegel for his part is clear that the proper subject of a contractual relationship, including exchange, is property in the form of a 'single external thing'.[23] It is important for Hegel (for reasons upon which we shall elaborate) that contracts are a product of arbitrary will (*Willkür*). The parties do not have to exchange and an exchange will only occur if both parties are able to realize thereby their own particular ends, in which case they will have established a contingent 'common' will. Any such exchange implies no alteration in the relationship between the parties; they start and finish their interaction as 'independent property owners' or 'immediate self-subsistent persons'. At the more explicitly social level of civil society the same contractual process and assumptions are at work. The very first reference to civil society indicates this when it is described as 'an association of members as self-subsistent individuals ... an external organization for attaining their particular and common interests'.[24]

A simple example will bring out the crucial similarity between Marx and Hegel here. Suppose X has two knives and Y has two forks and suppose further that each in order to satisfy her own needs requires one fork and one knife. The conjuncture of these two suppositions enables an exchange to take place. That this is merely contingent can be appreciated if X is, instead, supposed to have two knives and one fork while Y still has two forks. In this latter circumstance X can satisfy her needs although Y cannot. But since Y has nothing that X wants then there is no basis for exchange, no common will between them. It is for this contingency in the face of need that Marx attacks political economy.

Adapting our example to Marx's terminology he points out that X's knife is an object of Y's need but that as far as X is concerned Y's need or will is impotent. Moreover, Y would be placed in the humiliating position of a beggar whose supplications X would see as impertinence.[25] The upshot is that instead of Y's need having power over X such that X supplies her with a knife, X has acquired power over Y. That this is a perverse inversion for Marx can be seen by examining his own alternative to the argument presented by the economists.

Marx distinguishes between what he calls human relationships and estranged (*entfremdete*) relationships. The latter, which are what the economists deal with, are the relationships between property owners that are mediated by money. The former relationship is the human one of human to human with man himself as the mediator.[26] Since to Marx 'the essence of man (*das menschliche Wesen*) is the true community of man' then men 'by activating their own essence, produce, create this human community (*menschliche Gemeinwesen*)'. Thus 'true community' is not the product of reflection but emerges directly out of human activity, out of the need and egoism of individuals.[27] Understood in this way a process of exchange can be seen as the direct mediation of human to human so that it is 'equal to the species-activity and the species-spirit (*Gattungsgeist*) whose real, conscious and authentic existence (*wahres Dasein*) consists in *social* activity and *social* enjoyment (*Genuss*).[28] Elsewhere Marx explains this putatively positive sense of exchange when he remarks that if we assume man's relation to the world to be a human one then 'love can be exchanged only for love, trust for trust and so on'.[29] But if, following the economists, we assume typically that exchange or barter is the 'abstract relation of private property to private property' then men are no longer conceived as relating to each other directly as men.[30] In that case their exchange relationships are the manifestations of their alienation or estrangement[31] and do not serve as a confirmation or objectification of their human nature.[32]

If we return to our example then at a properly human level X would have used her production of a knife to satisfy Y's need since in human terms Y's needfulness is a sufficient reason for X to supply the deficiency. In the 'true human community' X would recognize that Y's 'human nature necessarily implies an intimate relationship' with her 'human production'.[33] Instead, therefore, of confirming human nature the premise of private property results in the estrangement of human nature: an estrangement that is manifest when X's possession of a knife enables her (should she so wish) to extract some service or some thing from Y in return for the knife. We shall return to the meaning of 'human production' on page 127 but first we must continue to follow the 'logic' of private property.

Exchange, or contract more generally, is thus a relationship undertaken by two self-interested parties, each of whom aims to realize his own particular ends. Once contract is comprehended in these terms, then, as Hegel points out, it 'remains at the mercy of wrong'.[34] If Y has nothing to exchange for X's knife then the *same motive* that would have prompted an exchange, that is, Y's desire to satisfy her own interests, is that which could prompt Y simply to appropriate X's knife. Marx, though, is not interested in the relatively straightforward relationship of theft, merely referring in passing to the possibility of physical force making direct plunder possible.[35] What does interest him is how, once force has been neutralized, the two parties attempt to delude each other ('*so suchen wir uns wechselseitig einen Schein vorzumachen*') or how the appearance (*Schein*) of exchange in fact is based on deceit (*Betrug*). He expresses Hegel's point about the connection between contract and wrong as 'since our exchange is self-interested on your side as well as mine and since every self-interested person seeks to outdo the other we must necessarily strive to deceive (*zu betrügen*) each other'.[36]

We can reuse our example to elucidate Marx's reasoning to that conclusion. The possibility of exchange (the market) makes the division of labour feasible so that now X specializes in the production of knives and Y in the production of forks. X intentionally produces more knives than she needs but this surplus is one only in appearance since, in fact, she has produced with the aim of attaining by exchange forks from Y. In similar fashion Y in her turn has *appeared* to produce surplus forks but really has produced an object for self-interested exchange, has produced for the sake of attaining knives. Hence, while in appearance (*Schein*) it is a mutual supplementing of needs, in truth (*Wahrheit*) it is a mutual plundering as X and Y each try to get the better of the bargain, to get more in exchange for less. The system that foments this also makes them both endeavour to create new needs (say, knives with serrated edges or forks with longer prongs) with the aim of forcing the other to make a new sacrifice, to become newly dependent. Each new product is a 'new potentiality for mutual fraud (*Betrug*) and pillage'.[37]

While Hegel himself does devote most attention to wrong in the form of coercion (*Zwang*) he does have a section on fraud (*Betrug*) and examination of this section reveals that Marx's language is redolent of Hegel's own technical vocabulary. Hegel remarks that the common will shared by the contractors, since it rests on *Willkür*, is only an 'appearance' (*Erscheinung*) of right and becomes in wrong a 'show' (*Schein*).[38] In a fraudulent relationship a 'false disguise' (*falscher Schein*) is given to the thing exchanged[39] in that one party to the contract makes a show (*einen Schein vormachen*) to deceive the other party.[40] Fraud, moreover, is a wrong which is to be found primarily in contract because although reciprocation (an exchange) has occurred – unlike the unilateralism of theft – the defrauded party has been saddled (*aufgebürdet*) with what she is asked to believe is right.[41]

Marx and Hegel on Human Need

We noted above how for Marx without the alienating circumstance of private property 'human production' would be possible. In this case X's production of a knife for Y would have given X immediate satisfaction because this production would have 'gratified a *human* need' (Marx's emphasis) and in so doing would have 'objectified human nature (*menschliche Wesen vergegenständlicht*)'. Y would now acknowledge X as a complement to her own being and X would know herself to be confirmed in Y's thoughts and love. Hence X's realization in her production of her own individuality would also have confirmed her 'authentic nature', her 'human communal nature'. The same would apply equally to Y in the production of a fork for X – their productions 'would be as many mirrors' from which their 'natures would shine forth'.[42]

A crucial step in this argument is the identification of human production with the satisfaction of 'human need'. In the contemporaneous *Economic and Philosophical Manuscripts* Marx is more forthcoming about this notion of human need. There Marx distinguishes 'crude practical need' from human need.[43] At the root of this distinction lies a familiar contrast between animals and humans. If, like the modern proletariat, man is confined to crude need then this is a 'bestial degeneration (*viehische Verwildrung*)'.[44] A little later Marx significantly refers to a regress to an 'unnatural simplicity of need'[45] and, similarly, the crude communism of Cabet and others is rejected by Marx because it merely negates the world and seeks, instead, to return to the 'unnatural simplicity of the poor unrefined man who has no needs (*des armen und bedürfnisslosen Menschen*)'.[46] This man has not yet progressed sufficiently to develop human needs.[47]

For Marx, the common factor in crude animalistic needs is their egoism[48] but human needs are those that have transcended that perspective since they have other humans for their object. In that circumstance the individual 'in his most individual existence is at the same time a communal being'.[49] Whereas animals produce one-sidedly to satisfy their own (or their young's) immediate physical needs, humans produce truly when free from such needs. This free production is the 'objectification (*Vergegenständlichung*) of the species-life of man'.[50] This objectification is only possible when private property has been superseded (*aufgehoben*). With this supersession need loses its egoistic character so that the senses themselves become 'human senses' (which is achieved when they have as their 'objects' (*Gegenstände*) the 'objective world' (*gegenständliche Welt*) of human production.[51]

As is clear from his rejection of crude communism Marx sees this as a historical process. It is in this context that he remarks that the stage of development (*Bildungsstufe*) that mankind has reached can be gauged by the character of the relationship of man to woman.[52] Of all human relationships this is the most natural, where 'natural' means pertaining to human nature or 'the natural species-relationship'. Accordingly, for males to treat females as objects of lust is not human-natural but rather is an 'infinite degradation'. Lust is an animalistic or crude need,[53] whereas to see the female as another human being is 'to grasp (*erfassen*)' oneself as also human so that the need for the other has become a human need.[54]

Once again resorting to Hegel can provide some clarification. It will be recalled that Hegel was most precise about the proper scope of contracts. The reason for this precision was his opposition to the extension of contractarian language and assumptions beyond their proper arena. He had two illicit extensions particularly in mind. One of these was the contractarian theory of government, the other was the idea that marriage could be understood in contractual terms. It is this latter opposition that is of interest.

Although marriage might begin in contract, this is a contract 'to transcend (*aufzuheben*) the standpoint of contract'.[55] In marriage we no longer have the circumstance of two self-subsistent units entering externally into some contingently limited relationship. Such an understanding of marriage would make it no more than an association bound by 'mutual caprice (*gegenseitige Willkür*)'.[56] Instead the married couple are conscious of themselves as a unity and this union is their 'substantive aim' manifest in their 'love, trust and common sharing of their entire existence as individuals'.[57] The partners in a marriage thus 'renounce (*aufgeben*) their natural and individual personality'.[58] This renunciation is a liberation. One aspect of this liberation is the liberation from 'dependence on mere natural impulse'.[59] What this signifies is the transition from lust to love. The 'sensuous moment' or 'physical passion' is placed within an 'ethical framework'.[60] Viewing oneself and one's marital partner as together constituting one person removes the relationship from 'the contingency and caprice of bodily desire'.[61] Furthermore, this unity of personality expresses itself in common property. The arbitrariness (*Willkürlichkeit*) of the particular needs, and the selfishness of the desires, of a mere individual property-owner are transformed into labour and care for a common possession (*Gemeinsames*).[62] In sum, in Hegel's terms, the true relationship between man and woman means transcending the level of selfish sexual gratification in order to attain the recognition that the partner is not an alien other. In achieving this transcendence we are realizing our essence, our 'substantive self-consciousness'.[63] This self-consciousness means the renunciation of selfish isolation and the 'knowing of myself as the unity of myself with another and of the other with me'.[64]

Despite the fact that Hegel is here talking of husband–wife relationships and Marx refers to that between man and woman this does not signify a sharp division. Two factors can be cited to support this judgement. First, Marx's context is a criticism of 'rude unthinking communism', one consequence of which is to make women common property. This, however, is no advance and, in language that we have already met, this universal prostitution expresses in a 'bestial form' (*thierische Form*) the inadequacy of this type of communism.[65] The relationship that Marx has in mind is therefore one that is more than selfish animal/sexual gratification. Second, Marx's positive reference to the man–woman relationship is that this relationship is 'the immediate, natural, necessary (*unmittelbare, natürliche, nothwendige*) relation of human being to human being'.[66] This is evocative of Hegel's references to the family relationship as 'immediate or natural' (*unmittelbar oder natürlich*)[67] and to marriage, more particularly, as being the 'immediate type of ethical relationship'.[68] The recurrence of this terminology supports the case for there being here some conceptual affinity. In Hegel's philosophical system 'immediacy' is a logical relation. He remarks in the *Encyclopedia* that 'immediate knowledge is to be accepted as a *fact* (*Tatsache*)'[69] and that one mode of this knowledge is intuition (*Anschauung*). In line with the presence of this conceptual affinity Marx says that the man–woman relationship reduces to 'an observable fact (*anschaubares Factum*)' the extent to which 'nature has become the human essence for man'.[70]

It is central to Hegel's programme that familial relationships for all their transcendence of individualism, remain, because they are indeed immediate relationships, at the lowest level in the development of ethical life. Since in Hegel's schema the moment of the family gives way to civil society and to the 'system of needs' then we are, in a sense, back at our starting point. There is, however, one final aspect to take up in the light of the journey that we have undertaken.

Conclusion

We observed in passing that Marx does allow that the process of exchange *qua* species-activity arose directly out of the 'need and egoism of individuals' and that the political economists correctly saw that property is alienated (*entäussert*) out of necessity and need.[71] Once again the conceptual move is made by Hegel who sees the alienation (*Entäusserung*) of property leading to contracts which are entered into, *inter alia*, 'by need in general'.[72] But although the economists might be correct here they are, for Marx, unable to accommodate the change from egoistic need to human need. The economists remain fixed at a conception of need understood solely in egoistic terms. However, though fixed in this respect, the economists do draw attention to the increasing differentiation of these egoistic needs. This now accounts for the point made earlier when the process of mutual deceit and plundering was identified by Marx as stimulating egoistic producers into creating 'new needs' which they can then satisfy for their own selfish ends.[73] Despite this expansion these needs remain 'crude'. Additionally, this multiplication of needs, and of the means of fulfilling them, gives rise to a lack of needs and means (*die Bedürfnisslosigkeit und die Mittellosigkeit erzeugt*) on the part of the worker (a process Marx claims to have demonstrated from the writings of the economists themselves).[74] Hence in an estranged exchange-economy money makes (creates) the difference between effective and ineffective demand. Without money for travel my need to travel is ineffective. Since my need (without money) is not recognized then it is no more than a figment of my imagination, lacking reality. This is now part and parcel of my estrangement for it means in effect that because I have no money for travel then I have 'no need, that is, no real, self-realizing need, to travel'.[75]

That civil society has an inner dynamic to multiply needs and the means of their satisfaction *ad infinitum* was stressed by Hegel.[76] This dynamism reaches a point when luxury coincides with want (*Not*) and where the means with which to satisfy these needs, because they are the exclusive property of some, are barred to the propertyless 'needy man'.[77] Hegel also recognizes that what constitutes a 'need' is itself a social process and he is reported to have remarked that the limitless need for 'comfort' is suggested by those who 'hope to make a profit from its creation'.[78] Despite this, however, Hegel's assessment of needs differs (not unexpectedly) from that offered by Marx.

For Marx the multiplication of needs within an exchange economy is merely an additional manifestation of dehumanization; the estranged wage-labourer is determined by 'social needs alien (*fremd*) to him' which 'act upon him with compulsive force (*Zwang*)' and to which he must submit 'from egoistic need'.[79] For Hegel, on the other hand, this increasing multiplication, abstraction and social determination of needs reflects the increasing liberation of mankind from the 'strict natural necessity of need'.[80] The source of this liberation lies in human nature itself. The needs of man, as *denkender Geist*,[81] are conceptually distinct from those of animals.[82] Whereas Marx used the distinction between human and animal need to indict market society for reducing man to less than an animalistic existence,[83] Hegel sees, even in the worst excesses of civil society, a manifestation of human freedom. Hence the 'rabble of paupers' that civil society can generate is constituted essentially by a 'disposition of mind' (*Gesinnung*) and loss of 'self-respect' (in England the poorest believe they have rights).[84] That Hegel can in this way see some 'reason in the cross of the present' is symptomatic of his basic endorsement of the value of political economy. Marx, of course, knew this full well and, indeed, he declares at one point that Hegel 'adopts the standpoint of modern political economy.'[85]

To Hegel, what the economists reveal is an underlying rationality of how the particularity of self-interested action necessarily implicates the actions of others and thus establishes a system of interdependence which represents (in Hegel's terms) the first glimmerings of concrete universality. But Marx can only see in this endorsement of political economy the endorsement of the rupture between public and private life, between civil society and the state. Hegel's attempted reconciliation by emphasizing the need for mediating institutions and processes between the individual and the state is rejected.[86] One passage in the *Economic and Philosophical Manuscripts* is revealing in this regard, namely, where Marx declares that political economy is self-contradictory because, on the one hand, it points to the division of labour and exchange as indicative of the 'social nature' of its science while, on the other hand, it sees society established through 'unsocial particular interests'.[87] Neither Adam Smith's 'invisible hand' nor Hegel's 'cunning of Reason' are allowed for by Marx. It is worth observing in conclusion that this antipathy to mediation persists throughout Marx's career. Communist society will be a transparent society. While in the early writings this takes the form of the transcendence of all dualism,[88] in the later work it is evident in, for example, *Capital*, when he writes that 'the veil is not removed from the countenance of the social life-process, i.e. the process of material production, until it becomes production by freely associated men, and stands under their conscious and planned control'.[89] The association of free producers not only will be able to arrive at a settled plan but also will be able to carry it out because their production will be geared to human need which necessarily has transcended the egoism of a market economy. While Hegel's thought remains at the level of a market economy it nevertheless provided Marx with some of the tools with which he constructed his vision of a human community.

Notes

1. J. Ritter, *Hegel and the French Revolution*, trans. R.D. Winfield, (Cambridge, MA, MIT Press, 1982); M. Riedel, 'Tradition und Revolution in Hegel's *Philosophie des Rechts*', *Zeitschrift für Philosophische Forschung*, vol. 16 (1962), pp. 203–30 (this is available, along with other relevant writings, in M. Riedel, *Between Tradition and Revolution: The Hegelian Transformation of Political Philosophy*, trans. W. Wright (Cambridge, Cambridge University Press, 1984). For useful further comment see J. Schmidt, 'A *Paideia* for the "*Bürger als Bourgeois*": The Concept of "Civil Society" in Hegel's Political Thought', *History of Political Thought*, vol. 2 (1981), pp. 469–95. In using Riedel I do not commit myself to a complete endorsement of his thesis, which I think has to be qualified when extended beyond the context of German thought; see my review of

Between Tradition and Revolution in *History of European Ideas*, vol. 7 (1986), pp. 428–9.

2. G.W.F. Hegel, *Philosophy of Right*, trans. T.M. Knox (Oxford, Clarendon Press, 1952), para. 158 (all future references will be to paragraphs, with 'R' signifying remarks which are appended to the main paragraphs and 'A' signifying the additions gleaned from the reports of Hegel's lectures which are collated after the main text). I have used the German text, edited by J. Hoffmeister (Hamburg, Felix Meiner Verlag, 1955, 4th edn). This omits the additions for which I consulted G. Lasson's edition of Hegel's *Sämtliche Werke*, 2nd edn (Leipzig, 1921), vol. 6.

3. K. Marx, *On the Jewish Question* in idem, *EW*, pp. 212–41. I have used the German text in K. Marx and F. Engels, *Gesamtausgabe* (Berlin, 1982) Part I, vol. 2, pp. 141–69.

4. Marx, *EW*, p. 229.

5. Ibid., p. 227.

6. Hegel, *Philosophy of Right*, para. 190R.

7. Ibid., para. 189.

8. Marx, *EW*, p. 230.

9. Ibid., p. 229.

10. Ibid., p. 221.

11. Hegel, *Philosophy of Right*, para. 185. I have amended Knox's translation, giving 'misery' for *Elend* where Knox supplies 'want'. The view that individualism left to its own devices will produce chaos and violence was frequently made by Hegel; see *The Phenomenology of Mind*, trans. J. Baillie, (New York, Allen & Unwin, 1967), pp. 399, 504–5.

12. K. Marx, *Economic and Philosophical Manuscripts* in idem, *EW*, pp. 280–400; and in Marx and Engels, *Gesamtausgabe*, Part I, vol. 2, pp. 187–438.

13. Ibid.

14. See Marx, *Critique of Hegel's Doctrine of the State* in idem, *EW*, pp. 58–198; and in Marx and Engels, *Gesamtausgabe*, Part I, vol. 2, pp. 5–137.

15. Marx, *EW*, p. 191.

16. K. Marx, *Excerpts from James Mill* in *EW*, pp. 259–78; and in Marx and Engels, *Gesamtausgabe*, Part IV, vol. 2, pp. 447–66.

17. Marx, *EW*, p. 266.

18. Ibid., p. 274.

19. Cf. C.J. Berry, 'Property and Possession: Two replies to Locke – Hume and Hegel' in J. Pennock, and J. Chapman, eds, *Property* (New York, New York University Press, 1980), pp. 89–100.

20. Hegel, *Philosophy of Right*, para. 45R. See also para. 59R where such utilitarianism is termed a secondary 'modification'.

21. Marx, *EW*, p. 267.

22. Ibid.

23. Hegel, *Philosophy of Right*, para. 75.

24. Ibid., para. 157. See also paras 213, 217.

25. Marx, *EW*, p. 276.

26. Ibid., p. 260.

27. Ibid., p. 265.

28. Ibid. (emphasis in original).

29. Marx, *EW*, p. 379.

30. Ibid., p. 261.

31. Ibid., pp. 265, 374.

32. Ibid., p. 275.

33. Ibid.

34. Hegel, *Philosophy of Right*, para. 81A.

35. Marx, *EW*, p. 276.
36. Ibid., p. 275.
37. Ibid., p. 358. See also ibid., p. 265, where the credit system generates 'mutual deception (*Betrug*) and exploitation (*Missbrauch*)'.
38. Hegel, *Philosophy of Right*, para. 82.
39. Ibid., para. 88.
40. Ibid., para. 83A.
41. Ibid., para. 87A.
42. Marx, *EW*, pp. 277–8.
43. Ibid., pp. 353, 359.
44. Ibid., p. 359.
45. Ibid., p. 368.
46. Ibid., p. 346. This, too, echoes Hegel's critique of primitivism, the view that a supposed state of nature enjoyed by uncivilized (*ungebildete*) peoples is one of freedom and innocence (*Philosophy of Right*, para. 187R). Rather this is a state of unfreedom and savagery (ibid., 194R). Savages are confined to 'mere physical needs (*Naturbedürfnis*)' whereas the development (*Bildung*) of civilization into a system of needs incorporates the development of 'mental needs (*geistige Bedürfnisse*)' where man becomes concerned 'with a necessity of his own making alone instead of with an external necessity, an inner contingency, a mere caprice (*Willkür*)' (ibid., para. 194). In this development man transcends the restrictive animal realm of needs, but see text below.
47. See A. Heller, *The Theory of Need in Marx* (London, Alison and Busby, 1976), for a general discussion, especially p. 57 for the worker as 'a being without needs'.
48. Marx, *EW*, p. 352.
49. Ibid., p. 347.
50. Ibid., p. 329.
51. Ibid., p. 352–3.
52. Ibid., p. 347.
53. Ibid., p. 327.
54. Ibid., p. 347.
55. Hegel, *Philosophy of Right*, para. 163R.
56. Ibid., para. 161A.
57. Ibid., para. 163.
58. Ibid., para. 162.
59. Ibid., para. 149. Cf. Hegel's view of the development of needs as similarly a liberation out of natural immediacy (ibid., para. 187R) (see n. 43 above and text on pp. 123–4).
60. See the excellent discussion by M. Westphal, 'Hegel's radical idealism: family and state as ethical communities' in Z. Pelczynski, ed., *The State and Civil Society: Studies in Hegel's Political Philosophy* (Cambridge, Cambridge University Press, 1984), pp. 77–92.
61. Hegel, *Philosophy of Right*, para. 164R.
62. Ibid., para. 170. Cf. idem, *The Encyclopedia (The Philosophy of Mind)* trans. W. Wallace and A. Miller (Oxford, Oxford University Press, 1971), para. 519, where the sequel to the moral union of marriage is 'community of personal and private interests'.
63. Hegel, *Philosophy of Right*, para. 162.
64. Ibid., para. 158A.
65. Marx, *EW*, p. 346.
66. Ibid., p. 347.
67. Hegel, *Philosophy of Right*, para. 157.

68. Ibid., para. 161.
69. G.W.F. Hegel, *The Encyclopedia (Logic)*, trans. W. Wallace (Oxford, Oxford University Press, 1892), para. 66 (emphasis in original). I used the German text as in *Sämtliche Werke*, ed. G. Lasson, vol. 5.
70. Marx, *EW*, p. 347 (emphasis in original). *Anschaubar* could be rendered as 'intuitively evident'. Marx employs the technical term *Factum* throughout the *Manuscripts* and it is not without significance that he often uses it to refer to the premises of the political economists (see ibid., pp. 322–3). He criticizes the work of these economists because it 'assumes as facts (*Thatsache*) and events' what it should explain; it fails to 'comprehend' (*begreifen*) or 'grasp' (*begreifen*) its own laws and principles. What is needed instead is 'to grasp the essential connection' (*den wesentlichen Zusammenhang ... zu begreifen*) or 'necessary relationship' (*das nothwendige Verhältnis*) between, for example, the division of labour and exchange. All of this echoes Hegel's idea of philosophy as the articulation of the Concept (*Begriff*) so that the aim of *Philosophy of Right* is 'to apprehend (*zu begreifen*) and portray the State as something inherently rational' (Hegel, *Philosophy of Right*, p. 11). It is in accord with this that Hegel claims to show, for example, the 'necessary connection' (*Zusammenhang der Notwendigkeit*) between crime and punishment (ibid., para. 101R) unlike the theorist of the Understanding (*Verstand*) who deals with externalities and thus justifies punishment only contingently by its consequences (ibid., para. 99R). The economists are explicitly identified as such theorists (ibid., para. 189R) and civil society itself is 'the external state' or *Verstandesstaat* (ibid., para. 183).
71. Marx, *EW*, p. 266.
72. Hegel, *Philosophy of Right*, para. 71R.
73. Marx, *EW*, p. 358.
74. Ibid., p. 360.
75. Ibid., p. 378.
76. Hegel, *Philosophy of Right*, paras 190–1.
77. Ibid., para. 195.
78. Ibid., para. 191A. Hegel uses the English word 'comfortable'.
79. Marx, *EW*, p. 269.
80. Hegel, *Philosophy of Right*, para. 194.
81. G.W.F. Hegel, *Philosophy of Mind*, para. 381A (the Additions are not given in *Sämtliche Werke* ed. G. Lasson, but are in *Werke* ed. E. Gans *et al.* (Berlin, 1840) vol. 7 ii).
82. Hegel, *Philosophy of Right*, para. 190.
83. Marx, *EW*, p. 360. The normative nature of the notion of need in Marx's early writings is maintained by P. Springborg, *The Problem of Human Needs and the Critique of Civilisation* (London, Allen & Unwin, 1981), esp. pp. 98–109.
84. Hegel, *Philosophy of Right*, para. 244A.
85. Marx, *EW*, p. 386.
86. For discussion of this point see Jean L. Cohen, *Class and civil society: The Limits of Marxian Critical Theory* (Oxford, Martin Robertson, 1983), pp. 28 ff.
87. Marx, *EW*, p. 374.
88. Ibid., p. 348.
89. K. Marx, 1 *Capital*, p. 173.

9
Marxian Individualism

Ian Forbes

Introduction

Discussions about Marxism and individualism often present the two systems of thought as complementary in their adversity. Where Marxism is strong, there we find individualism weak; and where individualism looks robust, a corresponding inadequacy is said to exist in Marxism. But such presentations (and they are provided by ideologues of both persuasions) generally reduce Marxism and individualism to their crudest and least convincing forms. A further difficulty stems from uncertainties over which Marxism and which individualism is being mooted or attacked. Also, there are various levels at which the argument can be conducted, ranging from propositions concerning the proper conduct of social scientific enquiry (for example, individualism versus holism) to normative and prescriptive issues (for example, individualism versus collectivism).

This paper enters this field by focusing, first, on the relationship that individualism has to radical social thought, and analysing the relevance of attacks on the anti-individualism and collectivism of Marxism. This will lead to an account of the ways in which Marx can legitimately be associated with some of the central concerns of individualism. A third section reviews a wide variety of claims made in respect of the content and intent of Marx's thought *vis-à-vis* individualism. To conclude, some remarks are made about the need for an explicitly 'Marxian' individualism, both to augment Marx's theory of change in society and to develop the ideological defences of his critical social theory.

Individualism in Social Theory

It can be argued that the variety of conceptions of individualism in existence facilitates our analysis rather than makes it more complex. The term, although it has a distinct ideological tone, cannot be said to have any intrinsic property of ambiguity, and the differentiation between modes of individualism by, for example, Lukes, demonstrates that it is not possible to rely upon a single explanatory and/or descriptive framework. The context of its use, therefore, is the central issue, and particular attention will be paid to the manner in which 'individualism' is deployed against Marxist thought. The reasons why it is thus deployed are not so very problematic. Conspiracy theory need not be invoked, although there are probably elements of this, nor would false consciousness provide an entire explanation for individualist attacks on Marxist theory and practice. In other words, there are particular problems with the treatment of 'the individual', in that he or she appears to be ignored or devalued in theory and practice.

Those problems are, inevitably, the focus of rhetorical as well as substantive attacks by liberals. As such, and as Markovic points out, 'we, who would like to do something theoretically and also directly, practically towards the realization of democratic and humanist socialism, find ourselves having to wage a battle against liberalism, as the ideology of a society still in existence'.[1] The key claim of liberalism, the one which is used consistently and to great effect, is that individualism counterposes itself to collectivism in the way that freedom is distinguished from slavery. Liberals, therefore, insist that the question of individualism or collectivism can have only one answer. Marxists must respond to such a charge, but in so doing are often drawn into an argument on quite unfavourable terms. Partly, this stems from the possible definitions of the concepts themselves. For Fritzhand:

> The answer to the question 'individualism or collectivism' would pose no difficulties to the Marxist if these notions were used only in the meaning accepted by most Marxists. Life is not so simple, however: the terms 'individualism' and 'collectivism' have long since existed in the history of philosophical and political thought, and it is hardly surprising that at present they are given various meanings, and sometimes contradictory ones. Consequently, the controversy over collectivism and individualism cannot be confined within the limits determined by the meaning of these words as used by contemporary Marxism.[2]

It might be added that agreement on meaning is hardly likely among Marxists anyway. Nor can Marxism lay claim to proprietary rights over language, or define the kinds of difficulty with which social theory must contend. On the other hand, liberalism, too, has to contend with the changing currency of these terms. Thus liberalism is still able to function as 'a trend which defends the foundations of capitalism', but which also 'criticizes, from the viewpoint of the individual, the contemporary shape of capitalism', in the pursuit of 'respect for human rights, a vast field for the creative initiative of people, and respect for the principles of bourgeois democracy'.[3] Whatever we may think of these kinds of values, it is not unimportant that capitalism fails to realize them in practice.

While Fritzhand tends to dismiss the identification of 'the freedom of the individual with the freedom of the individual as shaped by the capitalist system' as no more than a residue of nineteenth-century liberalism, Pesic-Golubovic argues that 'in liberalism one can find the idea of the liberation of the individual as a person, and not just the liberation of man as an egoistic individual'.[4] In other words, there are some grounds for agreement between those who style themselves either individualists or collectivists.

Of greater moment, however, is the extent to which Marxists ought to be wary, not of individualism, but of collectivism. It is significant that such an admonition comes not just from the liberal-individualist West, but also, in a variety of forms, from the Eastern European Left.[5] Fritzhand, for example, warns that:

> some Marxists arrive at an absurd confusion of socialist collectivism with some of its non-socialist varieties, and usually with anti-socialist collectivism .... Nothing can do more ideological harm to Marxism than professing, on its behalf, the cult of collectivist idols and contempt for concrete people.[6]

In other words, there is the danger that the individualist critique may be well-founded, and that Marxism, like liberalism, can fail to have its values realized in society. Just as there are modes of individualism, so there are modes of collectivism. It is interesting to note that, implicitly, normative as well as descriptive factors are introduced to make possible the distinction between kinds of collectivism. Thus, given the inadequacies of bourgeois ideology, we must conclude that individualism and collectivism are equally problematic, whether they be invoked as defences or criticisms. Fritzhand's conclusion is that 'there are no reasons for Marxism to place collectivism above individualism', but this has limited pedagogical point if we have only just decided that both terms are unsatisfactory.[7] Kosik is more explicit, in that he specifies why Marxists should avoid precisely what kind of collectivism, and what kind of individualism.

> If we understand individualism as a priority of the individual before the collective, and collectivism as subjecting the individual to the interests of the whole ... the two forms are identical in that they deprive the individual of responsibility. Individualism means the loss of responsibility in that Man as an individual is a social being; collectivism means loss of responsibility insofar as Man remains an individual even in the collective.[8]

'Responsibility' is not simply the core value here. Rather, it expresses the relationship that exists between the individual and society, from whichever perspective. That is, Kosik attempts to dissolve the difference between individualism and collectivism.

Such an approach is particularly corrosive of individualist thought. Ontologically at least, all forms of individualism share the premise that the individual human person may exist, logically and in principle, independently of or in opposition to society. The real issue, however, emerges in the claim that individualist thought expresses a significant as well as commonsensical truth about social and political analysis. J.W.N. Watkins puts this point simply, stating that 'it is people who determine history, however people themselves are determined'.[9] Like Homans, Watkins believes in 'bringing people back in' to the centre of social theory.[10]

The intention, clearly, is to attack deterministic accounts of history and society, but it is not at all obvious that an appeal to 'people', 'however ... determined', achieves anything. In *The German Ideology*, Marx was, by comparison, very precise on just this point. For him, too, the first premises were 'real individuals, their activity and the material conditions under which they live, both those which they find already existing and those produced by their activity'.[11] These individuals are more than 'people' abstractly universalized and then given a hard, causal role in the world. Such individuals become recognizable as real only when the detail of their situation is provided, such that we begin with their existence as it actually is or might be. Yet the liberal individualist account generates an intuitive plausibility in two ways. First, as Bhaskar notes, 'it seems to touch on an important truth, awareness of which accounts for its apparent necessity: namely the idea that society is made up or consists of and only of people.'[12] Whether this amounts to anything more than a trivial truth has yet to be established, and there are many who argue that such a view is far from benign in its implication. Second, there is the perception of the nature of everyday existence arising from single individuals themselves. Dallmayr argues that,

especially in modern Western society, little effort is required to show that ego-references have become so strongly sedimented in ordinary experience as to function as taken-for-granted parameters. It seems to me that it would be pointless to deny the importance and effectiveness of individualism in given historical contexts – although one may very well question its ability, as a philosophical doctrine, to account for itself.[13]

Individualism, therefore, makes up in plausibility and effectivity what it lacks in theoretical adequacy, whereas Marxism expects to generate the former because it claims to be so sophisticated in the latter respect. That it fails to dominate even the argument about freedom demonstrates this point. O'Neill, for example, finds it 'a curiosity of scholarship that Hegel and Marx have come to be identified with a deterministic conception of history and the place in it of human freedom, whereas both conceived of history as the story of freedom'.[14] It has to be observed that there is a difference between the individualist view that people are making history now, and the Marxist view that people have the potential to make history, but the ideological battle is too easily reduced to the argument that the prime referent must be the individual, and not society. That the individualist doctrine holds such sway must be of concern, in the light of the disparity between the adequacy of the theories involved. As Bhaskar points out:

the real problem appears to be not so much that of how one could give an individualistic explanation of social behaviour, but that of how one could ever give a non-social (that is strictly individualistic) explanation of individual, at least characteristically human, behaviour![15]

The analysis of individualism, then, has to take into account the methodological as well as ideological components of the doctrine. This calls, first, for a historical approach to individualism, such that the inadequacies in the way that the concept has come to be understood and counterposed against other approaches can be revealed. Second, the underpinnings of individualism have to be considered, in order, first, to establish the regularities and consistencies in the ideas that characterize individualist thought, and second, to place those ideas in the contexts that differentiate one form of individualism from another. On this basis, it is possible to identify those modes of individualism which are most relevant to the discussion of Marx, in terms of the assumptions, claims and conclusions that are similar, contested, or open to interpretation. Individualist thought extends far beyond the premise of 'the single one', and advances at the same time 'a commitment to the moral primacy of the individual' and human autonomy.[16] Yet we can expect to find considerable overlap, since, as E.M. Wood adds, 'a host of additional assumptions must be made about man and his relationship to society before "individualism" ... can be made by definition to exclude "socialism" and "collectivism"'.[17]

Individualism does consist of more than a commitment to moral primacy and human autonomy, such that the distinction between individualist and non-individualist accounts of society is a real one. Wood is correct, moreover, to direct our attention beyond these key principles, for it is here that the modes of individualism become separable. However, it is argued here that the patterns of differentiation that emerge, and the 'host of additional assumptions', are not merely the indicators of proliferating theoretical defences. Rather, the initial raising of the twin standards of moral primacy and autonomy presupposes other, active and supporting, principles which cannot be dismissed simply because they are additional. These extra assumptions are concerned with the conception of human nature employed – more specifically, with the appropriate way to conceive of the relationship between human beings and society. This is no small question: a complete answer must amount to a general theory of society. Nor is it a question in which Marxists have no interest. Indeed, Marxist theory is very firm on the need to proceed from a proper understanding of the relationship between the individual and society.

Individualism's first answer to the problem of defining what it is to be human was clear, if lacking in depth. This is summarized by Lukes (and Marx before him) as the conception of the abstract individual, whereby 'the relevant features of individuals determining the ends which social arrangements are held to fulfil ... are assumed as given, independently of a social context'.[18] The existence of society is the recurring nightmare for this view. The representation of a fixed nature of individuals is devoid of any claim for the protection or realization of that nature, because this would require a society, and abstract individualism rules out even a tactical redrawing of the boundaries to permit a limited sociability. Thus the moral predicates of human dignity and autonomy, and the strategic ideals of privacy and self-development that accompany individualism, represent an attempt to give the human nature of individuals a prescriptive status, which cannot be sustained on the basis of its a priori content alone.

Society is problematic for abstract individualism in another way. The denial of a formative social context means that society can only be the sum of its atomistic constituents. This equation requires that values and ideals cannot be properties of society so defined, either in principle or in practice. Therefore, there is no power or content to those beliefs beyond the measure in which individuals socially coerce themselves and others to accept them. The abstract individual, to be consistent with first principles, must rely upon the operation of social forces, while rejecting the notion that they have any determining significance. In short, the creation and adoption of the values and ideals crucial for the postulation of abstract individualism depends upon a prior social understanding.

It is no surprise, then, that the moral and ideal notions of autonomy and primacy have survived more or less intact, whereas the reformulation of the idea of the abstract individual attests to its weakness. There are two main developments in this respect. The first method involves detailing the means by which the relationship between the individual and society is to be understood. Here we find that the concept of the abstract individual remains central, but is disguised and driven underground somewhat. The connections between individuals and society are articulated either by the attribution by description of qualities to the individual, or the generation of the principles of the explanatory model as a whole. Each element permits the development of much more sophisticated analyses of, for example, rights, obligation and justice. In this way, values and ideals are presented as universals, and still used to actualize the basic assumptions about individual human beings. In this class of individualism Lukes puts political, economic, epistemological and methodological individualism, to which can be added possessive, utilitarian and radical individualism.[19]

In the second method of dealing with the inadequacy of abstract individualism, the abstract individual disappears altogether. Instead, there is an alternative explication of the relevant moral categories, and a consequent reassessment of their force and logical and social status. Such values and ideals as are employed by the preceding doctrines are shown to be only provisionally acceptable as tenets of individual as well as social explanation. The appeal to non-social entities, extraneous to the individual, is untenable, on the one hand, because those ideals and values depend for their existence on the view of human nature, and on the other because they are also used to provide the necessary supports for that same view of an abstract human nature. Ruling out the abstract individual, but retaining the individual as the basis of explanation, means that this second form must address itself to theories of the mind and human behaviour. Instead of moral constructs dwelling in the consciousness of the individual, the operations of the mind, the way they are designed, become the focus. Included in this category are religious and ethical individualisms, attuned as they are to 'the historical and social influences on the individual mind'.[20]

Individualism against Collectivism

There is one similarity of particular importance between these two groups of individualist explanation. Both seek to acknowledge the significance of history and society, without undermining the essential claim that the individual remains the prime referent. Thus they are in opposition to determinist, collectivist and holist views of society. With respect to Marx, methodological and ethical individualism have the most specific application.

As we have seen, methodological individualism carries within it the notion of the abstract individual, with its attendant problems, yet it remains the most developed critique ranged against the Marxian enterprise. For Lukes, the key assertion is that 'all attempts to explain social (or individual) phenomena are to be rejected ... unless they are couched wholly in terms of facts about individuals'.[21] However, this presents the doctrine only in defensive and critical, rather than purposeful and positive, perspective. In Watkins's view, the core principle is 'that social processes and events should be explained by being deduced from (a) principles governing the behaviour of participating individuals and (b) descriptions of their situations'.[22] Watkins's presentation is much more conditional than Lukes's version, and there is a distinction made between procedure and evidence. That is, the information of the approach to social processes is outlined, and this is different from the way that relevant 'facts' are identified and separated from non-facts. Thus the 'principles' of (a) are discoverable and examinable facts, even though they will entail judgements about both human nature and behavioural patterns within society, whereas 'descriptions' under (b) are not facts in the same way, but contexts within which the facts must be placed and analysis occur.

Thus methodological individualism retains the abstract individual at the core, but does not seek simply to explain individual actions and intentions. Instead, the methodology is constructed such that the form and content of the mediating links between individual and society can be established. In this way, a social explanation can be the intent and the result, thus overcoming the objection that the conception of society has no substance or force by arguing that the impact of society on individuals is the crucial issue. In this way, methodological individualism is distinct from a more metaphysical account based on the absolute commitment to the idea that the individual can be perceived and understood without reference to society.

By contrast, ethical individualism is not a doctrine that purports to be an explanation at the level of grand theory, but is a view of the nature of morality. Here the individual is 'the source of morality', 'the supreme arbiter of moral (and, by implication, other) values, the final moral authority in the most fundamental sense'.[23] Although it may appear so, the notion of the abstract individual is not implicit in this doctrine. Morality is a social phenomenon, and the individual is related to it as both a creative subject and responding object. As such, ethical individualism concerns an aspect of social reality, and is explanatory and prescriptive in only this limited respect. The key idea here is autonomy, not simply as a right or quality that is inherent in each individual. Instead, there is a critical account of the role of morality as a form of social structure which, if not determining, certainly circumscribes and directs human thought and action. It becomes possible, therefore, to explain, in ethical individualist terms, what it is to be an individual in this or that society, and to postulate an alternative that simultaneously presupposes and makes a reality the autonomous individual.

Ethical individualism, in other words, is deeply concerned with history. Its development as a doctrine, unlike the development of methodological individualism, is not related to the attacks on the legitimacy of abstract individualism by other, usually determinist/collectivist/holist *Weltanschauungen*. Ethical individualism does not take the individual as given, but regards the individual as a cultural and social product, one, therefore, which emerges and changes in specific ways. Thus MacIntyre, for example, draws attention to the disordered and partial 'social processes of transition' during and after the Reformation, pointing out that, 'in every case, what emerges is a new identity for the moral agent'.[24] For Nietzsche, this was not only a pattern to be observed throughout history, but also a process with a specific end-product.

> If we place ourselves at the end of this tremendous process, where the tree at last brings forth fruit, where society and custom at last reveal what they have simply been the means to: then we discover that the ripest fruit is the sovereign individual, like only to himself, liberated again from morality of custom, autonomous and supramoral (for 'autonomous' and 'moral' are mutually exclusive) ...[25]

The individual, then, is a recent historical product, and it is not only Marxists who see that conceptions of the individual are equally historical. Moreover, the notion of autonomy cannot be regarded only as a universalistic ideal: it is in itself not given, but derives its form and content from historically placed individuals. Thus autonomy can be seen, in the light of the fresh identities that MacIntyre's 'moral agents' developed and in Nietzsche's historical and 'sovereign' individual, as an aspect of human social development.

Implicitly, ethical individualism is a superior doctrine to methodological individualism, and this is partly because it makes few grand claims and does not attempt to legislate against collectivism or social holism – the view that the whole is greater than its parts. If this is taken to mean that social wholes are ontologically more fundamental than individual people, then it is false. Watkins, of course, argues that methodological holism entails just this kind of extraordinary claim, in that it states:

> that the behaviour of individuals should be explained by being deduced from (a) macroscopic laws which are *sui generis* and which apply to the

social system as a whole, and (b) descriptions of the positions (or functions) of the individuals within the whole.[26]

But it is not the influence of social individuals that holism is rejecting, but the predominant influence of individuals qua individuals. Also, the view that social wholes involve something more than an aggregate of individuals can still be accepted, without any threat to the notion that individuals and the social entities constituted from them are interconnected in a mutually causal fashion. In Bhaskar's opinion,

> the properties possessed by social forms may be very different from those possessed by the individuals upon whose activity they depend. Thus one can allow, without paradox or strain, that purposefulness, intentionality and sometimes self-consciousness characterise human actions but not transformations in the social structure.[27]

At this point, it might reasonably be concluded that Marxism is being presented as the archetypal, even ideal, form of individualist theory. Indeed, D.F.B. Tucker seems to think that this is the way to perceive Marxism. He goes so far as to describe Marx variously as a methodological, ethical, ideal-regarding and humanist individualist, and he is clearly not trying to be offensive.[28] However, not all wish to defend Marx from the accusations that he ignored the fundamental importance of the individual in society. Some want to argue that this represents his most telling contribution to the scientific analysis of society.

Humanism and Individualism

There are sound reasons for Marxists to be suspicious of any form of individualism, in so far as the community is treated merely as a means for satisfying the private wants of individuals as their right, or as the individual regards personal interests as moral values. In these respects, collectivists are entitled to argue that 'individuals are axiological nonentities with respect to society; their individuality is of no consequence; what is important is not individuality, but the social model, to which they should always accommodate themselves'.[29]

However, the political implications of such a view are very easily presented in the form of a damaging critique. In the various defences of Marx and Marxism, however, we find conflicting views on the possible role of the individual in Marxist explanation, exemplified by the humanist and anti-humanist accounts of Marxian theory. Humanism, as a doctrine, has gone through a number of developments, from the Protagorean view that 'man is the measure of all things', to the Renaissance secularization of the study of human cultural and political achievements, to its more recent expressions. These are, first, the direct and negative response to religion, and second, the more interesting strand that

Williams identifies as incorporating a Hegelian belief in history as human self-development and self-perception.[30]

Nevertheless, humanism remains 'a theory or doctrine [that] is more concerned with man than with something other than man'.[31] The problem with this formulation, and with humanism so defined, is threefold. First, it rules out only the most vulgar kind of structural determinism, so ought not to be unacceptable, in principle, to Marxists. Second, this definition seems at the same time to echo the claim and purpose of methodological individualism, where individuals are deemed to be the prime consideration. This is clearly not acceptable to Marxists of any firmness. Third, the history and development of humanism appears to be closely linked to the birth and transformation of religious individualism into ethical individualism, with its belief in the moral autonomy and valuational power of the individual human being. It is necessary to keep in mind, then, whether a defence of Marx on humanist grounds necessarily implies an appeal to both, or either of, methodological and ethical individualism. In other words, is Marx's socialism also humanism, or vice versa?

Althusser is one who certainly thinks that this is not the case. For him, 'in the framework of the Marxist conception, the concept "socialism" is indeed a scientific concept, but the concept "humanism" is no more than an ideological one'.[32] Thus we are to conclude that it is the Marxist framework which ultimately decides that it is very much better to be scientific than ideological. If we follow Althusser here, we can agree that philosophical humanism could never be consistent with Marx's materialist methodology. At issue is the existence of human nature as a 'theoretical' concept, and the abstract individual, however conceived.[33]

Marx's theoretical anti-humanism means a refusal to root the explanation of social formations and their history in a concept of man with theoretical pretensions, that is, a concept of man as an originating subject, one in whom originate his needs (*homo economicus*), his own thoughts (*homo rationalis*) and his acts and struggles (*homo moralis*, *juridicus* and *politicus*).[34]

For Althusser, there is no knowledge to be gained in respect of human nature. Instead, we can only glean an understanding of the ideological role of concepts of human nature in respect of practical theoretical knowledge of the objective existence of structural features of society. This does not imply a simple economism, but it does entail a hard, but not vulgar, form of determinism. It is in this respect that Althusser's position can be criticized. His account of the notion of human nature cannot provide at the same time an account of the person, or individual, in society. There can be no doubt that Althusser correctly identifies Marx's break with philosophical humanism, but this by no means amounts to the quite different claim that the rejection of one, unsatisfactory, answer to the question of the individual invalidates the question itself.[35] It should be remarked, however, that, to Althusser's credit, some of the woollier positions of Marxist humanists have been exposed to searching criticisms. The characterization of Marx as an anti-humanist and anti-individualist must nevertheless be carefully formulated if it is not to do violence to the nature of his social and political theory, on the one hand, and the scope of his theoretical premisses, on the other. That is, his thought cannot be made to remove the problem of the individual in society – whatever the form of society – but must be used instead to provide an account of the individual. Both the liberal individualist and structural determinist views of Marx misrepresent his thought and misconceive the question of the individual in society, each in its particular way.

Therefore, the important question proves not to be whether Marx was an individualist or humanist. All that can be said is that he was opposed to certain forms of individualist thought that existed at the time. These forms, as we have seen, have changed, and we must expect a Marxian critique to develop in its own way. It has to be remembered that Marx's legacy is not the destruction of poor or previous modes of thought, but does detail the way to proceed. That legacy, however, is sometimes taken to mean that there exists a specific direction in which Marxian social science ought to proceed.

Marxian Individualism

If there can be such a thing as Marxian individualism, then it must be founded on a marked change in the way that individualism is currently perceived. Not at all strangely, individualism is seen by anti-individualists as a particularly unpleasant kind of doctrine, but this is not accompanied by a dispassionate appreciation of its merits or the structure of its relationship to historical change. Some collectivist thought, as Fritzhand argues, 'approaches individualism a-historically and condemns it wholesale, whereas Marxism conceives it in its historical development and distinguishes between its negative and positive aspects.'[36] This is, of course, humanist Marxism, which for Kosik 'does not entail either a negation of the individual in terms of a history consisting of suprapersonal forces or an interpretation of the individual as a means'.[37]

The combination of these views is expressed in Marx's view that individuality is of a higher order in communist society. Here we see that the individual, because he or she is a historical product, is an allowable concept in both a descriptive and prescriptive sense. In the same way, then, individualism is a historical product, and it can be argued that its emergence was progressive in the same way that capitalism represented a progression over feudalism.[38] If this is the case, then liberal individualism, in its many forms, is a precondition for the development of communist individuality, just as feudal communalism provided the basis for the development of social relations in capitalism.

This forms the rationale for the argument that the revolutionary potential of individualism should not go unacknowledged by a socialist critique. Keat, for example, maintains that capitalist

individualism ... involves the achievement of differentiation, of independent self-identities, by contrast with feudal community. Thus individualism is not to be simply opposed or 'negated' by the socialist advocate of community, since those of its features which represent the 'release' from feudal engulfment are to be preserved – though ... in a somewhat modified form.[39]

This means, first, that the significance of individualism as a historical product has also to be reflected in theory, such that Marxism does not have to rely on the possibility or the inevitability of a revolution in the means and relations of production to mediate a convincing discussion of the importance of the individual. As Kosik claims:

Individuality is neither an addition nor an unexplainable irrational remainder to which the individual is reduced after subtracting the social relations, historical contexts and so on. If the individual is deprived of his social mask and underneath there is no hint of an individual appearance, this privation bears witness only to the worthlessness of his individuality, not to his nonexistence.[40]

The Marxist must be aware of the progressive as well as regressive aspects of individualism, so that the negative expression of individuality that is confronted in contemporary capitalist society is not confused with the absence of any ability to achieve worthwhile expressions of individuality in the present, and despite the dominant social form.

Second, a socialist critique has to recognize that the process of individuation brought about by capitalist society carries with it a progressive character which, if ignored, can easily work against the realization of other goals of community, like solidarity and the unfortunately termed fraternity. If these communitarian concepts cannot incorporate a notion of the individual, and derive their meaning and strength solely from the ideal and practice of the collectivity, then their efficacy will always be limited by the need for redefinition according to the circumstances which remain the object of their action. In other words, collective action underpinned by collectivist thought must always be essentially defensive, whereas it needs also to be the essentially creative activity of individuals. If communitarian concepts do not 'see' individuals, especially flawed, bourgeois ones (like me!), then such individuals are unlikely to see any strong relation to that kind of communitarianism.

Marxian individualism, then, is not a specific model of individualism, but a theoretical practice which springs from accepting that the relationship between society and the individual is dialectical, and that such a relationship is not illuminated by attempting to establish the primacy of one or other of these categories. On this basis, the ideological battles between individualism and collectivism can be circumvented in favour of a political practice which is self-defining as well as other-legitimating. This is far from what Dallmayr calls the 'end of the individual', although it does bespeak 'an open-ended, non-possessive individuality enmeshed in, but not entirely congruous with, its surroundings'.[41] One normative element, it seems to me, must remain:

autonomy. This is to be understood not in the ethical individualist sense as a quality of humans, but in the Nietzschean sense of a created historical possibility which we may or may not realize. Marxian individualism is concerned that humans achieve autonomy in society, because it has become such a self-evident potentiality of each individual life – not in individuals *qua* individuals – locked, at present, within the increasing constraints of social life.

Notes

1. M. Markovic, 'The Possibilities and Difficulties of Overcoming Liberalism and the Present Form of Socialist Society', *Praxis*, no. 1 (1973), pp. 33–4. If this is true of Eastern European political movements, it is of even greater moment when the work toward the realization of socialism involves overcoming not just bourgeois ideology, but bourgeois society itself. See also idem, *Democratic Socialism: Theory and Practice* (Brighton, Harvester, 1982).
2. M. Fritzhand, 'Individual or Collectivism', *Dialectics and Humanism*, no. 3 (1980), p. 15.
3. Ibid., p. 18.
4. Z. Pesic-Golubovic, 'Liberalism as a Philosophy of Freedom', *Praxis*, no. 1 (1973) p. 101.
5. Examples would be movements such as Solidarnosc, feminism, the Greens and the development of critiques of state socialism.
6. Fritzhand, 'Individual or Collectivism', p. 20.
7. Ibid., p. 24.
8. K. Kosik, 'The Individual and History' in N. Lobkowicz, ed., *Marx and the Western World* (Notre Dame, IN, Notre Dame University Press, 1967) p. 189.
9. J.W.N. Watkins, 'Methodological Individualism: A Reply' in J. O'Neill, ed., *Modes of Individualism and Collectivism* (London, Heinemann, 1973), p. 179.
10. G. Homans, 'Bringing Man In', *American Sociological Review*, vol. 29 (1964), pp. 809-18.
11. K. Marx and F. Engels, 5 *CW*, p. 31.
12. R. Bhaskar, *The Possibility of Naturalism* (Brighton, Harvester, 1979), p. 37.
13. F. Dallmayr, *Twilight of Subjectivity* (Amherst, Massachusetts University Press, 1981), p. 138.
14. J. O'Neill, 'Scienticism, Historicism and the Problem of Rationality' in idem, ed., *Modes of Individualism and Collectivism*, pp. 12–13.
15. Bhaskar, *The Possibility of Naturalism*, p. 35.
16. E.M. Wood, *Mind and Politics* (London, California University Press, 1972), pp. 6–7.
17. Ibid.
18. S. Lukes, *Individualism* (Oxford, Basil Blackwell, 1973), p. 73.
19. Ibid., pp. 138–45; C. B. MacPherson, *The Political Theory of Possessive Individualism* (Oxford, Clarendon Press, 1963); and J. Rawls, *A Theory of Justice* (Oxford, Oxford University Press, 1973).
20. Lukes, *Individualism*. p. 140.
21. Ibid., p. 110.
22. J.W.N. Watkins, 'Ideal Types and Historical Explanation' in O'Neill, *Modes of Individualism and Collectivism*, p. 149.
23. Lukes, *Individualism*, p. 101.
24. A. MacIntyre, *A Short History of Ethics* (London, Routledge and Kegan Paul, 1967), p. 124.

25. F. Nietzsche, *The Genealogy of Morals: An Attack* (1887), (New York, Doubleday, 1967), Part II, Section 2.
26. Watkins, 'Ideal Types and Historical Explanation', pp. 150, 180.
27. Bhaskar, *The Possibility of Naturalism*, pp. 44.
28. D.F.B. Tucker, *Marxism and Individualism* (Oxford, Basil Blackwell, 1980), pp. 11, 61, 63, 65.
29. Fritzhand, 'Individual or Collectivism', p. 20.
30. R. Williams, *Keywords* (London, Fontana/Croom Helm, 1976) pp. 122–3.
31. A. Bullock and O. Stallybrass, eds, *The Fontana Dictionary of Modern Thought*, (London, Fontana, 1988), pp. 291–2.
32. L. Althusser, *For Marx* (New York, Vintage Books, 1970), p. 223.
33. Ibid., pp. 243–4.
34. L. Althusser, *Essays in Self-criticism* (London, New Left Books, 1976), p. 205.
35. Cf. L. Sève, *Man in Marxist Theory and The Psychology of Personality* (Brighton, Harvester, 1978).
36. Fritzhand, 'Individual or Collectism', p. 23.
37. Kosik, *'The Individual and History'*, pp. 195–6.
38. See also C. Gould, *Marx's Social Ontology* (London, MIT Press, 1978); and D.R. Gandy, *Marx and History* (Austin, Texas University Press, 1979).
39. R. Keat, *'Individualism and Community in Socialist Thought'* in J. Mepham and D.-H. Ruben, eds, *Issues in Marxist Philosophy* (Brighton, Harvester, 1979), p. 137.
40. Kosik, 'The Individual and History', p. 189.
41. Dallmayr, *Twilight of Subjectivity*, pp. 3, 12.

10
Marx, Engels and the Parliamentary Path

Michael Levin

Introduction

Students of Marxism will know all too well that the problems of Marx and Engels's intellectual development, of early *versus* late, or the placing of a supposed epistemological break, are among the most contentious issues in the secondary literature. Marx and Engels wrote prodigiously for about half a century and these writings bear clear witness to the impact of changing social, political and economic circumstances. In a number of ways the failures of the 1848–9 revolutions mark a watershed in their thinking. From that time they developed a politics of the long haul; a politics whose development was more thoroughly related to changes in economic circumstances. Thus began the intensive studies that later resulted in the *Grundrisse* and the three volumes of *Capital*. The *Communist Manifesto*, their most famous and influential short work, is a product of Marx and Engels's early and most optimistic period, which came to an end within a few years of its having been written. The so-called 'hungry forties' was a decade of hardship, poverty and lower-class discontent. Workers were without the vote. Trade unions were either illegal or barely tolerated. In this formative period for political Marxism it is hardly surprising that revolution on the 1789 model seemed a possibility. As the writings of Carlyle also testify, the spectre of the great French Revolution preoccupied conservatives and radicals alike. However, we shall see that even in the 1840s the parliamentary path was not discounted by Marx and Engels. Its possibilities appeared greater still when, in the late 1860s, the vote was extended to some working men in both Prussia and Great Britain. In this paper I shall examine Marx and Engels's analysis of the parliamentary option, of both its pitfalls and its possibilities.

The Nature of the State

Parliament is an institution of the state, so the critique of parliamentarism is a sub-section of the more general Marxist analysis of the state. This is sufficiently well known for us to sketch it out fairly briefly.

Marx's own work in this sphere commenced with the extended investigation of Hegel's *Philosophy of Right* which he undertook in summer 1843. Hegel, like Herder and Schiller, had been troubled by the basic divisiveness of modern society and was fascinated by the supposed wholeness of Greek civic life. Marx, too, shared this concern, but not Hegel's response to it: 'It shows Hegel's profundity that he feels the separation of civil from political society as a *contradiction*. He is wrong, however, to be content with the appearance of this resolution'. [1]

Hegel, then, whom Marx regarded as a representative of the modern state, had presented the state as the highest point of reconciliation between the individual and society, and saw particularity as being overcome by the institutions of monarchy, embodying the universal essence, and bureaucracy as a universal class. To Marx, in contrast, the powers granted to the state strengthen not its universality but its particularity. This was especially so when its personnel were recruited from an exclusive stratum, for in Hegel's system the landed gentry was 'summoned and entitled to its political vocation by birth without the hazards of election'.[2] State power, rights and privileges are exclusive to it and are thus implicitly defined as just those that the people do not possess. Thereby the disunity of modern society is reinforced rather than resolved, and instead of identifying with the universal as full citizens, subjects are condemned to the narrow idiocy and competitiveness of private existence. The state in fact represents an alienation of the powers of the whole community which will only be resolved when it no longer exists and society administers itself on a basis of full equality. Rather than attempt to separate the state from society, Marx looked for the hidden linkages.

> Everywhere it requires the guarantee of spheres which lie outside it. It is not realised power. It is *supported* impotence, it is not power over these supports but the power of the support. The support is the paramount power.[3]

From this realization it was just a short step to the notion of the class state. The state bureaucracy, courts, police and army appear henceforth not as neutral arbiters standing above social divisions and maintaining general law and order, but as the partisan instruments in capitalist society of bourgeois law and order. As Engels was later to put it, the state is

> as a rule, the state of the most powerful, economically dominant class, which, through the medium of the state, becomes also the politically dominant class, and thus acquires new means of holding down and exploiting the oppressed class.[4]

Another less acknowledged emphasis allows the state relative autonomy.

However, this also, in a different way, still detracts from notion of neutrality, for now the state becomes a mammoth, powerful yet parasitic excrescence on society with a primary commitment to itself. In the Rousseauesque sense it is a particular grouping likely to develop a particular will. Either way, as class state or particular interest, it is still a barrier to popular power, neither neutral and objective, nor the passive executor of the wishes of the legislature.

The Defects of Parliaments

Already in their analysis of the central political institution we have the core of Marx and Engels's critique of bourgeois democracy. It is that the state and also parliament and the entire political sphere do not occupy neutral ground in which success is obtained purely on the basis of cogent argument or numerical appeal.

The bourgeois constitution provides a universalistic statement of freedoms which become in practice class-based justifications of suppression. Commenting on the constitution of the French Republic, as published in November 1848, Marx noted:

> For each of these freedoms is proclaimed as the *absolute* right of the French *citoyen*. but always with the marginal note that it is unlimited so far as it is not limited by the *'equal rights of others* and the *public safety'* ... that is, the safety of the bourgeoisie, as the Constitution prescribes. In the following period, both sides accordingly appeal with complete justice to the Constitution: the friends of order, who abrogated all these freedoms, as well as the democrats, who demanded all of them. For each paragraph of the Constitution contains its own antithesis, its own Upper and Lower House, namely, freedom in the general phrase, abrogation of freedom in the marginal note. Thus so long as the name of freedom was respected and only its actual realisation prevented, of course in a legal way, the constitutional existence of freedom remained intact, inviolate, however mortal the blows dealt to its existence *in actual life*.[5]

This restriction of freedom Marx regarded as characteristic of a mentality that generally failed to acknowledge the narrow scope of what it presented as universal benefits. It was not just that the rights nominally pertaining to the political sphere were not actually manifested even there, for even were this remedied their scope would still be restricted, for the political itself was too narrowly defined. As just one more aspect of the division of labour, parliamentary politics was accepted as a specialist task practised only by the few. Political freedoms only related to the formal political sphere which itself formed only a segmented part of the social totality. Thus 'just as the Christians are equal in heaven, but unequal on earth, so the individual members of the nation are *equal* in the heaven of their political world, but unequal in the earthly existence of *society*'.[6]

The inequality by which paper freedoms emerge as actual restrictions derives from the division between owners and non-owners. The nominal rights of all can only be exercised by those with the means to do so. This facet was noted, *inter alia*, in the anachronistic forms and conventions of parliament, where the survival of a property-based franchise still indicated that access to wealth served as the primary qualification for political participation. As for the actual elections, in theory votes were won, but in practice they were bought. 'The traditional bribery of British elections'[7] was all too evident in the years before the secret ballot rendered it redundant.

> In the Tory Carlton Club and the Liberal Reform Club in London the representation of towns was positively auctioned to the highest bidder ....
> And on top of all this we must not forget the fine manner in which the elections are held, the general drunkenness amid which the votes are cast, the public houses where the electors become intoxicated at the candidates' expense, the disorder, the brawling, the howling of the crowds at the voting booths; putting the finishing touches to the hollowness of representation which is valid for *seven* years.[8]

The expenses of registration and electioneering, and the absence of a parliamentary salary still served to weaken the chances of working class candidates even after they had obtained nominal political rights. After Britain passed the third Reform Act of 1884 Engels could still conclude that 'Parliament is to remain a *club of the rich*'.[9]

For Marx and Engels the reality of the parliamentary system appeared systematically to curtail its pretensions; the class state for the neutral arbiter; paper freedoms for real political freedoms; and restricted political freedoms for general human emancipation. A similar characteristic applied to the prevailing theory of democratic political choice. Traditional social contract theory presented political forms as originating from the unconstricted choice of rational individuals. Tom Paine had presented the French Revolutionary epoch as signifying the Adam of a new world. This notion of political omnipotence overplays the significance of will and neglects the force of constraining circumstances. 'Are men free to chose this or that form of society? By no means',[10] Marx informed Annenkov in 1846. Ripeness as well as willingness curtails the realm of the possible, a law applying to liberal and socialist reformers alike, within parliament or without. A characteristic parliamentary malady mistakes legislative influence for basic social power and assumes that anything is possible, and any decision can be implemented, merely because parliament has so decreed. This disorder, termed 'parliamentary cretinism', was given its fullest clarification in Engels's account of the ill-fated Frankfurt parliament which, apparently, talked without being listened to in the happy conviction that the outside world awaited its every declaration with bated breath, whereas in reality it was merely a consultative body which mounted no real challenge to monarchical power and so eventually, when the latter was able to reassert itself, sank without causing even a ripple of attention or regret. At the height of its bravado it displayed the solemn conviction that the whole world, its history and future, are governed and determined by a majority of votes in that particular representative body which has the honour to count them among its members and that all and everything going on outside the walls of their house – wars, revolutions, railway-constructing, colonising of whole new continents, California gold discoveries, Central American canals, Russian armies, and whatever else may have some little claim to influence upon the destinies of mankind – is nothing compared to the incommensurable events hinging upon the important question, whatever it may be, just at that moment occupying the attention of their honourable House.[11]

Furthermore, the cosy club atmosphere of parliament leads all too easily to a politics of compromise which involves labour leaders in the betrayal of the class interests they are meant to represent. Such was the English situation where servile adherence to the Liberals contrasted so markedly with the creation of an explicit proletarian party in Germany. Coalitions are always precarious for their natural tendency is to blur and distort the separate real aims of the classes involved. However, they cannot always be rejected, for in certain situations they present the only means of progress. Compromise of ultimate class aims is what Marx and Engels most feared, but coalition without compromise is attainable between different social groupings who may for a limited period share the same short-term interests. During the 1840s Marx and Engels favoured an alliance of all progressive forces. Where certain remnants of feudalism survive, the communists even 'fight *with the bourgeoisie* whenever it acts in a revolutionary way, against the absolute monarchy, the feudal squirearchy, and the petty bourgeoisie'.[12] All progressive groupings are to be supported, but an ultimate aim for a marginal class will be merely a transitional one for the proletariat. Alliance without illusion, coalition without compromise, and unity without proletarian subordination were to be aimed for. Only the most oppressed class fights through until all oppression is removed. Thus the proletariat should never fall under the ideological or organizational sway of classes with limited aims, and, as the most unequivocal radical groupings, should always assume the leadership of any progressive alliance.

Such principles apply within parliament or without, but the corrupting tendencies and temptations already attending relations between different directly active mass organizations become even more enticing in a parliamentary context. This is because the whole atmosphere is one where labour leaders are too easily seduced into adopting the 'respectability' of their 'betters'. This tendency is the occupational hazard attending the closed parliamentary world. It can be countered only if a strong organic link between the masses and their representatives is maintained. Otherwise it continues unabated until 'some fine day the left may find its parliamentary victory coincides with its real defeat',[13] as happened to the French parliament of 1851 which voted to depose Louis Bonaparte but was 'finally led off in the custody of African sharpshooters'.[14] The general implication is that the bourgeoisie intend both parliament and the universalistically defined liberties for their own class use. In their rise to power their alleged principles helped gain widespread support for what in reality turned out to be narrow class aims. However, this tactic could be made to backfire by those who took liberal principles at face value and extended them beyond the use for which their nominal advocates intended them. When this happens the whole hard-won liberty package is redefined as 'socialistic' and thrown overboard. Liberty thus sinks below the surface so that political influence may rise out of reach above it. The bourgeoisie then cling all the more tenaciously to their economic and social power, and align themselves with upper-class political reaction. When, in the France of 1850, 'Universal suffrage declared itself directly against the domination of the bourgeoisie: the bourgeoisie answered by outlawing universal suffrage'.[15] The polite veil of parliamentary practice had been allowed to fall, and power clearly shown to rest upon bodies of armed men.

Parliament and Revolution

The above analysis leads too easily to the assumption that Marx and Engels regarded parliament as enemy terrain from which astute proletarian activists should keep a healthy distance, and that the proper location for them was either workplace trade union agitation or, better still, class revolutionary activism. It is easy to find highly publicized passages, particularly from the *Manifesto* and the March 1850 *Address*, which clearly envisage revolutionary violence.[16] These are sufficiently glamorous to have stolen the show. Supporters rejoice in the heady prospect of heroic deeds. Detractors are thankful to find Marx and Engels discrediting themselves in the eyes of all respectable opinion. Neither side sufficiently notices that they have mistaken a part for the whole. Marx and Engels did not envisage the labour movement's inevitably arriving at a historical juncture where the signpost to socialism reads *either* left towards the barricades *or* right through the parliamentary voting lobby. The notion that a revolutionary party has no interest in a bourgeois parliament finds no confirmation in the writings of Marx and Engels. For them the parliamentary and revolutionary paths were not mutually exclusive. If we examine their writings on Chartism, which had parliamentary aspirations, and the German SPD, which engaged more fully in parliamentary practice, we find criticisms of certain theoretical and tactical failures, but not of their parliamentary orientation as such.

The Chartists

It is truer of Marx and Engels than of most political leaders that silence implies consent, for were there ever analysts with a keener eye for deviations from political rectitude? Note the tendency to issue former associates with summary dismissal, to cut themselves off from and scorn the political groupings with which in many respects they seemed closest, to be suspicious of alliance and compromise, which they only enter into with an instrumental purpose that more than borders on the cynical, and to feel intellectually constrained by membership of party.

Yet of the Chartists hardly more than the most occasional and muted criticism can be found. From 1843 to 1850 Engels contributed to the Chartist *Northern Star*. In an 1847 speech he declared that he had 'lived in England for a number of years now and openly aligned [himself] with the Chartist movement during this period'.[17] A year earlier he and Marx had penned an adulatory 'Address of the German Democratic Communists of Brussels to Mr Feargus O'Connor', on the occasion of that Chartist leader's election to Parliament.[18] The Chartist Six Points, with their overwhelmingly parliamentary orientation, are explicitly referred to on a number of occasions. There were particularly compelling reasons why the later German socialist Gotha Programme was subjected to sustained heavy onslaught, but we can still conclude that in a more general sense Marx and Engels were not the people to let a formulated radical programme escape their careful critical scrutiny. Although tactical considerations always have to be borne in mind, we can still conclude that their 'failure' to criticize the Chartist Six Points was simply a consequence of their finding them generally unobjectionable. Chartism had its 'physical force' wing and it is inconceivable that Marx and Engels could have been unaware of it, but that aspect remained unmentioned and was not in fact represented in the Charter itself. This only looks like a fall from the lofty peaks of revolutionary zeal if one misunderstands Marx and Engels on the ambiguous concept of 'revolution'. Perhaps the primary image this term now evokes is of storming the Bastille or taking the Winter Palace. This aspect is definitely not rejected but neither is it the essence of the thing. For Marx and Engels the French Revolution was more than its most glamorous or notorious events – the Tennis Court oath, the 14th of July, the guillotining of the King. These were surface moments the essence of which was the destruction of feudalism and its replacement by a social system favourable to the full development of capitalism. Revolution is not so much the means as the consequences. By the same mentality Chartism and its demand for universal suffrage could be revolutionary to the extent that it furthered the process by which capitalism was to be replaced by communism. Thus democracy, rather than being an alternative to revolution, would be the first stage of it. Universal suffrage spelled the end of the prevailing order; it implied socialism. In contrast, Disraeli held that 'the wider the popular suffrage, the more powerful would be the natural aristocracy'.[19] He appears to have been more accurate than the Establishment pessimists whose basic analysis Marx and Engels for a time shared. For them, however, it was a source of hope. 'In England's present condition "legal progress" and universal suffrage would inevitably result in a revolution', declared Engels in 1842.[20] And two years later: 'These six points, which are all limited to the reconstitution of the House of Commons, harmless as they seem, are sufficient to overthrow the whole English Constitution, Queen and Lords included'.[21] Lest we seem to be relying too exclusively on Engels, from whom most of the writings on Britain derive, we should note that in 1848 Marx referred to 'the revolutionary might of the Chartists'[22] and four years later he pointed out that

Universal Suffrage is the equivalent for (*sic*) political power for the working class of England, where the proletariat forms the large majority of the population ... the carrying out of Universal Suffrage in England would, therefore, be a far more socialistic measure than anything which has been honoured with that name on the Continent. Its inevitable result here is *the political supremacy of the working class.*[23]

The achievement of universal suffrage in England would take place in a country already predominantly urban, whereas its previous unwelcome results in France were held to be the consequence of a social structure dominated numerically by a rural peasantry.

The Chartists were held to be 'the first working men's party which the world ever produced'.[24] In spite of a certain theoretical backwardness, their militancy, commitment and rejection of compromise placed them ahead of comparable socialist movements in Germany and France. Indeed in 1874 Engels complained that English labour leaders had fallen below the level of political maturity achieved by the Chartists a quarter of a century earlier.

Nobody holds it against the 'labour leaders' that they would have liked to get into Parliament. The shortest way would have been to proceed at once to form anew a strong workers' party with a definite programme, and the best political programme they could wish for was the People's Charter.[25]

German Social Democracy

It is also worthwhile considering Marx and Engels's treatment of German Social Democracy. The fledgling party was to be criticized for many things. The whole Lassallean credo of naive faith in the state, secret links with Bismarck, a projected alliance with the aristocracy, and the iron law of wages, all suffered the onslaught of their intellectual attack. Certain of their parliamentary tactics occasionally suffered similar treatment but *not* the actual practice of playing the electoral game and winning seats in the Reichstag.

In 1867 August Bebel and Wilhelm Liebknecht were elected to the Reichstag of the North German Federation. Liebknecht in particular showed what use could be made of such a forum and what costs had to be borne. Rather than succumb to the seductive allure of the parliamentary arena, he used his position to articulate a policy of uncompromising hostility to chauvinism abroad and repression at home. The result was predictable. For opposition to the annexation of Alsace and Lorraine, for their vote against the war credits, and for their sympathetic attitude to the Paris Commune, Bebel and Liebknecht were imprisoned on the charge of high treason. During the trial 'the accused ... used the court room as a tribune for propagating social democratic ideas'.[26] Here we have a model for the practice of socialists in a bourgeois parliamentary context. Parliamentary representation, when properly fulfilled, is no soft option of security and status. It is rather a front-line position in the articulation of proletarian demands, and so draws upon itself the full force of repression available to the state apparatus. Imprisonment thus becomes an occupational hazard. The level of repression is both a pointer to the underlying reality of bourgeois parliamentarism and an index of the extent to which workers' representatives are doing their proper job of making demands incompatible with the prevailing socio-political order. There is no doubt that this form of parliamentary practice, even in the context of the backward Prussian constitution, was considered more useful than a heroic, glamorous, but ultimately futile insurrectionary gesture in conditions where real advance was either impossible or unsustainable.

In the 1874 elections the Social Democrat vote more than tripled its 1871 total. A delighted Friedrich Engels wrote to Liebknecht: 'The elections in Germany place the German proletariat at the summit of the European labour movement'. It is worth reiterating what put them there. The emphasis is not on their political militancy against the Prussian state, nor trade union activism against the employers, but rather 'the elections'. 'For the first time the workers voted *en masse* for their own people, and rely on their own party, and that over the whole of Germany'.[27] Not even the anti-socialist law seemed able to stem the apparently ineluctable avalanche of mass support. By 1890 the party had added more than a million votes to its 1874 total. The achievement of full political power appeared a certainty, at least to Engels.

> Today the party has 35 deputies and one and a half million voters, more voters than any other party could boast in the '90 election. Eleven years' Imperial proscription and state of siege have strengthened it fourfold, and made it the strongest party in Germany .... This party stands today at the point where one can ascertain, with virtually mathematical precision, the time at which it will achieve dominance.[28]

Johan Jacoby, active in the 1848 Revolution, had been elected to the Reichstag in 1874, but refused to take his seat. He could not envisage the parliamentary approach changing a military state into a people's republic. Marx and Engels's anger at this decision is instructive,[29] for it confirms the extent to which parliamentary practice was accepted as fitting. Not that they shared any illusion that Germany was as free as some of its major partners in trade. In the 'Critique of the Gotha Programme' Marx described it as 'nothing but a police-guarded military despotism, embellished with parliamentary forms, alloyed with a feudal admixture, already influenced by the bourgeoisie and bureaucratically carpentered'.[30] Engels was later to reiterate Liebknecht's designation of the Reichstag as merely 'the figleaf of absolutism'.[31]

It was particularly in this context that the old political tricks could be expected if a party of the left threatened to emerge above the level of a small sectarian clique. On the eve of the 1874 successes Engels rightly predicted that the state would assert itself against popular parliamentary effrontery. Repression commenced that very year, culminating later in the Exceptional Law against the 'universally dangerous endeavours of Social Democracy', which remained in force from 1878 to 1890.

The misuse of 'legality' against Social Democracy raises the question of the latter's attitude to the former. Does the adoption of parliamentary tactics preclude one from turning to less decorous means when necessary? Not so, according to Marx, who in 1880 presented SPD parliamentarism as a suitable tactic for a stage when the movement had not sufficient power and ability to mount a direct challenge to the regime.

> In Germany the working class were fully aware from the beginning of their movement that you cannot get rid of a military despotism but by a Revolution. At the same time they understood that such a Revolution, even if at first successful, would finally turn against them without previous organisation, acquirement of knowledge, propaganda .... Hence they moved within strictly *legal* bounds.[32]

Note here that the need for revolution is premissed upon there being a *military despotism* that has to be removed. What if, instead of this half-feudal form, socialists were confronted with a developed system of bourgeois representative democracy? If we refer to Marx's famous 1872 speech in Amsterdam we find that

> there are countries such as America and England, and, if I was familiar with its institutions, I might include Holland, where the workers may attain their goal by peaceful means. That being the case, we must recognize that, in most Continental countries the lever of the revolution will have to be force; a resort to force will be necessary one day in order to set up the rule of labour.[33]

This Amsterdam speech is frequently taken to be either an aberration or a change of mind, although it is not necessarily either. It would only become so if one assumed a mutually exclusive 'either-or' dogmatism on the question of paths to socialism. Our argument here, however, is that Marx and Engels were fairly pragmatic on means, which were dictated by the particular prevailing situation.

The implication that a sovereign representative chamber might allow a peaceful transition to socialism was made more explicit in Engels's critique of the 1891 Social Democratic draft programme.

> One can imagine that the old society could peacefully grow into the new in countries where all power is concentrated in the people's representatives, where one can constitutionally do as one pleases as soon as a majority of the people give their support: in democratic Republics like France and America, in monarchies such as England ... where [the] dynasty is powerless against the people's will. But in Germany, where the government is virtually all-powerful and the Reichstag and other representative bodies are without real power, to proclaim likewise in Germany, and that without necessity, is to accept the figleaf of absolutism and to bind oneself to it.[34]

The initial requirement in Germany, then, was to complete the bourgeois revolution by constitutional reforms that give the people's representatives legal sovereignty. This would work to the advantage of Social Democracy, which had the weight of numbers on its side. As the bourgeoisie are the most threatened by the rise of democracy, the question of the use of force should primarily be addressed to them. 'No doubt, they will shoot first',[35] for which reason the Social Democrats could not comply with the request that they renounce in principle the right to resort to non-legal means.

The most pronounced sign of adaptation to the parliamentary system appeared in Engels's 1895 reconsideration of the lessons of the Paris Commune. Now the old insurrectionary tactics appeared antiquated. The fire power at the disposal of the military was such that any popular uprising would be courting disaster. But as the balance of physical force became more adverse, the extension of the franchise more than provided compensation. The electoral process supplied a platform from which proletarian demands could be articulated and an accurate measure of the parties' respective strengths ascertained. However, in France, Spain and Switzerland universal (male) franchise had not been put to good effect. It remained for the German workers to set an example to others by their intelligent use of the suffrage. 'Slow propaganda work and parliamentary activity are ... the immediate tasks of the party'.[36]

We, the 'revolutionists', the 'overthrowers' – we are thriving far better on legal methods than on illegal methods and overthrow. The parties of order, as they call themselves, are perishing under legal conditions created by themselves. They cry despairingly ... legality is the death of us: whereas we, under this legality, get firm muscles and rosy cheeks and look like life eternal.[37]

Already in 1880 Marx had chided the English working class for their failure 'to wield their power and use their liberties, both of which they possess legally'.[38] In the *Manifesto* the sense of party had been decidedly weak but by the end of the century the context of working-class struggle had altered in a marked way. Working men were getting the vote and electing their own representatives to parliament. Engels's remarks on the need to make use of the possibilities that bourgeois society offered seem to mark a late adaptation to a changed situation but are in fact already latent and so merely expand and strengthen remarks made in his 1847 'Draft of a Communist Confession of Faith' and 'Principles of Communism'.[39] In the final version of the *Manifesto* Engels's comments on the establishment of a democratic constitution were emasculated into the brief and rather ambiguous phrase about winning 'the battle of democracy'.[40] To a large extent Marxism reached the European labour movement in the form Engels gave it. Thus the much derided reformism of the Second International should be seen less as a breach with Marxism than as the continuation of one of its tendencies.

Conclusion

From the Marxist standpoint it is not political representation as such but rather the particular form of it which is peculiar to the bourgeois state. The feudal system tended towards limited representation on the inflexible basis of the recognized Estates. In time bourgeois rule removed the remaining vestiges of this antiquated form and replaced it with the parliamentary system of liberal democracy. From Marx's few remarks on the Paris Commune we learn that representation under proletarian rule would not have a parliamentary form in the sense of a deliberative chamber formulating legislation for the nation as a whole. This would be replaced by an assembly of delegates, 'each delegate to be at any time revocable and bound by the *mandat impératif* (formal instructions) of his constituents'.[41]

Marx and Engels's critique of the parliamentary system and their notions of replacing it in a post-revolutionary situation lead all too easily to the belief that parliamentary representation was regarded as an alternative to revolution. It is this false assumption that we have attempted to remedy. To challenge bourgeois society it is necessary to make use of all the opportunities that it itself offers. A parliamentary system was preferred to a non-parliamentary one in that it provided a forum that could be used as *one aspect* of the struggle for socialism.

Notes

1. K. Marx and F. Engels, 3 *CW*, p. 75.
2. G.W.F. Hegel, *Philosophy of Right* (Oxford, Oxford University Press, 1983), para. 307.
3. Marx and Engels, 3 *CW*, p. 114.
4. K. Marx and F. Engels, 2 *MESW*, p. 320.
5. Marx and Engels, 11 *CW*, pp. 114–15.
6. Marx and Engels, 3 *CW*, p. 79.
7. Marx and Engels, 11 *CW*, p. 345.
8. Marx and Engels, 3 *CW*, p. 497.
9. K. Marx and F. Engels, *MESC*, p. 473.
10. Marx and Engels, 38 *CW*, p. 96.
11. Marx and Engels, 11 *CW*, p. 79.
12. Marx and Engels, 6 *CW*, p. 519 (emphasis added).
13. Marx and Engels, 7 *CW*, p. 179.
14. Marx and Engels, 11 *CW*, p. 180.
15. Ibid., p. 146.
16. But see Hunt's reminder that neither of these works was originally published under their authors' names, and his suggestion that they contained much to appease artisan impatience (R.N. Hunt, *The Political Ideas of Marx and Engels*, vol. 1, *Marxism and Totalitarian Democracy 1818–1850* (London and Basingstoke, Macmillan, 1975), pp. 151–2, 188, 190, 235, 236).
17. Marx and Engels, 6 *CW*, p. 389.
18. Ibid., pp. 58–60.
19. Quoted in S.M. Beer, *Modern British Politics* (London, Faber, 1965), p. 255.
20. Marx and Engels, 2 *CW*, p. 369.
21. Marx and Engels, 4 *CW*, p. 518.

22. Marx and Engels, 8 *CW*, p. 101.
23. Marx and Engels, 11 *CW*, pp. 335–6.
24. Marx and Engels, *AOB*, p. 380.
25. Ibid., p. 367.
26. W. Theimer, *Von Bebel zu Ollenhauer. Der Weg der deutschen Sozialdemokratie* (Bern, Franke Verlag, 1957), p. 26. Also see Marx, K., 'Die Presse- und Redefreiheit in Deutschland' in K. Marx and F. Engels, *Werke*, vol. 17, p. 283.
27. G. Eckert, ed., *Wilhelm Liebknecht. Briefwechsel mit Karl Marx und Friedrich Engels* (The Hague, Mouton, 1963), p. 184.
28. F. Engels, 'Der Sozialismus in Deutschland' in Marx and Engels, *Werke*, vol. 22, p. 250.
29. See August Bebel, *Aus meinem Leben*, ed. W.G. Oschilewski, (Berlin and Bonn-Bad Godesberg, Verlag J.H.W. Dietz, 1976) pp. 103, 208; Eckert, *Wilhelm Liebknecht. Briefwechsel mit Karl Marx und Friedrich Engels*, p. 185, n. 10.
30. Marx and Engels, *MESW*, p. 328. A more specific but still fairly brief account of the political system established in 1871 may be found in B. Russell, *German Social Democracy* (London, Allen & Unwin, 1965) pp. 83–8.
31. Marx and Engels, *Werke*, vol. 22, p. 233. See also p. 252.
32. Marx and Engels, *MESC*, p. 334.
33. K. Marx, *The First International and After* (Harmondsworth, Penguin, 1974), p. 324
34. Marx and Engels, *Werke*, vol. 22, p. 234.
35. Ibid., p. 251.
36. Marx and Engels, 2 *MESW*, p. 664.
37. Ibid., p. 666.
38. Marx and Engels, *MESC*, p. 334.
39. See Marx and Engels, 6 *CW*, pp. 102, 350.
40. Ibid., p. 504. In the spirit of Hunt one might regard this shift of emphasis as made to accommodate the artisan elements of the Communist League.
41. Marx and Engels, *MESW*, p. 288.

11
The Problem of Coercion and Consent in Marx and Gramsci

John Hoffman

Since the late 1960s there has been a substantial amount written on Marx's theory of politics, and more recently, this has become increasingly critical in tone. Some have indeed proclaimed a veritable 'crisis of Marxism', ascribing this crisis to the fact that what Marx had to say about politics and the state was either 'incoherent', 'contradictory' or 'extraordinarily weak'.[1] Four deficiencies in Marx's theory of politics are commonly pinpointed:

(a) the concept of politics as a superstructure arising from and ultimately determined by an economic base is a *reductionist* notion that makes it impossible to construct a specific theory of politics and the state;
(b) the view of the state as a committee for managing the common affairs of the whole bourgeoisie is *instrumentalist* in character since it implies that the state is merely a passive tool in the hands of a ruling class and has no dynamic of its own;[2]
(c) the assumption of an ever increasing polarization between bourgeoisie and proletariat as part of the inevitable collapse of capitalism suggests an economic *catastrophism* that makes the development of political theory redundant;[3]
(d) the concept of the state as an organ of coercion is a negative and restricted one which, in failing to analyse the ideological and cultural aspects of political power,[4] neglects the all-important question of *consent* in politics.

It is this last point, (d), which particularly interests me, for it is this criticism above all that invites attention to an aspect of the discussion which has been somewhat neglected, namely the relationship of Marx to Gramsci. While Marx is found guilty of a negative and restricted view of politics, Gramsci, it is argued, inaugurated a new chapter in Marxist political theory through his expanded view of the state: his insistence that politics involves not merely coercion, but also consent.[5] In the now celebrated formulation: 'The State is the entire complex of practical and theoretical activities with which the ruling class not only justifies and maintains its dominance, but manages to win the active consent of those over whom it rules'.[6]

This then is the question which is central to my paper: if, as Hobsbawm (among others) has argued, Gramsci was the pioneer of a Marxist theory of politics,[7] where does his position stand in relation to that of Marx? Marx seems to define politics narrowly in terms of coercion, while Gramsci analyses it broadly in terms of coercion *and* consent. Central to Gramsci's political thought (particularly in the *Prison Notebooks*) is his concept of *hegemony*: the aspect of politics which relates to consent rather than to coercion, 'intellectual and moral leadership'[8] rather than domination or dictatorship.

I want to argue in terms of three possible positions which can be adopted in an attempt to resolve the problem of the 'Marx–Gramsci relationship':

(i)   That Gramsci was indeed a pioneer who was the first to develop a full political theory within Marxism.

(ii) That Gramsci offered not a new theory of politics, but at most, a new reading of an old one, thus making explicit what had been implicit without actually departing from Marx's basic assumptions.

(iii) That Gramsci did a bit of both. His 'dual perspective'[9] involves both a new (and more interesting) reading of the Marxist classics *as well as* a new theory which 'breaks' from the past. This is a rediscovery of an older position and, at the same time, a reformulation of the question which from Marx's own standpoint, must be contentious and problematic.

I will seek to establish the following. While there is *prima facie* evidence for position (i), a rather stronger case can be made for position (ii). The latter, however, leaves a number of important problems unresolved so that position (iii) emerges as the most viable interpretation of the Marx–Gramsci relationship. Before elaborating on the above, one subsidiary point is worth making. Tackling the problem of coercion and consent in Marx and Gramsci has implications for analysing the other deficiencies claimed for Marx's theory of politics. The first three criticisms noted above all turn on the question of the relationship of politics to economics ('basis' and 'superstructure', 'ruling class' and 'state'). So in fact (although this point is less obvious at first) does the fourth – the problem which is the subject of this paper.[10]

Marx contra Gramsci: the Apparent Conflict

Marx's view of the state seems to focus essentially on the existence of a 'public force organised for social enslavement ... an engine of class despotism'.[11] Engels, for this reason, sets himself against all formulations of a 'free state' on the grounds that under socialism that state is only a transitional institution necessary 'to hold down one's adversaries by force'.[12] It is force which is emphasized in the definition of political power offered in the *Communist Manifesto* – 'the organised power of one class for oppressing another'[13] – and which is stressed when Marx tells Bakunin that the proletariat must use 'forcible means, hence governmental means'.[14] A political movement, Marx writes to Bolte in 1871, is a 'class movement, with the object of enforcing its interests in a general form, in a form possessing general, socially coercive force'.[15] Ralph Miliband writes (as an intended criticism of the classical approach) that for Marx and Engels, the state was 'above all, the coercive instrument of a ruling class'[16] and clearly these coercive-orientated definitions are continued in the Leninist, Trotskyist and Stalinist traditions.[17]

The contrast with Gramsci seems stark enough. Gramsci insists upon a 'dual perspective' which he traces back to Machiavelli's Centaur, half-animal and half-human, and Machiavelli's belief that 'there are two ways of fighting: by Law or by force ... as the first way often proves inadequate one must needs have recourse to the second'.[18] The doctrine of hegemony is specifically developed 'as a complement to the theory of the State-as-force'[19] and it is on the basis of coercion and consent that Gramsci proliferates his 'antinomies' between leadership and domination, the public and private and his 'two major superstructural levels', civil and political society.[20] Whether the definition of these antinomies is always consistent[21] is, from my point of view, less important than the fact that Gramsci's analysis is emphatically dualist in character. While Marx seems to be saying that politics is essentially coercive, Gramsci's argument is that 'two fundamental levels'[22] are involved. In the case of the liberal parliamentary regime, we have, says Gramsci, a system characterised 'by the combination of force and consent, which balance each other reciprocally, without force predominating excessively'.[23] How can we square this assertion with Marx's view that, even in liberal democracies, political power involves the organized oppression of one class by another?

Gramsci and Marx : A Deeper Consensus

There are a number of reasons for supposing that Gramsci, notwithstanding the arguments of position (i), is closer to the classical Marxist tradition than is sometimes suggested. I want to suggest at least three.

The first is the fact, not sufficiently emphasized in the Gramsci literature, that Gramsci does after all refer to the coercive aspect of politics as constituting *political* society and indeed, at times, Gramsci does speak of the state simply in these terms.[24] This might therefore be taken to suggest that, despite the dualist formulations, force or coercion is somehow *central* to the state. Certainly, as both Anderson and Femia have stressed, Gramsci took for granted the stress placed by the Marxism of the Comintern on the necessity of violence in the construction and destruction of states[25] and hence Gramsci's concern was to *supplement* rather than to supplant classical definitions. His earlier comment in 1919 that 'the principle of political power will wither away all the more rapidly under socialism' as the workers become 'more united and disciplined in the context of production'[26] fully accords with a coercion-centred view of politics.

The second reason for questioning the kind of contrast set out in position (i) arises from a more careful reading of Marx's own statements on the nature of politics, a reading stimulated no doubt by Gramsci's stress on hegemony-as-consent. While the centrality of Marx's emphasis on politics-as-force is undeniable, what emerges on closer inspection is that Marx is not equating politics with force *per se* but with force of a special kind. Political power, to recall the definition in the *Communist Manifesto*, is not merely the power with which one class oppresses another, but it is class power which has to be 'organized'. What does this organization involve? A political movement (Marx to Bolte) is a class movement 'with the object of enforcing its interest in a *general* form', a form 'possessing *general*, socially coercive force'.[27] The 'generality' of political coercion is also stressed in the reference to the state in the *Communist Manifesto* as the committee which manages the common affairs of the bourgeoisie as a whole. Why Marx's analysis of political coercion implies a vital ideological input is made particularly clear in *The German Ideology*, where it is argued that the class which is the 'ruling material force' must also establish itself as 'the ruling intellectual force' and this can only be achieved if such a class represents 'its interest as the common interest of all the members of society, that is, expressed in ideal form'.[28] This could certainly be interpreted in Gramscian terms as the need for a ruling class to win the consent of those over whom it rules, a task which could be facilitated by two further points noted by Marx. One is that the class making a revolution does, initially at any rate, express the 'common interest of all other non-ruling classes'[29] and the other – a point made by Marx in *Capital* – that state intervention in society involves both 'the performance of those common tasks that arise from the nature of all communities and the specific functions that arise from the opposition between the government and the mass of the people'.[30] It is presumably the role of 'ideology' to make it as easy as possible to confuse the two!

All this would suggest, therefore, that Gramsci is not alone in identifying an ideological or consensual dimension to politics. Marx's reference to the state as the 'official expression of civil society'[31] seems as expansive a definition as anything which Gramsci formulates. It is true that, for Marx, material and intellectual force are closely intertwined but so are they for Gramsci. Gramsci argues in the *Prison Notebooks* that his distinction between civil and political society (that is, consent and coercion) is 'merely methodological' and that 'in actual reality civil society and the 'State are one and the same'.[32] Hegemony should not be thought of as some kind of autonomous sphere which exists outside the class struggle. While hegemony, says Gramsci, is 'ethical-political, it must also be economic, must necessarily be based on the decisive function exercised by the leading group in the decisive nucleus of economic activity'.[33] The aspect of consent is intimately tied to what Gramsci calls elsewhere the 'aspect of force and economics'.[34] If this is so, then both Gramsci and Marx define politics in a way which incorporates both coercion and consent, and can it not be argued that Gramsci's great merit is not that he pioneered a new theory of politics but that his work has stimulated the rediscovery of an old one?

There is a third reason for arguing such a case. In the late 1880s Engels found himself confronted with versions of Marx's theory which presented historical materialism as an economic determinism: a 'meaningless, abstract, absurd'[35] presentation which Engels considered un-Marxist. At the same time, Engels did concede that in the general formulations of their theory, materialism had been stressed at the expense of dialectics. 'It is the old story: form is always neglected at first for content'[36] and although this was not the far-reaching confession of failure which some have assumed,[37] it did make the point that given Marx and Engels's preoccupation with debunking the idealists, they were 'partly to blame for the fact that the younger people sometimes lay more stress on the economic side than is due to it'.[38] Engels seemed to be saying the following: the substance of their theory (as far as politics is concerned) identifies the state as coercion and emphasizes the 'general dependence'[39] of the state on economic conditions. So much for the 'content', but what of the question of 'form' (a side of the theory which had not been neglected, Engels insisted, when it came to applying the theory in practice)?[40] The formal aspect points to 'the *particular* part played by political struggles and events',[41] the political movement 'endowed with relative independence' and 'with a movement of its own'.[42] In short, the state as coercion of a *particular* kind. Materialism pointed to the importance of the 'base'; dialectics to the irreducibility and efficacy of the 'superstructures'. If Marx was particularly concerned to emphasize the first, Gramsci developing his theory in a very different political context, was anxious to stress the second.

By 1924, Gramsci had become preoccupied with forging a strategy and tactics which would be 'more complex and long term than those which were necessary for the Bolsheviks in the period between March and November 1917'.[43] The main theoretical problem, as he saw it, was not philosophical idealism but a vulgar 'economism' which underplayed the importance of strategic political thinking and hence disarmed the communist movement in the face of Mussolini's fascism. In the *Prison Notebooks* great emphasis is laid on the importance of developing an 'autonomous science of politics' within the 'philosophy of praxis' (that is, Marxism) and we find Gramsci arguing that politics is at once 'borne on the "permanent and organic" terrain of economic life' (the materialist point) and at the same time, an activity 'which transcends' this terrain, bringing into play emotions and aspirations which 'obey different laws from those of organised profit'.[44] Is this not substantially the same point as Engels made to Bloch and others in the 1890s? Gramsci's concern with the autonomy of politics (its 'relative independence') rather than with its roots in economic life suggests, on this argument, less a theory which diverges from the positions of Marx and Engels than a divergent *context* – a concern with *historical* materialism rather than historical *materialism*. A more careful examination of Marx and Gramsci in the light of their particular (and contrasting) preoccupations reveals a deeper consensus which belies the argument of position (i).

Gramsci and Marx : the Problem of Dualism

There can be little doubt from the arguments advanced in position (ii) that both Marx and Gramsci have 'broad' conceptions of politics which embrace both coercion and consent. The problem, however, is this: while both coercion and consent are involved, it does not follow that both aspects are related to one another by Marx and Gramsci in the same kind of way. For Marx, the relationship seems to be this. Politics embraces coercion and consent because politics centres around coercion organized in a *particular* way which commands consent. A ruling material force requires a ruling intellectual force in order to present particular class interests in expansively general terms and thus win popular support for class rule. Interestingly enough, Marx and Engels, in *The German Ideology*, do speak of a class achieving 'hegemony'[45] but it is clear that the term 'hegemony' is merely a synonym for 'domination'.[46] There is nothing to suggest that political power can be broken up into domination or coercion, on the one hand, and hegemony or consent, on the other. For Gramsci, however, politics is more than just coercion which commands consent – force capable of persuading – it is coercion *and* consent. In what sense are these two different aspects separable?

This, in my view, is a serious problem in Gramsci. In the arguments around position (ii), I have already noted Gramsci's comment that 'in actual reality' civil society and the state are one and the same. The distinction, in his terminology, is 'methodological' rather than 'organic'. In practice, however, Gramsci finds this distinction difficult to sustain. In the famous comment contrasting society–state relations in East and West, Gramsci speaks of the state as 'an outer ditch, behind which there stood a powerful system of fortresses and earthworks'... 'when the State trembled a sturdy structure of civil society was at once revealed'.[47] This seems to imply an almost tangible separation between the two. One might be captured by revolutionaries but not the other. Indeed, this would appear to be the reason why Gramsci, in another, equally well-known comment, argues that a social group must become hegemonic *before* it attains governmental power.[48] Leadership first, then domination. Likewise, Gramsci argues elsewhere that when a ruling class loses its popular support, it becomes dominant without 'leading': it exercises coercive force alone.[49]

The contrast with Marx is compounded by the fact that not only does Gramsci appear to be saying that consent and coercion *are* 'organically' or empirically separable ('in actual reality'), but that some of his formulations might be taken to imply that, within the 'balance', decisive weight rests with *consent*. If, as Gramsci says on one occasion, the state is 'political society plus civil society: hegemony protected by the armour of coercion',[50] does this not suggest that consent is more central than coercion? One seems to be the core: the other merely the external plating.

If this construction is valid, then there is indeed an important difference in the way in which Marx and Gramsci handle the coercion–consent relationship. Gramsci appears to be saying that while the two aspects are both involved in politics, politics is *essentially* about moral leadership – a leadership reinforced or protected by the armour of coercion. In Marx, the emphasis is the reverse. Politics is *essentially* about coercion but about the kind of coercion which is organized in an idealizing, morally justifying manner. In other words, what is essential for the one thinker is contingent for the other. Form and content are diametrically opposed. Moreover, support for this argument can be found in the differences between Marx and Gramsci over what might be called the problem of agency in historical materialism.

In *The German Ideology*, Marx and Engels comment that 'in actual history, those theoreticians who regarded *might* as the basis of right were in direct contradiction to those who looked on *will* as the basis of right'.[51] Marx clearly sides with those who stress the primacy of 'might' or power. It is true that Marx speaks in 1844 of 'the principle of politics' as 'will' but he does so in order to castigate the 'political mind' as blind to the natural and spiritual limits of the will and thus 'incapable of discovering the real source of social ills'.[52] Central to Marx's theory of history (at least from *The German Ideology* onwards) is the premise that people enter into relations of production, relations which constitute 'the real basis of the state',[53] *independently of their will*. In this way Marx can be said to banish from his theory what might be called an independent voluntarism, that is, the existence of the will, politics, consciousness, purpose, and so on, as wholly autonomous factors in the making of history. Politics as will exists, to be sure, but always in a context in which people 'work under definite material limits, presuppositions and conditions independent of their will'.[54] The necessity of production, a historical act which 'must daily and hourly be fulfilled in order to sustain human life',[55] stands as the fundamental condition of history.

Gramsci was of course familiar with the broad outlines of Marx's theory and frequently quotes the comments on historical materialism in Marx's Preface to his *Contribution to the Critique of Political Economy* and yet his view of human agency differs significantly. In a critique of 'mechanical determinism', Gramsci speaks of the need 'to put the "will" (which in the last analysis equals practical or political activity) at the base of philosophy'.[56] It is true that this must be a 'rational will which corresponds to objective historical necessities'[57] but to say that the will *corresponds* to necessities is not the same as saying that (albeit in some complex, interactive manner) the will is a product of 'objective historical necessities'. Marx does say that people make their circumstances, they are free-willing agents, but is this not rooted in the fact that 'circumstances make people'?[58] The English editors of the *Prison Notebooks* note that, whereas Marx speaks of freedom with necessity 'as its basis', Gramsci develops a notion of freedom untrammelled by the need 'to take as its basis contradictions engendered in the world of material production'.[59] Since in the passage concerned the movement from 'necessity to freedom' is linked to the 'passage' from the 'purely economic' to the 'ethical-political moment', this is surely a point of some importance. Whereas for Marx even the freest of wills remains a determined determinant, for Gramsci, the will appears to become an autonomous agency which interacts with (rather than arises from) the material world. When Gramsci speaks of humans as 'concrete will', it is clear that the will is 'concrete' because it acts in and through the external world[60] and yet seemingly emanates from a source outside it. Just how Marx constructs a 'new materialism' which combines agency with structural determinism is a question for another paper, but one point is clear. If for Marx, politics is autonomous, it is autonomous because of the particular way the 'will' has been determined: there is not a 'balance' between a determining consent and its coercive determinant. For Gramsci, on the other hand, the consenting will breaks free from the world of coercive necessity. The philosophy of praxis is 'an absolute historicism'[61] and the world a 'historical nothingness' without the mediation of the will.

The arguments of position (ii) must yield to the arguments of position (iii). Gramsci does help to make us aware of the fact that Marx's view of politics is broader than is often supposed. At the same time there is a break with the classical conceptions. Consent for Marx arises in politics as part of a movement 'possessing general, socially coercive force'. In the case of Gramsci, a residual idealism leads him to suppose that the consenting will inhabits a separate world of its own.

Notes

1. L. Althusser, 'The Crisis of Marxism' in Il Manifesto, eds, *Power and Opposition in Post-Revolutionary Societies* (London, Ink Links, 1979), p. 234; E. Altvater, and O. Kallscheuer, 'Socialist Politics and the "Crisis of Marxism" ' in *The Socialist Register*, R. Miliband, and J. Saville, eds (London, Merlin Press, 1979), p. 105; F. Claudin, 'Some Reflections on the Crisis of Marxism', *Socialist Review*, vol. 45 (May–June 1979), p. 137; B. Jessop, 'Marx and Engels on the State' in S. Hibbin, ed., *Politics, Ideology and the State* (London, Lawrence and Wishart, 1978), p. 41; B. Jessop, 'The Gramsci Debate', *Marxism Today* (February 1980), p. 23.

2. A. Hunt, ed., *Marxism and Democracy* (London, Lawrence and Wishart, 1980) p. 40; A. Cutler, B. Hindess, P.Q. Hirst and A. Hussain, *Marx's 'Capital' and Capitalism Today* (London, Routledge and Kegan Paul, 1977), vol. 1, p. 172.

3. P. Anderson, *Considerations on Western Marxism* (London, New Left Books, 1976), p. 116; V. Perez-Diaz, *State, Bureaucracy and Civil Society* (Macmillan, London, 1978), p. 87.

4. R. Miliband, *The State in Capitalist Society* (London, Quartet Books, 1973), p. 8; idem, *Marxism and Politics* (Oxford, Oxford University Press, 1977), p. 43.

5. See, for example, E. Hobsbawm, 'Gramsci and Political Theory,' *Marxism Today* (July 1977), pp. 205–13; C. Mouffe, ed., *Gramsci and Marxist Theory* (London, Routledge and Kegan Paul, 1979); C. Buci-Glucksmann, *Gramsci and the State* (London, Lawrence and Wishart, 1980).

6. A. Gramsci, *Selections from the Prison Notebooks* (London, Lawrence and Wishart, 1971) p. 244.

7. Hobsbawm, 'Gramsci and Political Theory', p. 207 .

8. Gramsci, *Prison Notebooks*, p. 57.

9. Ibid., p. 169

10. It is worth noting that those who are most enthusiastic about Gramsci's 'expanded' view of politics, generally take the position that he is also able to avoid the sins of reductionism, instrumentalism and catastrophism (for example, Jessop, 'The Gramsci Debate', p. 25; Buci-Glucksmann, *Gramsci and the State*, p. x).

11. K. Marx, *The First International and After* (Harmondsworth, Penguin, 1974), p. 207.
12. Engels to Bebel, March 18–28, 1875, in K. Marx and F. Engels, *MESW*, p. 335.
13. K. Marx and F. Engels, 6 *CW*, p. 505.
14. Marx, *The First International*, p. 333.
15. K. Marx and F. Engels, *MESC*, p. 255.
16. Miliband, *The State in Capitalist Society*, p. 8.
17. See, for example, V.I. Lenin, *Collected Works*, vol. 25 (Moscow, Progress Publishers, 1966), p. 397; R. Blackburn, 'Marxism, Theory of Proletarian Revolution', *New Left Review*, no. 97 (May–June 1976), p. 18; Buci-Glucksmann, *Gramsci and the State*, p. 13.
18. Gramsci, *Prison Notebooks*, p. 170.
19. Ibid., p. 56n.
20. Ibid., p. 12.
21. P. Anderson, 'The Antinomies of Antonio Gramsci', *New Left Review*, no. 100, (November–January 1977), pp. 5–78.
22. Gramsci, *Prison Notebooks*, p. 169.
23. Ibid., p. 80n.
24. For example, ibid., p. 160.
25. Anderson, 'The Antinomies of Antonio Gramsci,' p. 46; J. Femia, 'Gramsci, the Via Italiana and the Classical Marxist-Leninist Approach to Revolution', *Government and Opposition*, vol. 14 (1979), p. 83.
26. Marx to Bolte, 23 November 1871, in Marx and Engels, *MESC*, p. 328 (emphasis added).
27. Buci-Glucksmann, *Gramsci and the State*, p. 155.
28. Marx and Engels, 5 *CW*, p. 60.
29. Ibid., p. 61.
30. K. Marx, 3 *Capital*, p. 508.
31. Marx and Engels, 38 *CW*, p. 96; F. Burlatsky, *The Modern State and Politics* (Moscow, Progress Publishers, 1978), p. 51.
32. Gramsci, *Prison Notebooks*, p. 161.
33. Ibid.
34. Ibid., p. 226; J. Texier, 'Gramsci, theoretician of the superstructures' in Mouffe, *Gramsci and Marxist Theory*, p. 67.
35. Marx and Engels, *MESC*, p. 394.
36. Ibid., p. 435.
37. J. Hoffman, *Marxism and the Theory of Praxis* (London, Lawrence and Wishart, 1975), pp. 112–15.
38. Marx and Engels, *MESC*, p. 396.
39. Ibid., p. 402.
40. Ibid., p. 396.
41. Ibid., p. 402.
42. Ibid., p. 399.
43. Gramsci, *Prison Notebooks*, p. lxvi.
44. Ibid., p. 140.
45. K. Marx and F. Engels, *The German Ideology*, ed. C. Arthur (London, Lawrence and Wishart, 1977), p. 66.
46. Indeed, in Marx and Engels, 5 *CW*, p. 61, the word 'hegemony' is dropped in favour of 'domination'.
47. Gramsci, *Prison Notebooks*, p. 238.
48. Ibid., p. 57. It may be thought that this proposition simply echoes the Leninist doctrine of proletarian hegemony (that is, leadership) in the struggle for democracy (see in particular, Anderson, 'The Antinomies of Antonio Gramsci',

pp. 16–17). Yet the difference is this: Gramsci speaks of political leadership in terms of a dichotomy between coercion and consent leadership as *opposed* to domination that would be difficult to square with Lenin's view of proletarian 'discipline'.

49. Gramsci, *Prison Notebooks*, p. 275.
50. Ibid., p. 263.
51. Marx and Engels, 5 *CW*, p. 329.
52. Marx and Engels, 3 *CW*, p. 199.
53. Marx and Engels, 5 *CW*, p. 329.
54. Ibid., p. 36.
55. Ibid., *CW*, p. 42.
56. Gramsci, *Prison Notebooks*, p. 345.
57. Ibid., p. 346.
58. Marx and Engels, 4 *CW*, pp. 130–1.
59. Gramsci, *Prison Notebooks*, p. 367n.
60. Ibid., p. 360.
61. Ibid., p. 463.

12
Marxism and Rights

Christopher Pierson

Marx and Rights

Characteristically, the socialist tradition has been seen to be divided in its attitude to law and, more particularly, to the practice of rights. On the one hand, for at least three centuries, the demand to be availed of one's civil, political and social rights has been a major element in the programmes and manifestos of the international labour movement and it is under this rubric that it has secured many of its most valued gains – for example, the right to form trade unions, the right to vote and the right to a minimum of social security. But of perhaps even longer standing is the counterposed associative disposition to hold the law at arm's length. This tendency takes a number of forms, ranging from a neo-anarchistic rejection of *all* forms of social regulation to the much milder belief that the law will become far less important once the adversarial legalism of a competitive market society gives way to the caring and curative practices of a socialist society.

In the past decade, this ambivalence towards the law – for long the butt of liberal and conservative criticisms – has come under increasing scrutiny from the representatives of 'libertarian socialism'. Singled out for especial criticism have been those recent neo-Marxist accounts which are seen to relegate law and rights (along with crime) to the class-divided circumstances of a capitalist society. In this paper, I want to consider the extent to which this view is, in fact, characteristic of Marx's own account of rights and to this extent deeply embedded in the very bases of Marxist politics.[1]

Rights and the Critique of Hegel

One commonplace view – that Marx only ever broke with his silence on rights to belittle them as a 'bourgeois sham' – can be immediately dismissed. Certainly, Marx was caustically critical of what he conceived to be the 'bourgeois misrepresentation' of rights as the consummation of political development and it is certainly possible to find examples of Marx expressing profound scepticism about the effectiveness of rights within the prevailing order. But, in fact, Marx did develop – in his early critique of Hegel's analysis of the state – a quite elaborate and sophisticated account of rights, occasional echoes of which can be heard throughout his more mature writings.

There is, in fact, much in Hegel's morphology of the state which Marx endorses, most notably the division between civil and political life, which both men characterize as distinguishing 'modern society' from feudalism. They both recognize that, under feudalism, economic and political life were intertwined, in what Marx styled 'the democracy of unfreedom' – where civil and political society were unified but the people were unfree – and they both contrast this unity with the separation of civil and political society which typifies the modern world.

It is in their differing evaluations of this civil–political division that the substantive difference between Marx and Hegel emerges. The core of Marx's critique is that Hegel, having recognized the separation of civil and political life as a contradiction, claims to find this opposition resolved in the form of the modern state, whereas, for Marx, it is the very *persistence* of this contradiction, characteristic of modern society, which calls into being the modern state. For Marx, 'the *constitution* of the *political state* and the dissolution of civil society into independent *individuals* – who are related by law... – are achieved in *one and the same act*'.[2] These two aspects of 'modern society' are but the two sides of one contradiction. The development of the political state is conditional upon and conterminous with the isolation of civil society, and the emergence of public life – the political state – is impossible without the concomitant development of private life – in civil society. Both issue simultaneously from the breakdown of the corporate life of feudalism. Political emancipation ensures the dissolution of the old order in which civil society has a directly political character. Similarly, as civil society became increasingly relieved of its former political constraints, the political realm, liberated from the 'adulteration of civil life', grew into 'the universal concern of the people ideally independent of [the] particular elements of civil life'. This process reached 'completion' in the French Revolution, following which '*class distinctions* in civil society became merely social differences in private life of no significance in political life'.[3]

In this way, Marx argues, the individual in the 'modern world' comes to lead a double life. Just as Christianity had taught of an inequality on earth but equality in heaven, so did the people become '*equal* in the heaven of their political world, though unequal in their earthly existence in *society*'.[4] Unlike the Christian, however, the modern citizen experiences not simply a divided consciousness, but indeed a divided reality – being, in political society, 'a communal being' (with communal interests), but, in civil society, a private individual struggling in the *bellum omnia contra omnes* of competing private interests. But Marx does not confine himself to the positing of the individual as divided and these two spheres of political and civil life as in opposition. Continuing the religious analogy, he gives it a Feuerbachian twist:

> The [political] state stands in the same opposition to civil society and overcomes it in the same way as religion overcomes the restrictions of the profane world, i.e. *it has to acknowledge it again, reinstate it and allow itself to be dominated by it.*[5]

For Marx, it is not just that under modern conditions civil and political society become the opposing poles of a single contradiction but further that civil society is the principal aspect of this contradiction – just as man's earthly existence is the principal aspect of the contradiction with his heavenly being.

'Political Emancipation': The Limitations of Rights

The consequence of Marx's position for an account of rights may become clearer if we pursue his own further breakdown of the civil–political division into two sets of related oppositions. As cited above, these are, first, 'the dissolution of civil society into independent *individuals* who are related by *law*', that is, the reduction of civil society into a sphere of atomistic and legally enabled individuals, capable of exercising justiciable rights under the rule of law, and second, 'the constitution of the political state', that is the more general estrangement of the state from (civil) society. We have already seen that Marx contends that the state cannot become the authentically universal sphere which Hegel envisaged because it is only called into being by (and is, as it were, the 'other side' of) the particularization of civil society. It is only the dissolution of civil society into mutually contending legal individuals which calls forth the modern state and it is only the persistence of the civil–political division which sustains it. Were this contradiction to be resolved, Marx argues, the very basis of the state would 'disappear'. Correspondingly, the general/universal interest which the state represents can be seen to constitute not an authentic (that is 'truly human') unity – for such a unity could only be found in an undivided person – but rather, the estranged expression of the general interest of civil society, that is the interest which each individual shares over against all the others in the *bellum omnia contra omnes*. The state does not overcome the contradictions and inequalities within civil society in establishing its realm of universal equality, it simply suspends them. Real differences in civil society are characterized as non-political and thus non-effective in the realm of the state.

Far from being the universal which overcomes the division between civil and political society, the state is then but the displaced representation of the general interest of civil society. This general interest cannot manifest itself directly in civil society, as this is the realm of dissociated and mutually competing individuals, but must rather find its abstract expression in the form of the state. However, since this general interest is formal and only obtained by abstracting from reality, 'the basis and content of such a "political society" inevitably remains civil society with all its economic divisions'.[6]

While civil society remains the unacknowledged and uncriticized premise of the political state, this state will continue to be 'shot through' by the contradiction within this displaced base. Civil society is the real basis of human life and the political state its ethereal projection. Thus, not only are political and civil life, citizen and bourgeois, seen to be dissociated but, Marx argues, the individual as bourgeois is held to be the more fundamental, unmediated and *natural* person, whose nature political life and the citizen exist to guarantee. But in fact, the freedom of such rights-bearing, legally enabled persons – for whom the political state acts only as a means, as guarantor of this freedom – is, for Marx, only the freedom of alienated, egoistic individuals, unmediated only in so far as the limitations of such a freedom have not been confronted and overcome. While 'man' is indeed recognized as 'a sovereign and supreme being', this is only 'man in his uncultivated, unsocial aspect ... man who is not yet a *true* species-being'. What is styled the freedom of the individual in civil society – the freedom to exercise one's rights under the law – is, in fact, the freedom of the individual's alienated life-activity. Thus, for Marx, the acknowledgement of the freedom of egoistic 'man' is rather 'the acknowledgement of the *unbridled* movement of the spiritual and material elements which form the content of his life'.[7]

The limitations of this 'partial' freedom and the possibility of going beyond it, Marx considers at length in his essay *On the Jewish Question*. Here he confronts the opposition of the Young Hegelian Bruno Bauer to the extension to the German Jews of the right to religious freedom. Such freedom was worthless, Bauer had argued, because it could yield only 'equality with slaves' – 'for the Germans were the slaves of the Christian state'.[8] The German Jews should rather join in the struggle for the more general emancipation of the German people and the displacement of the (oppressive) Christian state by a 'totally free state'.

Bauer's argument is flawed, Marx insists, because he has failed to recognize the real (and limited) nature of political emancipation (the extension of rights) and has erroneously identified it with fully *human* emancipation. For Marx, the supersession of religion – 'the devious acknowledgement of man through an intermediary' – is one aspect of a fully human emancipation. But it cannot be realized through a purely *political* emanication. This Marx illustrates through the experience of the United States, which proscribes state religion and yet which is 'the land of religiosity *par excellence*'.[9] This seeming paradox arises, Marx suggests, from the fact that political emancipation *of* religion does not mean complete and consistent emancipation *from* religion (which would be conterminious with fully *human* emancipation). Political emancipation of religion means only the right to worship as one chooses and not freedom from the superstition and alienation that religion is seen to express. In the 'free state' – under freedom *of* religion – the individual is liberated from religion only through the medium of the state and only in a political, and thus partial, way. This purely political annulment of religion, as of private property, consists only in declaring distinctions of religion/private property to be *non-political* – that is in confining these differences to civil society. Thus, 'the contradiction which exists between religious man and political man is the same as exists between the *bourgeois* and the *citoyen*, between the member of civil society and his *political lion's skin*'.[10]

The example of Jewish emanicipation, Marx argues, helps in the more general task of understanding 'where the limit of political emancipation lies'. For this

> splitting of man into his *public* and his *private* self and the *displacement* of religion from the state to civil society is not one step in the process of political emancipation but its *completion* .... The dissolution of man into Jew and citizen, Protestant and citizen ... is not a denial of citizenship or an avoidance of political emancipation: it *is political emancipation itself*, it is the *political* way of emancipating oneself from religion.[11]

'Truly Human Emancipation': Beyond Rights

Quite as important as this insistence upon 'the incompleteness and contradiction' of purely political emancipation is the universality claimed, by Marx, for 'truly *human* emancipation', with which the former is so often contrasted. While political revolution is '*limited* and *contradictory*', social revolution achieves 'a *total* point of view'. For Marx, 'the *man* is greater than the *citizen* and human life than political life'.[12] Correspondingly, in *On the Jewish Question*, Marx insists that while 'political emancipation is certainly a big step forward', it is not 'the last form of general emancipation'.[13] For the perfection of political emancipation is the perfection of the division into 'bourgeois' and 'citizen'. It is 'the reduction of man on the one hand to the member of civil society, the *egoistic, independent*, individual, and on the other to the *citizen*, the moral person'.[14] Thus, while the winning of the rights of the citizen represents a major advance over the structured inequalities of feudalism, freedoms of such a kind – secured to justiciable persons under the jurisdiction of the state – express, in themselves, the partial nature of this emancipation. The great limitation of this purely political revolution, Marx insists, is that 'it dissolves civil society into its component parts without *revolutionising* these parts and subjecting them to criticism'.[15]

To aspire to 'general human emancipation', it is essential to go beyond this purely political emancipation and, for Marx, this means resolving the contradiction between civil and political society. Having rejected Hegel's 'semblance of a resolution' through the mediation of a 'universal' state, Marx insists that this contradiction is only truly resolved when civil and political life are reunited, that is, when political society is reabsorbed by civil life. Only through this (renewed) coalescence of 'public' and 'private' life can the division of 'citizen' and 'bourgeois' give way to the individual '*real human being*'. For

Marx, 'only when man has recognised and organised his *forces propres* as *social forces* so that social force is no longer separated from him in the form of *political* force, only then will human emancipation be completed'.[16]

Marx characterizes this human emancipation through the unity of civil and political life as the realization of true democracy. Thus:

> Democracy is the solution to the *riddle* of every constitution. In it we find the constitution founded on its true ground: *real human beings* and the *real people*; not merely *implicitly* and in essence, but in *existence* and in reality .... Every other *political formation* is a definite, determinate, *particular* form of the state [in which] the political man leads his particular existence alongside the unpolitical man, the private citizen ... [But] in democracy the *formal* principle is identical with the *substantive* principle. For this reason it is the first true unity of the particular and the universal.[17]

Under this 'first true unity of the particular and the universal', rights practices would be increasingly irrelevant. Rights had been the cherished possessions of atomistic and legally constituted individuals, exercised under the aegis of the state within a society riven by the contradiction between civil and political life. Where this division between civil and political life was overcome, and the state's 'government of men' increasingly gave way to 'the administration of things', the logic of rights would be superseded. Inasmuch as true democracy heralded a society 'without the state', it also represented a society in 'circumstances beyond rights'.

Marx on 'The Rights Basis of Capitalism'

Assessing Marx's writings in the period to 1845, Lucio Colletti concludes that 'politically speaking, mature Marxism would have relatively little to add to this'.[18] While this position is probably overstated, it is clear that the advent of the materialist conception of history, with its disputed 'primacy of the economic' did yield a distinctive and often secondary account of the political, and such innovations as there were in Marx's political theory had comparatively little to do with an account of rights. It is true that, in his more sanguine moments, Marx's materialist premiss drove him to anticipate the possibility of revolutionary transformation effected through the exercise of existing political rights – as in 'The Amsterdam Address' or the 'Article on the Chartists' – but, just as often, he was driven to pronounce the same rights, under prevailing conditions, to be 'a farce'.[19] That, in fact, Marx continued to hold that rights were, in some sense, essentially bourgeois is made clear by a number of passages in *The Critique of the Gotha Programme* – which contains perhaps the most important commentary on rights in the late Marx. Here, writing of the rewards of labour within a society transitional between capitalism and communism, he draws attention to the continuing need of distribution based upon 'equal right' – which, he insists, remains 'a bourgeois right' vitiated by a 'bourgeois limitation'. For this equal right is 'an unequal right for unequal labour' and 'this right is thus in its content one of inequality, *just like any other right*'. He completes this account by insisting that only in developed communism 'can society wholly cross the narrow horizon of bourgeois right'.[20]

Rather than itemize the many and varying references to rights in the later Marx, I want here to concentrate upon what is probably the most coherent and developed treatment of rights in the mature Marx. This is to be found in the definitive status attributed to the exercise of rights in his mid-nineteenth-century account of liberal capitalism. Here, the emergence of a set of civil rights – habeas corpus, freedom of speech, thought and faith, and especially the right to own property and to conclude valid contracts – establishing an authentic though essentially formal and delimited sphere of equality and freedom, is seen to be one of the hallmarks of the transition from feudalism to competitive capitalism and a *sine qua non* of commodity production. In *Capital*, having established capitalism as a system of generalized commodity production, in which commodities (generally) exchange at their values, Marx poses the problem of how the capitalist, while both buying and selling commodities at their 'true' value, is still able to extract more value from the circulation of commodities than he initially invested in it. This riddle is solved for the capitalist by his finding 'a commodity whose use-value possesses the peculiar property of being a source of value', whose consumption is itself a creation of value. This 'special commodity' is labour power which appears on the market only when the labourer offers it for sale as a commodity, which, in turn, he can do only as 'the free proprietor of his own labour capacity, hence of his person'.[21] In this way, both equality (of exchange) and freedom (to sell one's own labour power) were seen, in Marx's account, to be structural requisites of competitive capitalism.

He was, of course, bitterly critical both of the limited and deceptive nature of this equality and freedom and of their hypostatization by 'bourgeois apologists' as the ultimate and perfect embodiment of all freedom and equality. Under capitalism, the realm of equality and freedom is confined to a 'community of commodity exchangers', free to dispose of their commodities at will, and it is only as the proprietors of these respective commodities that capital and labour meet in a realm of untramelled equality and freedom. Using the familiar *Capital* leitmotiv of a 'surface appearance' masking hidden processes 'in the depths', Marx insists that this realm of equality and freedom, confined to the 'community of exchangers' within the market, is limited to society's 'surface process'. Beneath this, however, 'in the depths, entirely different processes go on, in which this apparent individual equality and liberty disappear'.[22] This division is given its classical expression in the closing section of Part II of Volume 1 of *Capital*. Here, Marx characterizes the sphere of commodity exchange as 'a very Eden of the innate rights of man ... the exclusive realm of Freedom, Equality, Property and Bentham'. But once we penetrate beneath the sphere of the simple circulation of commodities to expose the very process of production, Marx reveals a change in the 'physiognomy' of capital and labour:

He who was previously the money-owner now strides out in front as a capitalist; the possessor of labour-power follows as his worker. The one smirks self-importantly and is intent on business; the other is timid and holds back, like someone who has brought his own hide to market and now has nothing to expect but – a tanning.[23]

This 'paradox' of co-resident (formal) equality and (real) inequality is, for Marx, an essential structural feature of capitalism and it is here that he isolates the rights basis of capitalism – that is, the corpus of civil rights which ensures that all individuals, conceived as legal persons, shall meet as free and equal agents within the realm of exchange, irrespective of all differences and inequalities outside this sphere. It is this development which Marx contrasts with the structured and formal inequalities of feudalism, with its restricted trading practices, and the direct and explicit expropriation of surplus labour (the *corvée*), politically or religiously legitimated. For once capitalism has been fully established there is no need, under normal conditions, of an extra-economic coercion to extract surplus value. For capitalist appropriation it is necessary only for commodities to circulate on the basis of freedom and equality within the 'community of exchangers'. Direct coercion may still be employed, from time to time, but 'in the ordinary run of things, the worker can be left to "the natural laws of production"'.[24]

However, Marx insists, capitalist relations of production did not always present themselves as 'the natural order' and the bourgeoisie was not always able to rely upon this 'dull compulsion of economic relations'. The conditions which would permit of free and equal commodity exchange had first to be established by 'freeing' the labourer from ownership of the conditions of his or her own production. It is in their suppression of these historical origins of existing rights and freedoms that Marx locates the second great deception of the 'apologists' of the bourgeois order. For bourgeois historians, Marx argues, concentrate exclusively upon the 'positive' aspects of the emancipation from feudalism – the release from serfdom and the overcoming of the restrictions imposed by guilds – while they ignore the 'negative' aspects in which these newly-emancipated men and women became sellers of their labour power only because 'they had been robbed of all their own means of production' and denied the traditional guarantees of existence afforded by a (paternalistic) feudalism. The history of this expropriation, upon which the primitive accumulation of capital depended, is, for Marx, 'written in the annals of mankind in letters of blood and fire'.[25]

Marx identifies much the same 'eternalization of historical relations of production' in the characterization of individualism and individual freedom to be found in both natural rights theory and in classical political economy. He criticizes the misrepresentation of 'isolated individualism' in these theories as a 'return to a misunderstood natural life' or a return to the (contractual) orgins of society. Rather, this individualism is an *historic* form, indeed a *modern* development appropriate to the emergence 'in the eighteenth century' of a distinct 'civil society'.

For paradoxically, 'the epoch which produces this standpoint, that of the isolated individual, is also precisely that of the hitherto most developed social relations' and, correspondingly, the individualism of natural rights theory and of eighteenth century political economy must be seen to be not natural but socially and historically determined.[26] While it serves the bourgeoisie to present its laws of political economy as natural and thus unalterable and to characterize the (possessive) individual as natural man, 'not as a historic result but as history's point of departure', Marx insists that these constructs are as much the result of a particular mode of production, and are thus as epoch-bounded (and transitional), as those of any other. With the further development of the productive forces, the claim that 'free competition equals the ultimate form of the development of the forces of production' will be exposed as an attempt to pass off 'middle class rule' as 'the culmination of world history'.[27]

Conclusion

It is quite possible to see how these claims of the later Marx might be represented as a criticism of rights as a 'bourgeois sham'. This is clearly in Marx's mind when he writes, half-ironically, of the workers' 'freedom from' ownership of the means of production or of the workers' 'selling themselves and their families into slavery and death by voluntary contract with Capital'.[28] Nor, in the light of the historical resistance to factory legislation, to the legal control of the labour contract, and so on, is this scepticism wholly misplaced. However, in this conclusion, I want to suggest that Marx is not generally confined to condemning rights as a 'bourgeois sham', and further, that his often much more elaborate account of rights is, in fact, itself seriously flawed.

I began my discussion by outlining the most important premises of the early Marxian critique of rights. We saw that this critique turns on the somewhat abstract distinction between a 'complete' human emancipation and 'partial' political emancipation, so that, while 'political emancipation is certainly a big step forward', Marx is insistent that this is a *definitively* restricted form of emancipation. Nor is this restriction to be understood simply as a matter of degree. Rather, Marx argues that where emancipation is political and vested in the institution of political rights, this, in itself, expresses the failure to overcome that division between civil and political society which is the barrier to 'true' democracy and 'truly human' emancipation. Political emancipation is indeed to be preferred to political slavery but its achievement, which Marx tends to associate with the ascendancy of the bourgeoisie over feudalism, is typically associated with the severance of civil and political society – under which circumstances, he further insists, the exercise of these political rights does not and cannot constitute a threat to the prevalent bourgeois order. Thus we saw that Marx characterized the French Revolution as 'establish[ing] juridical and political equality only upon the basis of a new and deeper inequality' and that in 'the contradiction between the democratic representative state and civil society' he located 'the perfection of the classic contradiction between the public commonwealth and slavery'. Thus the holder of rights – the citizen – can exist only where divided from and contrasted to the 'bourgeois' individual.

I subsequently turned to the later Marx's account of the rights basis of capitalism in the *Grundrisse* and *Capital*, in which Marx insists not only that there is an authentic realm of freedom and equality under the rule of the bourgeoisie but that this freedom and equality – indispensable to the operation of the capitalist mode of production – is definitively restricted. Under 'the money system', Marx insists, 'equality and freedom prove to be inequality and unfreedom ... it is not individuals [but] capital which is set free'.[29] In this way, Marx tends to identify rights, including political rights, as a part of the juridical structure of capitalism. They have a progressive aspect, associated with the progressive role of the bourgeoisie in displacing formalized feudal inequalities, but at the same time they tend to be identified with the legal apparatus of enforceable rights of contract – itself the basis for the 'concealed' expropriation of surplus value – and cannot form the basis for the securing of true democracy/socialism.

We saw that, for the early Marx, at least, this limitation of rights was open to a radical resolution. In the resumption of the unity of civil and political life under true democracy, the rationale of both an independent state and a practice of rights was to be overcome. For this democracy, in Marx's account, was not only 'the solution of the riddle of every constitution', it was also, in some sense, 'the solution of every riddle of the constitution'. Thus, classic problems of the political authority of the state, the difficulties of representation, the limitations of parliamentarism, simply ceased to exist where the individual resumed his or her 'true self'. The state, representation and rights had been an expression of a divided individual and a divided society – where this division was overcome, these problems ceased to exist, yielding, if not 'an end of politics', then at least 'a society beyond rights'. While no comparable account of the overcoming of rights is to be found in *Grundrisse* or *Capital*, there is sufficient evidence in the more political writings of the later Marx – notably in *The Critique of the Gotha Programme* – to allow us to anticipate that a classless, communist society is also seen to be a 'society beyond rights'.

'Bourgeois Rights'?

I would suggest that while this Marxian critique of rights is interesting and suggestive of very real limitations, it is also vitiated by at least two substantial weaknesses. Marx tends to associate the institution of rights too closely with the rise of the bourgeoisie and with the juridical structure of capitalism – a position that is particularly clear in the *Grundrisse* and *Capital*. While there is strong historical evidence to associate the early development of civil and political freedoms with the emergence of a capitalist market economy, this cannot be held to justify the claim that the conception of rights is unproblematically and irredeemably a feature of this bourgeois polity. For the struggle for and securing of rights has never been confined simply to the struggle to secure those freedoms essential to the operation of a market economy. While some such rights – free movement of labour and capital, freedom to enter into legally enforceable contracts – may indeed be indispensable in establishing such an economy, the winning of political rights also represents an authentic popular conquest and, perhaps most importantly, a means of exercising constraint on overweening political authority. Nor should rights be too readily associated with a 'bourgeois interest'. Much of the history of the (international) labour movement could be written in terms of the attempt to generalize (formally) bourgeois rights. Not only the universalization of the franchise but other civil rights – for example, rights of association and combination – have all, at times, been fiercely contested by the representatives of the bourgeoisie. Similarly, any attempt to posit a straightforward identity of capitalism and formal freedoms is bound to seem historically insecure. Capitalism has not always been associated with the fullest civil and political freedoms – it has not always been essential to fathom around beneath the 'surface process' to identify a 'hidden' mode of exploitation.

'The Overcoming of Rights'

Of course, a defender of Marx's position might be willing to concede some or all of these objections by insisting that they do not materially affect the force of his argument. Indeed, they only become critical when related to a second major weakness in Marx's account – his expectation that, whatever the particular nature of these rights, the whole problematic of rights was to be overcome in the inception of (true) democracy or communism. The precise historical and categorical status of rights was in some sense a moot point because those differences of interest and problems of political authority which generated the necessity of rights would be 'resolved' in democracy based on the reunification of civil and political society and with it the 'overcoming' of politics.

It seems, then, that, for Marx, rights were only valuable under capitalism, because only here did there exist the 'potential for the serious infringement of the freedoms' these rights were held to guarantee.[30] This potential for infringement existed only where power was exercised over individuals, and such circumstances could only arise out of the differences of interest entailed in the division of civil and political society or, in later accounts, in the existence of classes. Where these circumstances no longer existed, there would be no need of rights as guarantees against an exercise of power that would be obsolete. However, the grounds for accepting Marx's expectation of passing 'beyond the circumstances of rights' are extremely uncertain. To accept it, we should have to accept some, if not all, of the following propositions: that

> all social conflicts can ultimately be derived from the institutions of private property and the class structures created by it. With the abolition of that institution social conflict loses its essential basis;[31]

that, correspondingly, all disputes over which it makes sense to appeal to rights would be eliminated with the transcendence of class society; that under communism there will be no specifically political institutions over which it would be appropriate to exercise rights of constraint or control; that under communism it will be possible to ensure such an abundance of production that all competition over scarce goods and resources will be rendered obsolete; that the harmony engendered by the elimination of classes and the resumption by 'man' of his 'true self' will eliminate disputes over the allocation of resources and reveal 'man' as a naturally co-operative animal. It is difficult to see how these several claims could be maintained. To take but one of them, it now seems that the expectation of abundance is extremely improbable, especially in a world perceived to have finite resources, and certainly the threshold of abundance that would eliminate all disputes over allocation of resources is almost unimaginable. Similarly, the expectation of 'a stateless society' is open to increasing theoretical criticism, even among socialists. Claus Offe's claim that 'socialism in industrially advanced societies cannot be built *without* state power and it cannot be built *on* state power' is characteristic of this more recent thinking.[32] Not only are these claims for the overcoming of rights in a post-class society exaggerated, there is in fact good reason to suppose that the sanction of these rights might be still more important under a socialized economy. On the one hand, the 'constrained' but two-edged freedoms of the capitalist mode of production – for example, contractually free labour and the free movement of such labour – represent a very real means of restraint that could be lost after socialization. On the other, where the market principle ceased to operate, the allocation of resources might well represent a new seat of authority against which it might be appropriate to seek to exercise rights. These reservations are made still more acute when one recognizes the likelihood of socialization under other than optimal conditions.

One might seek to ease Marx out of this tight corner by insisting that the 'overcoming of rights' is an expectation he confines to a fully communist society – a position for which there is textual support in *The Critique of the Gotha Programme* – and that, where the conditions for the establishment of communism are not met, rights may continue to be important. But such a concession would radically alter the Marxian perspective on rights. For it has become clear that the conditions for such a 'fully communist' society are, at least in the envisageable future, almost unattainable and it is correspondingly difficult to anticipate the circumstances under which 'the overcoming of rights' might be realized. Such a concession also raises what now looms as a massively important and long-standing problem – the nature of rights in a *socialist* (that is, not fully communist) society. On this pressing question both Marx and much of the Marxist political tradition are conspicuously silent.[33]

Notes

1. E.P. Thompson, 'Introduction' in State Research Collective, eds, *The Review of the Security of the State: Vol. 1* (London, Julian Friedmann, 1978), p. xi.
2. K. Marx, *On the Jewish Question*, in K. Marx, *EW*, p. 233.

3. K. Marx, *'Critique of Hegel's Doctrine of the State'* in idem, *EW*, p. 146.

4. Ibid., p. 233.

5. Marx, *On the Jewish Question*, p. 220 (emphasis added).

6. L. Colletti, 'Introduction' in Marx, *EW*, p. 35.

7. Marx, *On the Jewish Question*, p. 233.

8. Introductory material by Colletti in Marx, *EW*, p. 211.

9. Marx, *On the Jewish Question*, p. 217.

10. Ibid., p. 221.

11. Ibid., p. 222.

12. K. Marx, *Critical Notes on 'The King of Prussia'*, in Marx, *EW*, p. 419.

13. Marx, *On the Jewish Question*, p. 221.

14. Ibid., p. 234.

15. Ibid.

16. Ibid.

17. Marx, *Critique of Hegel's Doctrine of the State*, pp. 87-8.

18. Colletti, 'Introduction' in Marx, *EW*, p. 45.

19. K. Marx, *The Chartists*, in K. Marx and F. Engels, 11 *CW*; K. Marx, *Speech on the Hague Congress* [The Amsterdam Address], in idem, *The First International and After* (Harmondsworth, Penguin, 1974).

20. K. Marx, *Critique of the Gotha Programme* in idem, *The First International and After*.

21. K. Marx 1 *Capital*, pp. 270–1.

22. K. Marx, *Grundrisse*, pp. 244–5.

23. Marx, 1 *Capital*, p. 280.

24. Ibid., p. 899.

25. Ibid., p. 875.

26. Marx, *Grundrisse*, p. 84.

27. Ibid., p. 652.

28. Marx, 1 *Capital*, p. 416.

29. Marx, *Grundrisse*, p. 650.

30. E. Kamenka, *Marxism and Ethics* (London, Macmillan, 1969), pp. 29–30.

31. Ibid.

32. C. Offe, *Contradictions of the Welfare State* (London, Hutchinson, 1984), p. 246. For a further discussion of recent developments, see C. Pierson, 'New Theories of State and Civil Society', *Sociology*, vol. 18, no. 4 (November 1984), pp. 563–71.

33. For a careful and well-considered recent analysis of the relation between socialism and a practice of rights, see T. Campbell, *The Left and Rights* (London, Routledge and Kegan Paul, 1984). See also D. Lane, 'Human Rights under State Socialism', *Political Studies*, vol. 32, no. 3 (September 1984), pp. 349–368.

13
Rational Choice Marxism[1]

Alan Carling

In 1977 and 1978, Paul Hirst and Barry Hindess published with their collaborators the two volumes of *Marx's 'Capital' and Capitalism Today*. In the latter year Gerald Cohen published *Karl Marx's Theory of History: A Defence*. In retrospect, it is possible to see in these events a turning point for Anglo-Saxon Marxist theory, and the latest evidence of the remarkable capacity of Western Marxism to renew itself, despite everything. Hirst and Hindess, who had been for almost a decade the most influential English exponents of Althusserian Marxism, seemed to announce in 1977 their utter despair at systematic social thought in general and Marxist theory in particular. It appeared that the Althusserian project, initially promising nothing less than a total reconstruction of history and politics on a new basis of social science, had lapsed and crumbled into dust.[2] The virtues of Cohen's work only served to throw this denouement into a somewhat sharper relief. It might be said tendentiously that while Althusserians talked a great deal about rigour, Cohen actually practised it. His argument was careful, painstaking: chock-a-block with nice distinctions other people hadn't dreamt were there.[3] It proceeded stepwise, analytically. It was no longer a case of gathering Marxism into some great mass to be swallowed whole or not at all. Instead, Marxism was to be sorted into a list of distinct claims: each one deserving its own interrogation for meaning, coherence, plausibility and truth. The logical relation between claims became an explicit topic of the theory, so that it became more open to judgement which parts of a complex Marxist corpus stood or fell together.

A Cumulative Shift

Despite the peculiar authority of his own work, Cohen was never alone in making the analytical move. It is now possible to see a range of other writers, especially John Roemer and Jon Elster, but also Norman Geras, Allen Wood, Adam Przeworski, Phillipe van Parijs, the later Erik Olin Wright, Robert Brenner and all those of us who have bobbed about in the wake of Michio Morishima and Ian Steedman, as contributing in different fields to a cumulative shift in the accents of Marxist theory. Something of a parallel shift is apparent in the development of a 'critical human geography' by Doreen Massey and her collaborators, and also in the work of anarchist inspiration produced by the inimitable Michael Taylor.[4]

Inevitably, it is easier to detect that a decisive shift has taken place than to say in what exactly it consists. Precisely because the shift is analytical in the sense suggested above, one would not expect to find a new consensus of opinion across the whole range of concerns brought into a new focus: historical materialism, the labour theory of value, class structure and exploitation, the relation between the individual and the social, conceptions of reason and human nature, the historical reference and general relevance of moral judgements, and much else besides. If complex topics like these are to be picked apart and probed and worried as a deliberate – almost obsessive – policy of method, it is not surprising that a variety of competing views quickly becomes evident. This sense of variety will only be enhanced by an accompanying determination to face rather than evade the legacy of awkward questions the history of the twentieth century has bequeathed Marxist theory – above all, the painful failure of revolution in the West and the almost equally painful success of revolution in the East.[5]

It is, of course, perfectly true (and important) that the attempt to assimilate this history has distinguished Western Marxism as a whole, but this assimilation has often proceeded rather obliquely.[6] Sometimes it has paid homage to canonical texts with an extravagance disclosing the real distance travelled from them. At other times it has moved into fields very important in their own right but set apart from the main interests of classical Marxist social and political theory: fields such as epistemology and metaphysics, literary and cultural theory, theories of ideology and aesthetics, the encounter between Marxism and psychoanalysis, and so on. Given the displacements making up this intellectual history, the analytical turn can be represented both as a continuation of the concerns of Western Marxism by other means and a critical return to the classical agenda.[7]

This sense of a return with fresh eyes is equally evident in Cohen's defence of a newly sophisticated version of technological determinism, in Steedman's and in Roemer's critiques of the labour theory of value, in Geras's reflections on the *Theses on Feuerbach*, in Elster's presentation of Marx as a pioneer in the theory of collective action, and in Wood's persistence in that deceptive and classical question 'What's wrong with capitalism?' This line of thought might suggest 'neo-classical Marxism' as an appropriate title for the new tendency. Other suggestions already in the field include 'analytical Marxism', 'game-theoretic Marxism' and – stretching a point – post-post-classical Marxism. To the extent that a name is important, I would prefer to use the term *rational choice Marxism* in order to collect the new work under a single heading, and to suggest why a single heading may be appropriate. For if there is one distinctive presupposition of the intended body of work it must be the view that societies are composed of human individuals with resources of various kinds attempting to choose rationally between various courses of action.[8]

This view is a commonplace of that broad sweep of conventional economics and philosophy conducted in the liberal tradition. What makes the difference (and it is a dramatic one) is the joining of this presupposition with the classical agenda of Marxist theory. In the most schematic terms, the result is the subversion of a received dichotomy between social pattern and individual choice. That is, fundamental social pattern comes to be represented as the (usually unintended) outcome of choices made by deliberating agents. This approach is liable to prove as unsettling for those Marxists who have come close to the denial of individual choice as it will be for those anti-Marxists (or Marxist anti-theorists!) who have come close to the denial of fundamental social pattern. It has often seemed, in other words, as if there is one box, marked 'agentless structure' in which one peers to find modes of production, grand historical designs, epochal social change, ideological hegemony, sociological analysis, determinism and constraint, while one looks to another, marked 'structureless agency', to find the individual, volition and choice, moral judgement, politics-as-it-is-lived and history-as-it-is-experienced. If these options were the only two on offer, Marxists would indeed face a cruel dilemma, since their basic mental equipment ought to alert them equally to the existence of structured inequality, the efficacy of political action and the importance of the concrete historical process.

At least in specific domains of theory, rational choice Marxism opens up the third, transcendent box. It becomes possible to grant individual autonomy without abandoning thereby structured inequality (Roemer) or historical pattern (Cohen). No longer does the choice lie between agentless structure and structureless agency. What the structure is is a structure of human agency.[9] And it then seems possible to sum up this whole change of perspective in a phrase: the reinstatement of the subject.

Cohen on History and Social Structure

In *Karl Marx's Theory of History* Cohen committed Marx once again to the view that history has a pattern and that the pattern results from human deliberation in the face of scarcity. Accordingly, human rationality joined with historical scarcity creates a pressure to improve productive technique (raise the level of the forces of production) which is ultimately unstoppable. Rationality works directly in the development and choice of productive technique and indirectly in the choice of social relations most suited to the further development of productive technique, given the level of productive technique already reached. This latter gloss of Cohen's is intended to bypass the standing counter-example frequently used to oppose straightforward technological determinism – namely the effect that the relations of production undoubtedly have on the development of the forces of production (never more so than under capitalism). If one goes on to assume (as an empirical premiss) that any given set of (pre-communist) relations of production will be unable to cope with forces of production developed beyond a certain level, a periodic choice of new economic structures is almost certain to occur.[10] Such revolutionary transitions divide historical epochs. The pattern of history is given in the corresponding sequence of economic structures, culminating in that high, unfettered regime of productive technique that communism is (supposed to be).

This bald view (very baldly stated here) has been subjected to considerable refinement and amendment in the debates since 1978. It has been said by Levine and Wright that Cohen's reconstruction still relies on too individualistic and transhistorical a concept of human rationality. Cohen has entered doubts himself concerning Marx's 'one-sided anthropology' and about the simple-minded view of 'fettering' the earlier theory seems to presuppose. Elster has called for much closer specification of the mechanism through which the choice of new relations of production is registered in history; contributing thereby to the important and wide-ranging debate on the possibility of functional explanation in the social sciences which Cohen's treatment has inspired. Van Parijs has advanced a solution of the 'primacy puzzle' in terms of a 'slow dynamics' (of forces of production) 'embedded in [a] fast dynamics' of changing relations of production when the latter are in contradiction with the former. Both Elster and Levine and Wright introduce in different ways the role of political organization and timing in enhancing or frustrating the revolutionary transitions basic to the theory – thus introducing within the new theoretical context all the old questions revolving around the distinction between class-in-itself and class-for-itself. Brenner has gone further in suggesting that the logic of the situation of the pre-capitalist peasantry often inclines them directly against the development of the forces of production.[11]

For present purposes, however, I wish to focus on Cohen's enduring reorientation of the 'theoretical object' in the chapters preceding his original statement of the theory itself. First, Cohen emphasized the distinction between the *material* and the *social* as basic to Marx's thought. This contrast introduces non-standard connotations of both terms. In the new contrast with the 'social', 'material' loses its ordinary contrast with 'mental'. The motive for this change is that knowledge (a mental phenomenon) is clearly central to the development of forces of production.[12] If the definition of the latter excludes knowledge, then Marx's theory of history cannot be materialist, whatever else it may be. Further, productively useful knowledge must be conceptually distinct from relations of production (from the 'social') in order for the theory to gain any empirical leverage. This does not, of course, mean that the creation, dissemination and use of productively useful knowledge is independent of relations of production. Quite the contrary, the theory is at bottom *about* the interdependence of social relations of production with the creation, dissemination and use of productively useful knowledge (in order to overcome scarcity).

If 'material' loses its ordinary contrast with 'mental', then 'social' loses its ordinary contrast with 'individual'. In Cohen's view, Marx uses the term 'social' in a special, power-denoting sense. Recall that the basic elements of Marx's theory are people and things people need (use-values). The basic topic of the theory is the relationships obtaining among people and use-values as these evolve through history. But these relationships do not set 'the individual', on the one hand, against 'society', on the other. The 'social' denotes these people, things and relationships under power-laden descriptions. The 'material' denotes these people, things and relationships under power-neutral descriptions.[13] In this, the ordinary language distinction between the 'social' and the 'individual' breaks down because individuals (or things) are importantly described by their relational properties, and these may include social relational properties. That is, the same physical individual may be described alternatively in material terms as a computer operator (which is not purely 'physical' since it has reference to mental qualities – 'skill') and in social terms as a wage-earner. The person is evidently no less an individual under the second kind of description than under the first.[14]

These points would not be so important for the subsequent development of rational choice Marxism were it not for the general redirection of the sociological imagination that they entail. Visually, the effect is *to set societies back on the level*.[15] That is, the reinstatement of societies as sets of relationships among individuals (and things) undermines the deeply ingrained habit of seeing societies in terms of hierarchies, pyramids, diamonds, heaps, layer cakes, jellies, blancmanges and other party pieces of social stratification.[16] Where it has not shared directly in this impression that people go around standing on each other's shoulders, recent Marxist theory has still used a metaphor of levels powerful enough to tear people apart and distribute them to the four ends of the social earth – to the political, the economic, the ideological and (for the favoured few!) the theoretical. It seems, in other words, that there are three ways in which the base–superstructure metaphor has been used misleadingly. The first is in its more familiar role as an explanatory paradigm, for which Cohen's original work, and the subsequent debate with Elster and others, has done a great deal to clarify the issues at stake. The second and third abuses are concerned more with the strategic impression of a society which the metaphor has helped to sustain.

In Althusserian hands, the model of levels and instances was used both to banish 'the individual' as any kind of integral actor from a base–superstructure complex which was thought to constitute the whole object of social enquiry (apart from that residual patch allowed to the benighted followers of Edward Thompson: the 'conjuncture'), and at the same time to introduce into this object a division between the upper (political and ideological) and the lower (economic) reaches. By his decisive – almost triumphant – 'refutation of the legend' that Marx denied the existence of human nature, Norman Geras is able to rescind the second abuse. He re-establishes with full classical credentials the integrity of the human actor as an animal of a particular kind: an animal with unique and elastic powers, whose uniqueness in fact resides in the elasticity which its natural powers provide. This human animal is restored to the centre of the social stage, so that 'historical materialism itself, this whole distinctive approach to society that originates with Marx, rests squarely upon the idea of a human nature'.[17]

It remains to rebut the third abuse of the base–superstructure metaphor, since the reintegrated individuals might still be thought to dwell at different levels of the social structure, rather like the inhabitants of a tower block, whose floors might be marked in ascending order – economy, family, party and (in the penthouse suite, no doubt) philosophy. As far as the pedigree of any such thought in Marx is concerned, it should be enough to point out that the social structures of *Capital* are sets of relationships between whole individuals exchanging, buying, selling, owning, producing and consuming use-values. In the topography of *Capital*, there are no vertical levels, but only horizontally disposed sites – market, factory, home – between which people move in conducting their characteristic business.[18] In these commutations, people are not moving between base and superstructure, as if they were stuck in the lift between floors or as if they concentrated for one moment on their feet and the next had their head in the clouds. Putting it another way: the state, say, lies in the *background*, just over the horizon of the capitalist economy. It does not hover above it. It was said before that rational choice Marxism involves a critical return to classical views. In the matter of social structure, there is a return to views cured of the stratification fever caught from twentieth-century sociology.

From the Theory of History to the Analysis of Capital

In Marx there is a rich – seemingly inexhaustible – vein of theoretical insight, but there are only two theories, and one of those is hardly more than a sketch. The sketch implies a long range theory of history of the kind elucidated by Cohen. This might be called the general theory of historical materialism. In addition, there is the special theory of historical materialism adumbrated in *Capital*. This is the theory of the capitalist regime of production alone.[19] It is true that the two theories are supposed to be related, since the laws of motion of capitalism ought to exemplify the principles of the general theory, and the transition from capitalism to socialism ought to stand in a (shortish) line of similar transitions from previous historical epochs. But it is also true that the general and special theories have theoretical presuppositions which generate radically different 'fixed points'.

In the case of the general theory, the fixed point will necessarily be transhistorical, since the general theory claims to be an overall theory of historical change. Anyone who thinks it is the first rule of Marxist science that history disqualifies fixed points had better abandon the search for a general theory right here. In Cohen's reading, as we have seen, the fixed point is supplied by human rationality facing a somewhat stable schedule of (largely physical) needs and goals across the long run of history. This reading can survive the objection that human capacity and motivation are influenced, rather than formed altogether, by social and historical circumstance, if it is plausible to think that a certain kind of technological rationality is sufficiently widespread, sufficiently urgent and insufficiently hampered or blocked for the forces of production to progress in every kind of society (or perhaps in at least one kind of society in each epoch!).[20] This assumption is not utterly outlandish, but it is nevertheless a large and controversial one – as any assumption sustaining a general theory of history is bound to be.

With the special theory, the situation is considerably easier. In Marx's version, the fixed point of the theory is the set of social relations constituting capitalism – strictly, the circuit of industrial capital. Given this fixed point, it is perfectly plausible to assume that the kind of human motivation obtaining is the one that the general theory also happens to presuppose. Indeed, the social relations of capitalism seem peculiarly adapted to foster the spirit of technological rationality, and to incline the interests of those who already hold resources in favour of technological development. This correspondence is so striking as to raise the suggestion that the presumed general theory may be an illicit projection from the special theory backward into history.[21] In any case, the problem in Marx's work is that the presupposition of the special theory – the class relation of capital – is left largely ungrounded in the general theory. There is, of course, a narrative account of the historical genesis of the class relation (primitive accumulation) and an historical-cum-logical reprise of the development of the forms of value leading up to capital, but no systematic theoretical link is forged between the class action portrayed in *Capital* and the transhistorical action envisaged in the general theory. It is not shown why capitalism had to emerge when it did from a long-run environment structured minimally in terms of productive technique and human capacity.

Marx's special theory proceeds by offering a complex answer to the following question: How is it that a regime of class division and exploitation can arise from the interplay of market transactions freely conducted under norms of equality?[22]

There are two possible lines of attack on this question, leading theory and politics in somewhat different directions. First, it may be allowed that capitalism involves a measure of freedom (and equality), and reasons may be sought for the transformation of these qualities into the opposite experiences (domination and exclusion) in the lives of most people who live under capitalism. Roemer's work in particular belongs in this line of thought, and its great merit is to sharpen considerably the answer Marx was able to give in this direction. In this view, classes emerge precisely from the conditions of freedom that market institutions promote. Alternatively, criticism may proceed essentially through a denial of the description of market transactions contained in the question. This is to look for the source of the problem in the misrepresentation of itself offered by capitalism. It may be suggested, for example, that what passes for freedom under capitalism is a covert form of oppression because of the manipulation of tastes, the promulgation of false needs or the generally illusory character of the choices on offer.

The heavy artillery of ideology is often wheeled in at this point to depict a realm of mystified surface appearance radically at odds with the deeper and grimmer reality of capitalist class relations. Now while it would be foolish to deny that manipulations and distortions of preferences occur under capitalism, and that their extent offers grounds for criticizing capitalism, the most important question is the weight to be assigned to these processes in the overall indictment of capitalism. The judgement is important because the first line of attack points towards a theory of the macroscopic properties of capitalism which aspires to be true of capitalism, and in that sense scientific, while the second line of attack implies a more philosophical and literary critique of received ideological forms. The two lines of attack are further related to distinct recommendations for socialism, since, broadly speaking, if capitalism is recognized as being in part genuinely free and equal, we want more of the very things capitalism now provides, while if the freedom and equality of capitalism are entirely chimerical, we want none of the things that capitalism now provides, since we want the reality and not the mere semblance of freedom and equality, and the endorsement of the appearance is likely to take us further away from the achievement of the reality.

This question is further complicated because Marx's critique of capitalism – his version of the special theory – pursues both lines of attack on his motivating question. He wants to tell it like it is and how it appears to be. The two lines are also frequently entangled in his work, in part because he adopts the methodological principle that science is achieved through the critique of ideology, that is, that the critique of false (ideological) representation opens the path to true (scientific) representation. Since Marx finds systematic misperception due to capitalism in two main areas, it is important from both a theoretical and a political point of view to determine whether the elucidation of these misperceptions invalidates or partially endorses the claims made by capitalist ideology concerning freedom and equality. This is particularly the case with regard to freedom, as far as the rational choice approach is concerned, since the reality of freedom is inscribed in its basic assumptions.

The Sources of Misrepresentation

The first area of systematic misrepresentation Marx located in the political economy of his day. His theory of value led to a new representation of capitalism as a system of exploitation rather than the thoroughgoing system of equal exchange its apologists portrayed. But this part of Marx's critique, which connects distortion specifically to the realm of circulation (for this purpose, 'appearance') as distinct from production (alias 'reality'), does not rely on the denial of the fact or significance of choice (hence freedom) in the realm of circulation. Instead it posits a confusion in one crucial case over the *object* of choice – over *what* is being exchanged in the labour contract. Nor does it deny that *commodity* exchange is equal exchange. Inequality arises because the relevant exchange is not a commodity exchange, given the confusion about what is and what is not a commodity. In capitalist ideology, the worker is liable to believe that what she is exchanging at its value (labour-power) is something else (labour) for which she is denied adequate compensation. The fraud on labour may be concealed by the fair trade in labour-power.[23]

The second source of systematic misperception was analysed by Marx under the heading of 'fetishism'. Economic fetishism (which certainly exists under capitalism, but to an extent Marx may have exaggerated) involves the false attribution of economic powers either to unaided bits of matter or to unaided commodity forms – especially the spectacular forms of money in isolation from the networks of social and/or material relations which are in fact responsible for the economic powers they appear to enjoy.[24] Yet the powers in question do exist in the said networks, so that, as Cohen explains, the illusion of fetishism is like that of a mirage or the pre-Copernican cosmology (in which knowledge of the source of the illusion does not destroy the appearance which gives rise to the illusion) and not like that of a hallucination or the emperor's new clothes (in which the appearance disappears with the knowledge of the illusion).[25] The misperception of (economic but not religious!) fetishism is not the perception that something exists when it does not, but the perception that something which exists is other than it is.

What effect, then, will Marx's disclosure of the mirage-image have on those who inhabit capitalist relations? Will the knowledge that economic power truly resides in the ensemble of social and material relations of itself restore to the agents previously subject to the illusion the freedom to use their part of the powers in unalienated fashion? It seems unlikely that a merely cognitive process could wreak such havoc with capitalism, if only because those who command resources have powers and interests other than the power and interest at the focus of Marx's critique of capitalism – each person's labour power and its creative expression. Ruling classes might be quite happy to exploit the alienated labour-power of others in order to satisfy their material requirements, thereby releasing their own creative powers for expression in a non-economic domain called 'culture'.[26] This is not an implausible picture of the creative achievement of historic leisure classes, corrupted and confined as this achievement is (in an inevitable Marxian view) by its continuing dependence on the exploitation that makes it possible.

If we now turn to the exploited group itself, whose material interests and creative powers are thwarted alike under capitalism, the diagnosis of the mirage looks like an indispensable part of any programme of social change designed to restore economic powers to their rightful owners. Without the awareness of the illusion, it is not clear how the requisite change could be conceivable, let alone conceived as desirable. Diagnosis of the mirage is a liberating act in its own right: those no longer in thrall to the mirage are freer than they were before – or at least they are certainly not less free. Reversing the direction of comparison, one can say that those still subject to the illusion are really (in truth, that is) more free than they think they are when they falsely attribute economic motive force to money and unaided bits of matter. But, in this case, Marx's diagnosis of economic fetishism offers the worst possible paradigm for the converse situation – frequently invoked by the critics of consumer capitalism – in which people think they are free when they are not really (in truth) free at all.[27]

I conclude that those who would entirely debunk the freedom enjoyed under capitalism will find no comfort in the classical critique of capitalist ideology. They will also have to confront the position, implicit in their claims about capitalism, that the freedom to which socialists aspire is somehow above and beyond the mundane variety we currently experience. On this account, socialist freedom is not to be equated in any way with the greater freedom we seem to enjoy in a North American than in a British supermarket to buy not just milk, but milk with six levels of fat content and two styles of pasteurization, each offered in eight different flavours. Socialist proposals corresponding to the two lines of attack on Marx's question then involve the suggestion either that everyone, and not just the privileged minority, should be offered the choice between chocolate and strawberry milk, or, the contrary suggestion, that the choice is not worth having since no one in their right minds would choose either, especially when wholesome, regular milk is there for the asking. The contradiction between these proposals has not prevented both being entertained simultaneously, as an understandable hedging of bets, or perhaps, because if the first proposal is not viable under socialism (or is viable already under capitalism), resort must be made to the second, reserve proposal in a process Elster would include under the heading of Sour Grapes.

I believe that socialists should be predisposed towards the first proposal, and the maximization of freedom subject to two kinds of constraint: the technological constraint and the version of egalitarianism which rejects exploitative social relations.[28] The second proposal seems to me dispirited because it delivers at one stroke the ordinary vocabulary of freedom and most experience of common sense to the enemy camp. By judging that capitalism is not right only where it is not as it seems to be, it risks the concession that nothing seems to be wrong with capitalism. Ironically, for an approach which starts out looking very radical indeed, much more is conceded to capitalism than the classical response to capitalism concedes. In my view, the main burden of the latter response is that the rich get the pleasure and the poor get the blame not because the freedom of capitalism is an illusion, but because it is real. Or, putting the matter more precisely, the marketplace really is a free space. What is constitutionally unfree is the state-place, which upholds property. What is consequently unfree is the workplace, where those without property find it is in their best interest to labour for their daily bread. This is the consequence Marx took for granted, but Roemer seeks to prove, assuming the state, private property and the market.

Roemer on Class and Exploitation

Roemer's work may be introduced by a slight adaptation of the model which he chooses to make his central point concerning the relation between class and exploitation. Imagine there are two people whom for the sake of vividness we suppose to be located on two different islands, called Woman Friday and Man Crusoe respectively.[29] Each has the same need of subsistence, which is, say, one bushel of corn per week. Each is also rational, and wishes to gain this subsistence with the minimum possible expenditure of effort. But there is one important difference between Friday and Crusoe, or, more precisely, between the island environments they inhabit. Friday only has available a labour-intensive (LI) technology which requires no material input apart from labour, and so can be operated from scratch, but requires that she work six days a week to produce one bushel of corn. Crusoe, on the other hand, has access to a superior, capital-intensive (CI) technology which uses an amount of material input (seedcorn), but which only requires three days' work to produce the output of one bushel of corn, and also reproduce the amount of seedcorn necessary to get the process going. We also assume that Crusoe has on hand a stock of twice the amount of seedcorn necessary to run the CI technology for a week. All the material parameters of the subsistence model have now been set. They constrain what is jointly possible for Friday and Crusoe. It is worth noting, first, that what distinguishes the two technologies is their respective productivities, the CI technology being exactly twice as productive as the LI technology. It is this difference which is critical to the subsequent argument, and it corresponds precisely to the fact that the level of development of the forces of production is higher (twice as high) on Crusoe's than on Friday's island (according to the classical definition of these terms in Friday's case and the only plausible extension of classical usage in Crusoe's).[30] Second, the pictures of the production process on the two islands – one without constant capital and one with it – correspond to the Volume 1 and Volume 3 models of *Capital*. It follows that Roemer's results lie beyond the scope of Marx's Volume 1 analysis, in which it is necessary to assume the class relation Roemer is able to deduce.[31]

We now ask what Crusoe and Friday make of their respective situations. So long as they exist in isolation from each other, Crusoe simply works three days a week and Friday is stuck with working six. This is the limit of Robinson Crusoe economics, in Marx's pejorative use of the term. Once their mutual isolation is breached, a number of new possibilities open up. These possibilities involve the social relations that might be established in the given material environment.[32] Recall that Crusoe has more seedcorn than he needs for his own subsistence. He could double his weekly output by working six days instead of three, but there is no point in his working beyond three days since his needs are satisfied after three days and he would be stockpiling useless corn. (Trade in produced commodities cannot occur in a one-sector model.) So a generous, public-spirited Crusoe might simply give his extra stock of seedcorn to Friday. Friday could then switch to the CI technique; both islands would have three-day economies, and the net benefit of the two people would be equalized. In this egalitarian (petty bourgeois or socialist) outcome the gains of productivity (and of the initial capital stock) are equally distributed between the two parties. Notice that once the initial endowment of capital is made, the two economies can reproduce themselves independently and indefinitely, since Friday will have sufficient surplus above subsistence after the first week to start production in the second.

But now suppose that Crusoe does not give Friday what she needs, but offers her a deal. Crusoe offers Friday the opportunity to work for pay of one bushel per week using Robinson Crusoe's stock of seedcorn and the CI technology. The crucial question is how long Friday will have to work, and therefore how much she will produce. If both parties are rational, and we assume that the transaction is a voluntary one, there must be incentives for both parties to make the agreement. Crusoe's incentive is obvious enough. He will certainly not make a deal involving less than three days' work by Friday, since this will not even reproduce the wage he pays, and he will find his capital stock running down (though he could easily afford its being run down to half its original level, in a drip-drip rather than one-shot gift to Friday). Nor will he be interested in making a deal beyond six days, since Friday can produce enough for both parties using the CI technology in this time, and we have assumed that Crusoe has no interest in surplus for its own sake. But if Friday works any time between three and six days, the number of days above three will be the number of days that Crusoe can reduce his own working time and still end up with his net subsistence for the week. This is a clear incentive. But does Friday have an incentive to enter employment under such terms? She does, and this is the key moment of class reproduction according to Roemer's brilliant insight. As things stand, Friday is working six days for her subsistence, so that she has an incentive to work any time less than six days for a subsistence wage. It follows that if a deal is struck anywhere between three and six days, both parties will benefit from the deal, given their respective situations. In the most extreme case, if Crusoe is able to maintain a 'take it or leave it' attitude to Friday's predicament, or, as Roemer assumes in his original presentation of the example, there is an industrial reserve army in the labour market and no countervailing pressure on Crusoe to use the half of his capital stock which is surplus to his own requirements, Friday will be bid down to six days' working and Crusoe will be a pure capitalist, whose subsistence comes entirely from the work of other people.[33]

In terms of class formation, then, Friday is always a pure proletarian if she accepts any deal which yields a wage covering her subsistence, but we can see Crusoe moving monotonically from self-employment (from petty-bourgeois or peasant proprietor or whatever independent status) to an employing, capitalist status progressively more complete for any deal which involves Friday's working beyond three days up to the maximum of six. At any point in this interval, the gains in productivity available from the CI technology are distributed unequally. We know that the collective gain – which is also the true gain – is a doubling of productivity. But if one looks at productivity narrowly, as an answer to the question each individual might pose, 'how much corn does *my* labour yield?', then in the extreme case Friday's productivity appears not to have increased at all (since she is still working six days to bring home one bushel) whereas Crusoe's productivity has apparently increased to infinity (since he manages to bring home one bushel without working at all). No doubt Crusoe will be inclined to fetishize this magical result, attributing it to the extraordinary properties of his seedcorn, his skill in negotiation, his gender, his national origin or whatever was responsible for his having an extra supply of capital – virtue and judgement in any case rather than luck. But it is evident that these sterling qualities will avail him nothing unless he is able to induce Friday to accept his offer.

The Classical Construal

We now retell the story in the language of the classical theory of value, pointing up the conformity between Roemer's theory and the classical critique. The value of labour-power is defined to equal the value of the use-values required to reproduce the labourer, whose (material) measure in this example is always one bushel of corn for both Friday and Crusoe. But the value of this material basket of goods alters. Under the LI technology, the value of labour-power is evidently six days whereas under the CI technology it is three days, made up of just less than three days' working to produce a net output of one bushel, together with the balance of three days' total working necessary to reproduce the constant capital required to operate the CI technology. These are the direct and indirect labour components of the value of labour-power in the CI regime. (In the LI regime, there is no indirect labour.) Under the LI regime, the value of labour-power completely exhausts the total value added by Friday (six days), whereas in the CI technology, there is some remainder, depending upon the amount of time beyond three days that Friday works. This is surplus value, corresponding to the value of the net output above one bushel that Friday is able to produce in working beyond three days. In the extreme case of pure capitalism, surplus value is three days; the total value (still six days of Friday's working) is split equally between the value of labour-power and surplus value, and a transfer of value (three days' worth) has occurred between Friday and Crusoe. This is classically construed exploitation of Friday by Crusoe, and the rate of exploitation is 100 per cent, since each hour of Friday's net labour provides half an hour's worth of wages for Friday and half an hour's worth of profit for Crusoe. Putting it another way, three days' labour (by both parties) is the socially necessary labour time under the CI technology – it is the amount each person would have to work on his or her own – and Friday is working more than is socially necessary while Crusoe is working less than is socially necessary. And the person who is working more is the labour(-power) seller while the person who is working less is the labour(-power) hirer. In this correlation we have encountered for the first time Roemer's startling Class Exploitation Correspondence Principle (hereafter CECP) in its most classical form (the transfer of surplus value through the labour contract).

We have also followed classical usage by introducing the word 'exploitation' to characterize the unequal relation between Friday and Crusoe. If Crusoe is exploiting Friday we need to establish precisely what it is, in the circumstances portrayed by the example, that Crusoe is exploiting. First, and in a relatively non-evaluative connotation, both parties are making use of one or both of the technologies, hence exploiting whatever features of the natural world are responsible for the productivities the technologies have. But the use of the term 'exploitation' in the Marxian context also implies injustice, and it is unclear (to me, at least) what are the just claims of the non-human on the human world.[34]

Restricting the discussion to the social relations established between Friday and Crusoe, the most obvious, and traditional, suggestion is that Crusoe is exploiting Friday's labour. The problem with this suggestion is that Friday's labour for Crusoe only exists after the deal between them has been concluded – it is a corollary of the deal, so it cannot be something of which Crusoe makes use in order to clinch the deal. So either the deal is exploitative, but it is not Friday's labour that is exploited, or the exploitation of Friday's labour is a consequence of a deal which is not exploitative (at least, is not exploitative of Friday's labour). I take it that the second possibility strains the credibility of the Marxian indictment. The same argument applies, *a fortiori*, to the suggestion that Crusoe is exploiting the product of Friday's labour, despite the fact that Crusoe makes use of this product by eating it. (Does Crusoe exploit the corn by eating it when it is already in his hands?) It is nearer the mark, and in line with the classical emphasis on the distinction between labour and labour-power, to say that Crusoe is exploiting Friday's labour-power, since this is something which exists prior to the deal's being made. It is part of the environment from which exploitation is said to emerge. But there are two aspects of labour-power which are worth distinguishing – there is creativity and there is the sheer ability to slog. Now although the exploitation of the creativity of the majority is a fundamental feature of the Marxian critique of capitalism, it is excluded by the terms of this example, since it depends on the alternative uses to which Friday might put her creativity, and the only activities allowed here are corniculture and leisure (or high culture – not so corny culture?). There is thus no evidence that Friday would prefer to do something other than grow corn, and if her creativity is engaged in that activity, the basic pay-off structures change, since Friday will want to follow her natural bent for as many days as possible, contrary to the behavioural assumptions of the example. Crusoe and Friday will in fact compete to reward each other for access to any means of expression held by the other!

We are therefore returned for the answer to the slogging aspect of labour-power, which Friday will experience as a disutility when it goes into action, and try to avoid putting into action as much as possible. But we also have to ask what enables Crusoe to make use of this aspect of Friday's labour-power, since Friday assigns it voluntarily to Crusoe. We know from the example that this has to do with their differential access to the LI and CI technologies. So is Crusoe exploiting his own access to the CI technology? The answer is basically no, since it is not clear in general that a person can exploit anything that lies in his or her environment alone (can I exploit myself?), and it is clear from this example that if Friday had access to the CI technology (for example, via the 'egalitarian outcome'), Crusoe would have no means of inducing Friday voluntarily to enter terms of employment deemed exploitative. What Crusoe is therefore exploiting is the lack of access Friday has to the CI technology. And so we conclude that B exploits A when B takes unfair advantage of a situation in which A is placed by lack of access to resources.[35]

Private Property and the State

We can now make more explicit the cause of the lack suffered by Friday as a result of which it is in her best interest to be exploited. This was presented above in terms of a moral contrast, in which a generous, altruistic and socialist Crusoe would give Friday the access to resources a mean, egotistical and capitalist Crusoe would deny. But the more fundamental source of exploitation will be found in the social institutions which sustain the exclusion from resources. In this case, it is the institution of private property that lurks behind the market, and the institution of the state that lurks behind private property. It is this institutional complex which, one might say, allows Crusoe the opportunity to be generous or mean, and a rational if unreasonable Crusoe will be mean. So the source of exploitation has been traced to a situation of differential exclusion (from the means of production in this case) fortified by the institutions of private property and the state.

In what ways, and by what moral principle, is this outcome unfair, and thus finally an exploitation rather than simply an unequal exchange? Exploitation has been defined as taking unfair advantage of the situation of another person. The charge of unfairness cannot arise from the principle that everyone has a claim on the undiminished proceeds of his or her labour, since although the principle would deliver the required result in this case, there is a long list of classically honoured counter-examples, from the requirements of the young, the old, the sick and the handicapped to the requirements of investment, which tell against the application of the general principle to an adult, fit or present self. The principle must therefore be the negative one, that property ownership yields no valid claim on the proceeds of the labour of others. Respecting Cohen's distinction between productive and producing activities, we can say that capitalists as capitalists have no valid claim on any part of the product, even if their property ownership was in part responsible for the product being produced. In the language of the social and the material, no return is owed to a purely social contribution.[36]

But there is a further element in the evaluation. Exploitation is an unfair use of a situation of exclusion, but the situation which is exploited may be fair or unfair in itself. It seems appropriate to call a situation of unfair exclusion by the term 'oppression'. It is then easy to show via general counter-examples that oppression is neither necessary nor sufficient for exploitation, so that the issue of whether capitalism is oppressive must be approached independently of the question of whether it is exploitative.[37]

In terms of the present example, the question to ask is evidently whether Friday's initial exclusion from the CI technology was fair. The answer will turn on the story that is told about Crusoe's acquisition. On some accounts, such as one in which Crusoe's extra stock results from his extraordinary exertions in the previous week, the acquisition is not conclusively unfair (nor is it conclusively fair, according to the negative evaluative principle which is the only one so far allowed, and which only excludes title derived from property ownership of the means of production, saying nothing about title in the proceeds of my own, or anyone else's labour). The fairness of Crusoe's acquisition, and therefore Friday's initial situation, is thus far indeterminate, corresponding to the possibility of a 'clean path' of capitalist development. Suppose, then, that Crusoe's acquisition was clean and just by some unspecified principle. During the first week of production, Friday is not oppressed, but she is still exploited since Crusoe's just acquisition does not touch the justice in his use of what he has acquired – otherwise justly appointed judges could pass any sentences they liked.[38] But there is constant, non-fixed capital in this example, so that the whole of Crusoe's justly acquired asset in seedcorn is used up in the first week of working. If Crusoe is a pure capitalist, the whole of the constant capital for the next week's working will have been derived from Friday's surplus product of the previous week, acquired by Crusoe through his (just) ownership of the means of production in that period. But it now follows from the negative principle that Crusoe's title to means of production at the start of the second week is invalid: Friday's situation is unfair by Monday, and she is oppressed. Once capitalism gets into its stride, capitalism is oppressive as well as exploitative by a single principle of (un)just distribution. This is the heart of the Marxian indictment of capitalism, and its statement will serve to conclude the opening exposition of Roemer's theory.

Power and Exploitation

We shall now sketch some implications of Roemer's basic approach for the special theory of historical materialism. Discussion will focus on the question of power in Friday and Crusoe's two-island world, and then, very briefly, on Roemer's findings for models of capitalism beyond these two islands. The homily of the previous section omitted reference to power because the first task was to show how class division could come about through voluntary transactions. But what is commonly termed 'power' is still around here somewhere, and the relation of power to the example requires a careful analysis. This question is generally important because rational choice Marxism is a theory with an 'economic' and utilitarian pedigree, whereas the concept of 'power' draws on an alternative tradition of sociology and political science which has often been divorced from economic theory. Posing the question hints at a reconciliation between the two traditions.

Let us start by attributing power to Friday and Crusoe over their respective forces of production: Friday has power over her labour-power and Crusoe over his means of production (seedcorn) and labour power. We note first that power over a force of production is a social relation of production, and a mode of production in conventional Marxist usage is a set of social relations of production.[39] But Crusoe has (monopoly) power over means of production and Friday only has power over her own labour-power, so that the attribution of these powers sets up the capitalist mode of production as the power structure of this example. Roemer's results may then be interpreted as showing that the existence of the capitalist mode of production implies the existence of the capitalist class structure, given rational behaviour.

But what is meant, precisely, by the power that individuals are said to enjoy over forces of production? It is fairly clear that the relevant power is the capacity I enjoy to exclude you from access to my force of production against your will.

This is power in the sense of real ownership – effective control.[40] On this view, Friday and Crusoe are alike in having power, but differ in having power over different resources. Interaction between Friday and Crusoe arises because each party requires the resources of the other to reach an outcome preferable to his or her initial situation. The initial situation now figures twice in the analysis. It remains the starting point of the analysis, but is also a permanent resort for either party. The distribution of power specifies the current withdrawal options of the actors, and the definition of their powers allows each to withdraw without suffering consequences apart from those entailed by the withdrawal itself. But this means that both parties enjoy power *over* the other since, if each respects the power of the other, either can deploy his or her resource to affect the pay-offs available to the other.

We now illustrate how the *extent* of the power (colloquially, the power) I enjoy over you depends on:

i)   the needs and preferences (the interests) of us both;
ii)   your power;
iii) my alternative to interaction with you.

It will be useful first to define the extent of the power each enjoys over the other by the maximum damage each could do to (the interests of) the other, should he or she so wish. Interestingly, this is three days' labour in each case, since Friday can penalize Crusoe by three days' work with respect to Crusoe's best option if Friday should withdraw, and Crusoe can penalize Friday by three days' work with respect to Friday's best option if Crusoe should withdraw. These penalties evidently depend on the interests represented by the pay-off structure (point (i)). The limits of the power of each over the other are therefore given by the ultimate sanctions each can bring to bear on the other, using the powers which define their position within the relations of production.[41] The threat of these sanctions appears in the example at two points. First, in a real case the implied threat may help to determine the point at which the agreement is concluded between three and six days' working. This point is indeterminate as far as economic theory is concerned unless there is competition in the labour market, when Friday is bid down to six days' working or unless Friday has access to seedcorn from a source other than Crusoe, in which case she will work the minimum of three days. But these possibilities envisage other actors, or other resources of a kind which render the sanctions available to each party against the other ineffective. Both continue to enjoy power over resources, but they can no longer translate this power into power over each other (point (iii)). In the case of a competitive labour market, Friday loses her power over Crusoe, and in the case of superabundant seedcorn (cf. the 'open frontier') Crusoe loses his power over Friday. This also establishes the general relation between the power of B over A and the dependence of A on the resource of B. If alternative possibilities are excluded and there is interdependence, it must be assumed that Friday and Crusoe reach some compromise agreement between three and six days' working.[42]

The Enforcement Problem

Now the question arises whether the agreement will be honoured. If Friday is guaranteed a subsistence wage at the end of the week, she has no incentive to perform any work, since it is no longer her business where her corn wage is going to come from. Conversely, if Crusoe is guaranteed the work, he has no incentive to pay the wage (or pay it in unadulterated corn). Given these incentives to default, can the agreement be enforced? Friday's enforcement problem has been solved historically by the abolition of the truck system, and the opening of alternative sources of supply through the money wage and competitive consumer markets (although a form of the problem reappears with inflation). Crusoe's problem has been solved historically by the factory system, and the domination of Friday within the labour process. In the tradition of Marxist sociology of which Braverman and the early Olin Wright are recent standard-bearers, exploitation is rooted in this domination of the worker, and the corresponding proposals for the socialist alternative emphasize the importance of industrial democracy. Without questioning in the least the significance of coercion at the point of production in the life of the worker, or the desirability of the countervailing socialist demand, Roemer's approach tends to make this form of coercion secondary to the powers already contained in the relations of production. The capitalist's problem is that, unlike other commodities, labour-power remains attached to the person of the labourer, and although the labourer has assigned it to the capitalist as an act of will, the use of labour-power in the interest of the capitalist requires the continuous, and not just once-for-all, co-operation of the labourer. This might suggest that power in the workplace is supplementary to the powers defining the relations of production, so that the two loci of power demand two independent critiques. But the worst that either party can do (the most damaging sanction either party can bring to bear) for non-performance of the agreement that constitutes the class relation is the threat of breaking the relation – the strike by Friday; the sack or the lock-out by Crusoe. And these ultimate sanctions coincide with the extent of the powers defining the relations of production. In particular, the sanctions available to Crusoe which would normally be considered under the heading of 'factory discipline' all fall within the scope of the powers defining his ownership of the means of production.[43]

This point can be clarified by supposing that the powers are infringed, so that the current withdrawal options are no longer available. Suppose, for example, that an accumulation-minded feudal Crusoe (more plausibly, an accumulation-minded Crusoe with a feudal ally) were to impose corvée labour on Friday in the LI technology. Friday would have no reason to consent to this arrangement, which infringes her effective control over her labour-power and decreases her utility. But such an infringement would also render it in her interest to work longer than six days for a subsistence wage. So the attribution of effective control of (power over) labour-power sets the upper limit of exploitation. But now suppose that a socialist Friday expropriated half of Crusoe's seedcorn, infringing the ownership of the latter. The effect is, of course, the same as in the previous case in which Crusoe lost *monopoly* power because Friday had an alternative source of seedcorn. In either case, there is no way Crusoe can induce Friday to be exploited, so long as Crusoe is unable to expropriate the seedcorn back – that is, so long as Friday enjoys power over the seedcorn she has expropriated or otherwise acquired. This illustrates point (ii) – that the extent of your power over me depends on my power. Also, and significantly, the attribution of powers (the claim that a particular mode of production exists) bounds the outcome of interaction in a precise sense – between three and six days' working in this case – just as it bounds the sanctions available to the interactors. Vary the distribution of powers, and the outcomes range from Friday working for Crusoe as much as is compatible with her physical reproduction and the converse outcome in which Crusoe works to the limit for Friday (if Friday expropriates all the seedcorn and becomes a capitalist). These extreme distributions of utility over outcomes are set by material parameters, and not by social power. In summary, the power structure sets inner bounds to the outcome of interaction, whose outer bound is set by material constraints. The arena of interaction is circumscribed by material possibilities, and then, more narrowly, by the power structure. I believe that this result accords well with our general intuitions about 'power', and conforms in theoretical practice to the distinction between macro-sociological analyses which focus on the power structure at the expense of the interaction, and economic analyses which focus on the interaction at the expense of the power structure.

For the sociological analysis, an important further question will then arise: what secures the power structure? In virtue of what are the powers properly attributed to Friday and Crusoe? The general Marxian answer has already been given: because a state exists. It is a defining characteristic of a *capitalist* state that it will intervene with the resources over which it has power to prevent the infringement of the powers which define the capitalist relations of production. It is this intervention which will confound a feudal Crusoe or a socialist Friday, although it must be said that actually existing capitalist states have been more punctilious in this respect in relation to Crusoe's than to Friday's powers.[44] And the institution that so intervenes is a *state* because of the range of resources – unique in a given society – over which it has control (finance, real estate, labour-power, legal enactment, means of representation, armed forces), and especially because of the extent of its legal use of the last resource on the list.[45] To attribute powers to Friday and Crusoe is therefore to make implicit reference both to a third party (the state) and to other resources (especially armed force) which are excluded from the analysis of the interaction which gives rise to classes under capitalism.[46] This is a perfectly reasonable procedure for a special theory, which respects the contours of power existing in a given social formation. It will not be so reasonable for a general theory of history, in which there is no longer a struggle on the basis of power, but a struggle *for* power – a struggle to redefine the contours of power in a given social formation, generating a new distribution of freedoms and rights for the actors in the social formation. If this idea will guide the criticism of Roemer's attempt to interpret the general theory of historical materialism in terms of an equally general theory of exploitation, it remains to indicate what reservations about the special theory of exploitation lead Roemer himself to adopt the generalization he does.

Roemer's Complex Models

Up to now, the classically inspired special theory has been presented in an impossibly restricted setting: a particular two-person one-sector subsistence model. The reader will want to know: whether surplus-value exploitation only and always arises in such a model. What happens to the basic results (especially the CECP) in a more complex theoretical universe?

In order to answer these questions Roemer introduces a veritable battery of n-person, m-sector linear models whose parameters vary in the following three ways:

(i) *Behavioural assumptions*. In the *subsistence models*, rationality implies minimization of effort (labour-time) to obtain a fixed bundle of consumption goods from given endowments (Friday/Crusoe). In the *accumulation models*, rationality implies maximization of revenue (through production and exchange) from given endowments. In classical notation, this is the difference between the C-M-C and the M-C-M' (where C = Commodity, M = Money and M' = More Money) chains of commodity production and exchange.[47]

(ii) *Behavioural options*. Actors always have the option of self-employment and trade in produced commodities (means of production and consumption goods). In addition, they may be given access to a labour market or a credit market. In the Friday/Crusoe world, there was an embryonic labour market, but no credit. (Trade was excluded by attenuation to a single produced commodity – corn.)

(iii) *Technology employed*. This is either the Leontief technology familiar from neo-Ricardian price theory or the more general activity analysis or convex cone technology.[48] They all involve constant returns to scale.

In all cases, agents in the economy are alike in being rational, but differ in their initial endowments. Endowments (and therefore agents) are ranked by wealth, measured as the market value of agents' physical stocks at prices corresponding to the reproducible competitive equilibrium for the economy in question. (Crusoe had wealth in seedcorn, and Friday none, though there were no prices in the one-sector model.) An equilibrium represents an individual optimum for each agent. Agents are further distinguished (and ranked) by the amount of time they work at equilibrium, and by their class position. The latter is a qualitative (set-theoretic) notion depending on whether or not agents at equilibrium are self-employed, are employed by others, or employ others. These possibilities are not mutually exclusive and Roemer shows that in general agents sort themselves into a fivefold class decomposition: big capitalists (pure employers), small capitalists (employers/self-employed), petty bourgeoisie (purely self-employed), semi-proletarians (self-employed/employed), proletarians (purely employed). We encountered all these class positions in the Friday/Crusoe example, except the semi-proletarian, which would have occurred if Friday had some wealth in seedcorn, but not enough to run the CI technology for three days.

A CECP arises when there is a correlation between wealth and class position (the resource-rich optimize consistently at class positions made 'higher' by the correlation) and a further correlation between wealth and exploitation status. The latter is measured by the balance between the labour performed and the labour content of subsistence goods in the subsistence models, and by the balance between the labour performed and the labour the agent could command by purchasing goods out of revenue in the accumulation models. A favourable balance defines an exploiting and an adverse balance an exploited status. In the accumulation models, the 'modal' definition of the balance implies that a 'grey area' of agents may exist who are neither exploited nor exploiting.[49] The general logic of derivation for a CECP is this: unequal wealth in resources plus common orientation as rational actors implies differential class position with covariant exploitation status. It is worth noting that this derivation reverses the sequence found in Althusserian sociology: here, individuals create class positions; there, individuals are created for class positions.

It now transpires that so long as the definitions of labour value (hence exploitation) are suitably adapted to the requirements of the successive models, the CECP is essentially preserved (strictly, a different CECP is provable for each model). The Friday/Crusoe case is no *ad hoc* construction. This is good news for the classical intuition. Indeed, it is an astonishing tribute to Marx's genius. (It doesn't reflect badly on Roemer, either.)

The bad news comes in three large doses. First, some orthodox positions on the labour theory of value must be sacrificed in order to preserve the CECP. In particular, values depend on prices for the most general linear technology.[50] Second, it is impossible to make classical sense of the notion of exploitation if labour is radically heterogeneous. This is because it is impossible to rank actors by their labour contributions at equilibrium and an alternative attempt to rank actors according to equilibrium wage rates results in the loss of the essential correlation between wealth and class position. The problem of skill cannot be handled within this framework.[51] Third, the classical focus on the labour market is logically misplaced, because the transfer of surplus labour through the labour market is neither necessary nor sufficient for surplus-value exploitation. It is not necessary because the transfer of value can take place either through product markets alone or credit and product markets together. Roemer uses the first case to examine unequal exchange and a corresponding 'world division of labour' brought about by free trade between self-employing national economies – imperialism without empire.[52] In the second case, isomorphism theorems connect one-to-one the decomposition into credit classes with the decomposition into employment classes found when labour markets exist.[53] The sufficiency of labour-market labour extraction for exploitation fails in view of a special three-person counter-example according to which surplus labour is performed by one employed actor when the initial wealth, and subsequent welfare, of all three actors is identical, and so the question of exploitation cannot arise.[54] It is partly in the hope of resolving difficulties such as these that Roemer proposes his second, general theory of exploitation.

History and Exploitation

The avowed purpose of Roemer's major work is to provide a general taxonomy of exploitation: to escape from capitalism into history, socialism and beyond. This programme brings the general theory of exploitation which he proposes into close relation with the general theory of historical materialism. It offers a frame of reference for interpreting the past and, perhaps, for changing the future. To this end, Roemer proposes the following deceptively simple definition of exploitation:

> A coalition S, in a larger society N, is exploited ... only if: (1) There is an alternative, which we may conceive of as hypothetically feasible, in which S would be better off than in its present situation. (2) Under this alternative, the complement to S, the coalition N–S=S', would be worse off than at present.[55]

The references to 'better off' and 'worse off' generalize the form of inequality essential to the intuition of exploitation – in principle extending the scope of the theory to cover any dimension of social life for which a criterion of rankable benefit is plausible. The conjunction of (1) and (2) is intended to capture the interactive element in the intuition: the sense in which the welfare of the exploiting coalition S' depends upon the poor fare of the exploited coalition S.[56] This way of identifying the inequality together with its presumptive source evidently relies upon a comparison between the status quo and the 'hypothetically feasible alternative', which is, in the first instance, a construction of thought experiment. Usually, Roemer takes the alternative to involve new social arrangements pertaining after the resources available in the status quo have been redistributed in some fashion. Two dimensions of generality then open: it is possible to extend the list of types of resource investigated under the definition, and to imagine different rules for redistributing the same kind of resource. At this point, the general theory connects directly with politics, because a political movement might be concerned with the consequences of maldistribution of a particular kind of resource in the status quo, and its programme of action might be informed by the attempt to achieve the redistribution of that resource specified by an appropriate rule. Any such redistribution rule will define a withdrawal option for the exploited coalition S. The pay-offs under the 'hypothetically feasible' alternative are those available supposing that the exploited coalition escape the status quo with some portion of some variety of resources it does not enjoy at present, and organize itself independently on this basis.

It is then possible to speak in the plural of forms of exploitation under the status quo: each one wired to a different escape route for potentially distinct coalitions of people exploited in different respects within the status quo. It follows that when different observers return different answers to the question: which are the exploited coalitions in the society? or the question: is a given coalition exploited? there may not be disagreement about what exploitation is, but about the particular alternative to the status quo the observers have in mind.[57] On the other hand, each withdrawal option is liable to be associated with some differences of ethical standpoint, since withdrawal under terms set by the redistribution rule promises to overcome the injustice (the specific form of unfairness) which makes the comparative distribution of benefits and burdens in the status quo exploitative. The general theory might finally connect with a delineation of needs (of human nature), since it may be the resources required to satisfy a particular order of needs whose maldistribution leads to a particular form of exploitation in the status quo and whose frustration the alternative regime promises to overcome.

If the horizons of the general theory are thus potentially as broad as the utilitarian tradition of social thinking, it is necessary to show in what sense it remains distinctively Marxist. It does so largely because the surplus-value theory of exploitation occurs within it as a special case, wherever the restrictive assumptions of the classical theory are allowed (above all, the homogeneous labour assumption). To confirm this it is necessary to show that a CECP will typically satisfy the two conditions in the general definition. But this is already clear from the correspondence principles: if wealth is equally endowed to all, there is no decomposition into distinct classes, and agents will all work socially necessary labour time at equilibrium. So, comparing the pay-offs in the equilibrium under equal endowment with the equilibrium in an unequal endowment status quo, the exploited would work less and the exploiters would work more in the alternative regime, satisfying the general definition. The redistribution rule involves the exploited coalition withdrawing with its proportional (usually per capita) share of available social assets. Since this involves a redistribution of property rights, the general theory is also called the 'property-relations approach' to exploitation. In the classical case at issue here the relevant property is property in what Roemer calls 'alienable assets' (especially means of production). This rule serves to define *capitalist exploitation* in the general theory. If the general theory and the classical theory coincide for the central case, the general theory is not limited to surplus extraction through the labour market, since we have seen that a CECP applies where there is trade and credit and a Wealth Exploitation Correspondence Principle where there is trade in produced commodities. Moreover, the general theory renders the appropriate verdict ('No exploitation') for the counter-example to the sufficiency of surplus extraction for exploitation, and the general theory can go on to accommodate cases in which the labour-value approach is ill-defined.[58]

The most important of these involves skill, and the extension of the resource list to include non-alienable alongside alienable assets. To model this case,

Roemer assumes not that different kinds of labour are offered, but that absence of skill restricts the technology that can be worked by a given agent. This restriction in the status quo may lead the unskilled to do worse and the skilled to do better than either would do if the knowledge required to work the whole matrix of technology were equally available to all. For example, if Crusoe gave Friday the seedcorn, but not the knowledge required to plant it, Friday would be in the same predicament as before, but out of a different variety of exclusion from productive assets. Roemer calls this case *socialist exploitation*, since it is a form of exploitation consistent with equal distribution of capital, and possibly characteristic of actually existing socialism. To complete the list of exploitation types, there is *feudal exploitation*, most conveniently thought to result from an unequal distribution of labour-power: serfs are deprived by feudal obligations of the ability to trade or otherwise optimize the output from a part of their personal unit of homogeneous labour-power. (Slaves are similarly deprived of the whole unit.)[59] In addition, there is *status exploitation*, derived from differential returns to a bureaucratic position independent of any genuine expertise the bureaucrat may possess. (If bureaucrats have such expertise, they are not let off the hook, since they may then become guilty of socialist exploitation.)[60] Finally, there is *needs exploitation*, resulting from the differential welfare of the needy when income is equalized in respect of every other difference between agents. The redistribution rules which make these cases exploitative under the general definition involve respectively restoring every serf (or slave) to the enjoyment of a full unit of their labour power, eliminating bureaucratic differentials and distributing resources to ensure equality of welfare.

As the terminology implies, these forms of exploitation may be viewed in a sequence corresponding to the sequence of regimes of production given by the theory of history and a progressive sociology of knowledge in which the forms are reflected successively in thought (capitalist ideology attacks feudal exploitation, socialist ideology attacks capitalist exploitation, communist ideology attacks socialist (and ultimately needs) exploitation...). But the succession of forms of exploitation may also be held to settle the long-distance political agenda, according to which the historical task of each epoch is to eliminate one form of exploitation before moving on to confront the next. In Roemer's view, the historical process resembles an onion, in which the removal of each skin reveals the next deeper skin. The end of progressive politics is the elimination of the onion. If one cannot tame Tawney's tiger stripe by stripe, one has to tackle his onion layer by layer, and you cannot peel an onion from the inside out.[61] This is how the historical process selects time-bound 'historical tasks' of emancipation for the progressive social movements. In this way, Roemer snatches orthodoxy from the jaws of heresy.

It should be made clear at once that the general theory of exploitation is offered here only as an *interpretation* of the Marxist theory of history. It is parasitic on the latter rather than a substitute for it, unlike Roemer's special theory of exploitation (itself now embedded in the general theory) which is a full substitute for the classical labour theory of value. It is therefore unsurprising to discover that the difficulties of Roemer's interpretation centre around the two concepts at the heart of current debates on the theory of history itself: power and rationality. I have argued above that it is possible to connect the special theory for each mode of production to a definition of each mode which attributes power to actors over resources and thereby specifies the *current withdrawal options* of the actors. These options may be used as threats in current bargaining situations. We have seen that the general theory also specifies a withdrawal option, but this time it is a counter-factual *withdrawal option*, and the facts to which it runs counter are above all the facts of power. The redistribution of power over resources envisaged under the 'hypothetically feasible alternative' lies on the other side of an immense social revolution. It is the difference between Friday's threat to strike and her threat to expropriate Crusoe.

This distinction is connected to rationality, because there is a corresponding distinction to be made between proximate rationality (optimization given power) and long-distance rationality (optimization over the distribution of power). In order to achieve the latter optimization, exploited agents will have to be convinced that there are long-distance benefits to be had and then overcome the free-rider problem of collective political action in order to dislodge those in power before claiming the presumed benefits. In different ways, and different historical contexts, Elster, Przeworski, Brenner and Taylor all raise the challenge that long-distance rationality may not be rational at all, or that, if it is rational, it is so only under certain special circumstances which make proximate and long-distance rationality coincide.[62] Subject to these challenges, a Cohenesque version of the theory of history is considerably weakened, and with it the historical attachment and political implications of Roemer's general theory of exploitation.

Besides these reservations, there is plenty of evidence internal to Roemer's discussion of this element of his theory, and one massive piece of evidence from outside, that it is inappropriate to consider forms of exploitation as sequential rather than pertaining to options of social organization which remain significantly open in principle. The great merit of the general theory of exploitation is to place these options on the same table. The effect of close attachment to the general theory of history is to sweep some of them under the carpet again.

To be more specific: the three most important forms of exploitation in Roemer's account are capitalist exploitation, socialist exploitation and status exploitation. The forms of social organization corresponding more or less clearly to these kinds of exploitation are the market, a regime of decentralized workers' co-operatives, and a centralized planning mechanism. If you eliminate the market and therefore capitalist exploitation, you may run into incentive problems, or problems of technical innovation which reduce the projected pay-offs of those exploited under the market regime. If you allow a regime of workers' co-operatives free rein, then those co-operatives which develop special skills and knowledge may pull ahead of the rest and become socialist exploiters. If the co-operatives are joined by fully-fledged free-market relations, and can capitalize their advantages, there might be a return to capitalist exploitation.[63] But if you redistribute their surplus through a mechanism of central planning, you may just be substituting status exploitation for socialist or capitalist exploitation. Or consider the international context: the relations among the three worlds are very likely characterized by differential access to skills and to capital, working out their logic via the terms of trade and the international credit and labour markets; the whole compounded by more or less direct forms of political domination. This suggests that a rich mixture of capitalist, socialist and status exploitation exists between the First and Third Worlds, with the Second perhaps poised somewhere in between. It would take a brave commentator to assert an unequivocal trend in the development of those relations.[64]

One might suppose that feudal exploitation at least had been left behind for good and all, but there is more than a passing family likeness between feudal exploitation and status exploitation. The exploiters in both cases owe their position to 'extra-economic' resources, despite the fact that personal advancement in one system is the result of birth and warfare, while in the other advancement may be due more to political reliability (to the extent that it is independent of true expertise). Loyalty and respect for hierarchy (with the odd stab in the back to keep everyone on his or her toes) seem important principles of co-ordination in both cases.[65] And if this family likeness between feudalism and bureauracy offers some clues about the ability of Russian society to abridge the capitalist stage, then what are we to make of the Japanese transition from feudal forms to highly advanced capitalist ones? In any case, the modern capitalist corporation is a monument of rewards to position, alongside ownership and skill.[66] In short, the historical process may resemble an onion less than a balloon: exploitation is suppressed in one place only to pop up somewhere else. Roemer's application gives too much away to an unreconstructed classical vision of progress.

If these points are largely internal to Roemer's own discussion, massive evidence against the linear chronological conception is supplied by the example of gender. Here

> we need a historical understanding of the ways in which gender and class have become so intertwined in capitalist society .... The recognition of the different origins of class and gender oppression need [not] blind us to either the gendered character of class under capitalism or to the importance of struggling for a socialism that has been redefined in the light of feminism.[67]

This point is evidently of universal historical relevance. Part of what needs redefining by its light is John Roemer's *General Theory of Exploitation and Class*.

Let Several Flowers Bloom

I have introduced rational choice Marxism not as an assortment of remote specialist interests, but as a fully-fledged paradigm, which deserves to take its place beside the two other constellations of theory currently discernible within the broad spectrum of progressive social thought – namely, post-structuralism and critical theory. Rational choice Marxism qualifies as a paradigm because of the scope of its interests, and the elements of a common approach identifiable across these interests. Indeed, it is now only within the rational choice context that some of the leading items on the classical agenda of Marxist theory – historical explanation and the delineation of social form, the collective dynamics of class struggle, the evolution and evaluation of capitalism – can be fruitfully discussed. In these areas, rational choice Marxism has inherited the mantle of Althusserian structuralism. But it is not the linear descendant of Althusserianism, since it seems to have developed in wholesale reaction against, rather than in critical engagement with, the Althusserian legacy. I take post-structuralism to be precisely the linear descendant of Althusser – at least in regard to the characteristic cluster of problems associated with the concept of ideology. The third paradigm – critical theory – has rejuvenated itself in the work of Habermas, on a route of intellectual history that has bypassed Paris via the Rhine, rather than via Oslo Fjord and the North Atlantic.

With all this variety and vitality of intellectual culture, and with the example of Althusserianism before us (or behind us), it would be wrong to make overweening claims for any one paradigm. We should therefore conclude by exploring certain limitations of rational choice theory and the practice of rational choice Marxists. First, because rational choice explanation offers a particular kind of bridge for outcomes to a background distribution of values, beliefs, interests and resources, it is always possible that extra-rational motivations such as habit (if habit is a motivation) or emotion may render the bridge defective. It is also true that the background distribution itself remains unexplained, as in the case of the distribution of power and the historical process. In addition, rational choice explanation is inherently vulnerable to its own form of microscopic teleology, in which the behaviour leading to the outcome risks being treated as the principal evidence for the beliefs and values which would have made the behaviour rational. This is rationalization of action rather than rational explanation of action. But those who would write off the rational choice approach on this account should first consider the analyses of preference formation within a rational choice framework made by Elster in *Ulysses and the Sirens* and *Sour Grapes*,[68] and then reflect on the consequences for Marxism of abandoning the bridge between property distribution and class position constructed by Roemer.

Gender Difference

A second objection is more specific, perhaps symptomatic: namely, the sensitivity of the paradigm, as developed so far, to questions of gender division. The initial issue is one of language. The three leading lights of rational choice Marxism continue to use the masculine forms in generic contexts. This includes reference both to the true generic set (humankind) and, often, to a proper subset.

For Cohen, for example, 'If an artist creates a beautiful object out of something which was less beautiful, then we would find it natural to say that he creates beauty' (wouldn't it be more *natural* to say that he or she creates beauty? or indeed that she or he creates beauty?).[69] Elster also has one or two asides and examples which I find slightly obtuse, to put it no stronger.[70] Although I have not searched out every last quotation, the usage is as far as I know unacknowledged and unexplained except in the bizarre case in which Cohen speaks of the 'sexist personification of humanity which Marxists have not always avoided', and then goes on not avoiding it.[71] It is true that rational choice Marxism has an intellectual background in philosophy and economics, which are the two backwoods disciplines in these respects. So it may be unfair to tax individuals with a collective fault. But the longer it goes on, the less the usage looks like adherence to a discredited convention and the more it looks like some kind of political statement. Where have these great men been for the last 15 years?

Alongside these commissions, there is a remarkable – seemingly total – omission of reference either to feminist theory or the general topic of sexual difference.[72] It is true that no one (not even three ones) can be expected to say something about everything. It is also hazardous, as Althusser discovered, to infer presences from absences. The case nevertheless seems to move from pardonable silence to purblind paralysis at the point when the discussion is led to the very brink of an illuminating connection with another (I thought, roughly adjacent) body of thought – and nothing is said. Let us examine two spectacular examples. In the course of 'Reconsidering Historical Materialism', Cohen describes as follows a human need to which 'Marxist observation is commonly blind':

> A person does not only need to develop and enjoy his powers. He needs to know who he is, and how his identity connects him with particular others ... [This is] a need to be able to say not what I can do but who I am, satisfaction of which has historically been found in identification with others in a shared culture based on nationality, or race, or religion, or some slice or amalgam thereof.

But not gender? Is it not beyond question that gender is a rather early and significant point of reference for 'who I am' and do I not share a culture with people of my gender as well as, and probably before, I share one with people in my slice of the amalgamated union of nationality, race and religion? I have in mind's eye a snapshot of my son being chased terrified down a Bradford street, escaping, in the company of a Muslim boy friend, from three girls: one Muslim, one Sikh and one a Christian, his sister. And like those of nationality, race and religion, do gender identifications not 'generate, or at least sustain ... bonds whose strength Marxists systematically undervalue', not in this case 'because they neglect' but in spite of not neglecting 'the need for self-identity underlying them'? Here, perhaps, we see the theoretical consequences of that widespread elision between the male and the species whose more innocent expression is the use of the generic pronoun.[73]

The second example involves Roemer's concept of *status exploitation*. Here, at last, one might think, is the recognition that the existence of exploitation is an open question for every dimension of social division. In it lies the promise of a generalization adequate to the complexity of the real social world. But is this how Roemer intends the theory of 'status exploitation' to be taken? Not a bit of it. We have seen 'status' interpreted in an excessively literal – one might almost say, official – sense: to cover the exploitation of a bureaucratic position, independently of the alienable and non-alienable resources the status holder may also command. So the only status that can be exploited is one of formal occupational position, as if there were no other dimensions of status generally recognized across the entire range of social interaction: tending to seal the fate of individuals within it.[74] Of these, the most important are surely gender, ethnicity and age.

In the case of gender, it is difficult to miss the parallel between classical Marxism and second-wave feminism. Recall that the theory of value sets out with a group – the proletariat – and an intuition that their lot is not as just and happy as the official doctrine prescribes. The theory then recasts the distribution of benefits and burdens, representing the capitalists as doing less and getting more than they claim, while the workers are doing more and getting less than they are told to believe. It is characteristic that the current situation of the putative disadvantaged group is represented as worse than the disadvantaged group may currently think it is. This is the radical politics of the long face. But the classical theory of value also holds out the alternative of a better world in which the currently apparent balance and real imbalance will be converted into a real balance.

What else has feminist theory set out to do? It has derided some of the activities and functions dear to the self-importance of men, and represented a range of other activities in which women are heavily engaged as workers, carers, nurturers and supporters as both more important and more burdensome than conventional wisdom allows.[75] And feminist theory has also held out the alternative of a better world – a world in which there are no men as we commonly understand male behaviour, just as socialism envisages a world without capitalists, as we commonly understand capitalist behaviour. In the terminology of the general theory, we will have to say that women are *oppressed* as women so long as they are unfairly excluded from opportunities of satisfaction because of their gender (and there is a strong presumption that the exclusion will be unjust whenever it is caused in this way). They are *exploited* if they unfairly assume disproportionate burdens to the benefit of men as a result of the exclusion. Their counter-factual withdrawal option involves the elimination of the status differential – including the sexist practices defined as such by the maldistribution of resources or benefits which they entail.[76] Of course, we are not yet out of the woods, because it is true that women can be oppressed or exploited without being oppressed or exploited as a result of gender division (Friday was such a case). But this truth does not imply the converse proposition too easily taken for granted by Marxists: that whenever women are oppressed or exploited they are not oppressed or exploited by gender, but rather as members of a social class. The possibilities for two bases of social division X and Y are as follows: individuals are neither X or Y oppressed or exploited; X but not Y; Y but not X or both X and Y oppressed or exploited. These possibilities range independently over a potentially extensive list of resources, needs and criteria of benefit in the context of a variety of social institutions. In addition, there is the opaque but hopefully not impenetrable screen established by representation and ideology, in that an individual may be X while appearing to be Y oppressed or exploited (and all the other possible combinations of X, Y appearance with X, Y reality).

Ethnicity and Exploitation

We can illustrate these points from the qualification that Cohen immediately enters to the perspective opened up by his assertion that Marxists ought to recognize the independent basis of the need for social identification:

> I agree with Frank Parkin that what I would call divisions of identity are as deep as those of class, and that they cannot be explained in the usual Marxist way. But I think he is wrong to suppose that this weakness in Marxism casts doubt on its treatment of domination and exploitation as centring on class conflict .... For racial exploitation and class exploitation are not two species of one genus. Racial exploitation is (largely) relegation to an exploited class because of race. And if, as Parkin thinks, Protestants exploit Catholics in Northern Ireland, then the exploitation is economic, and not in a comparable sense religious. Catholics are denied access to material values, not religious ones ...[77]

Let us take up the example of Northern Ireland. The use of the phrase 'relegation to an exploited class' suggests the opposite possibility 'promotion'. Promotion to what? To a non-exploited or exploiting class, presumably. So the phrase seems to suggest at first sight that if a person were not a Catholic, he or she would not be in an exploited class. This might happen either because being a non-Catholic was, in itself, a sufficient condition for not being in an exploited class, or perhaps, that being a non-Catholic was a sufficient condition for owning some productive asset, with the consequence (endorsed by Roemer's work) that such a person could not be in an exploited class. But being Catholic or not seems to be the more fundamental feature of a person's situation either way, because in the first case the property variable has completely dropped out of the picture, and in the second it functions as an intermediate variable with no independent effect. If there is any exploitation, it is now an exploitation due to the ethnic rather than the ownership status of a person, and this was plainly not the conclusion motivating the choice of the phrase, or corresponding to the common Marxian thought about the kind of historical situation the conclusion was supposed to illuminate.

What is at issue here is obviously the relation between two features of an exploited person's situation – being Catholic and having no property (which are represented in theory under two descriptions of the same situation). Now if not having property is independent of being a Catholic, we have the converse problem to the one considered just now that not having property is, in itself, a sufficient condition for being in an exploited class. Contrary to the original claim, relegation has not occurred as a result of ethnic status. So what must be meant, and plausibly so in relation to the history of Northern Ireland, is that there is a distinction to be made among those without property between Protestants and Catholics, such that Catholics fare worse than Protestants (on average) and that they fare worse in this respect because they are Catholics. The opening claim is literally false, but can be amended to read with greater plausibility 'relegation to an especially exploited position within an exploited class because of race'. But now, remembering that there is only one person in one situation, described in two ways, being Catholic and not having property are both necessary conditions for the person's situation, but neither is sufficient on its own (that is, we are not dealing with a case of over-determination in which neither is necessary because either is sufficient).

It is worth remarking that this irreducibility of the ethnic (likewise the gender) component in material exploitation will be obscured by any tendency to see the distribution of class positions as pregiven in a social formation: positions to which different kinds of people are subsequently hailed and nailed. Once class positions are seen with Roemer as the outcome of interaction, there is little reason to refuse the suggestion that the overall distribution of class positions and their correlative material values might reflect processes of status discrimination working directly in the workplace or indirectly through the distribution of productive assets and the mechanisms of the market.[78]

But what of 'religious values', and Cohen's denial of their denial in Northern Ireland? It may not be possible to deny people ultimate access to religious values but their means of collective expression can certainly be heavily restricted. It is difficult to believe that this has not been the case in the long history of Catholic relations with Protestants in Ireland. This restriction will be oppressive so long as there is a presumptive right to the expression of religious values, or, more generally, of cultural values. But is there anything directly analogous to exploitation in the sphere of non-material values? An argument to this effect must link the Protestant identity with the Catholic identity in a constitutive way, so that the oppression of the Catholics arises from a dynamic of Protestant association and the related requirements of the Protestant sense of self. Here it is surely significant that the variety of Protestant consciousness which is fateful for the history of Ireland does not just register the better material circumstances Protestants enjoy, on average. It tends to read these advantages into a social myth according to which Protestant people are a higher form of life than Catholic people (but no longer on average, since the discourse of moral segregation rarely admits of shades of grey). As is the custom in such cases, the attribution of superior qualities to Protestants conveniently forgets that it is often action (and inaction) by Protestants which has left Catholics in a situation in which Catholics suffer the disadvantages to which the Protestant cause adverts.

But the very maintenance of the Protestant identity seems to depend upon this notion of inherent and not just contingent (historical and material) ascendancy. This is one reason why the Battle of the Boyne is still being fought in East Belfast.

Now it is true that every form of communal identification is in competition with every other, so that, at the very least, one might expect such identifications to jostle each other at the edges. It is also common, although hopefully not inevitable, that people feel good about themselves only in conjunction with feeling bad about somebody else. But there is a difference between feeling superior (which I am not here condoning in any way) and having a feeling of superiority whose security depends on some derogatory exhibition recurrently directed against those to whom you feel superior. A useful test of the distinction is the presence of flaunting, taunting and vaunting rituals designed to display the alleged superiority in terms so graphic that their meaning cannot be mistaken by the allegedly inferior group.[79] Especially when these flaunting rituals are backed by state power, those at the receiving end are placed in an unusually invidious position. If they do not respond to the ritual, they may appear to give (and will certainly be taken by the other side to give) a tacit endorsement to the sense of superiority – hence collude in a sense in the public recognition of their inferior social status. But if they resist, and are beaten back by the forces ranged against them, they risk the same outcome as before, but at a higher level, so to speak (with greater loss of life and limb). This is the challenge which lies behind the provocation that a flaunting ritual is.

I submit that this is precisely what has always been at stake in the Orange marches, and the tenacity with which many Protestants adhere to the rituals cannot be explained by the superior material circumstances they enjoy. Often these are not, in any case, obviously better than those of their Catholic neighbours. If the Protestants have been bought off, the purchase trades on their sense of self and not their balance at the bank. But then we are able to suggest that Protestants are exploiting the Catholic sense of communal identity (strictly, exploiting the fact that they do not (cannot) share the Protestant identity). Catholics are placed in a situation in which the best option the Catholics have (very likely, nearly every option the Catholics have) confers a benefit on the Protestants, even though the benefit in this case redounds to the Protestants' distorted sense of self-esteem, and nothing material (apart from missiles) passes between the exploiter and the exploited. The Catholics are trapped and made use of in their being, just as surely as the proletarians are trapped and made use of in their doing. There is thus a politics of communal association which is irreducible to, and yet shows certain features in common with, the politics of material distribution.

Out of the Woods

Suppose it is right to insist on the self-seeking character of human behaviour: both in the sense of seeking a sense of self and in the sense of seeking satisfactions for the sought self. Then concern with the character of social identification not only is a concession to social phenomena which have proved intractable to Marxist theory in the past, but also is intrinsic to the socialist project in the present and the future.

I ask you to imagine a group of people who have struggled together for as long as they can remember through a trackless and inhospitable forest, suddenly disgorged onto a vast, fertile plain transparent to their gaze. They break up and fan out across the new space. They expand somewhat, and no doubt relax a little. But after the first burst of enthusiasm, they look about them, and take stock. Their material circumstances have eased, to the full extent, if you will, that the realm of necessity lies entirely behind them. They are free and human, so they look for ways of expressing their essential creativity and meeting all their other needs. Some of these, we have assumed (and no doubt many more than at present) depend on the provision of resources immediately to hand, and have no repercussions for the activities of other people, save perhaps to supplement the goods which others can enjoy. But some kinds of expression (and probably not the least important of these) still depend on the provision of public goods, and the co-operation of other people. How do we know in advance that the provision of these public goods spontaneously corresponds to the newly released impulses of all the people concerned? How do we know that the supply according to ability matches the demand according to need? We cannot be sure, and so long as there is a potential dispute about the provision of public goods, there is a potential problem of social order, because the individuals, being human, are rational, and will be tempted to consume the public goods they need, whether or not the provision of all those goods was part of their first, unhindered action.

Let us suppose that they appreciate this, and they remember from their time in the forest that it will be foolish to nominate some of their number to be holders of state power, because it will be foolish to believe that any one among them is conspicuously immune from the corruptions of great power and high rank. So they will resort to a sense of collective identity, upon which the sanctions will bear which are necessary to resolve the problem of social order in the absence of a state.[80] All those who would take unfair advantage of the provision of collective goods by others will be admonished with respect to this sense of what the group is, and what it is about. We expect that the admonishment will be mild, by historical standards, since it is not undertaken in conditions of great scarcity and it is undertaken for reasons which everyone can approve. But it is necessary nevertheless to guard against the renewed exploitation of some by others. And the sense of identity itself must be non-exploitative – it must not make the sense of self-esteem enjoyed by some depend on the parade of superiority over others, since this is just one aspect of what the sense of collective identity is introduced to avoid.

But then the socialist is indeed like Ulysses. She has entered a formative commitment, according to which she will develop a sense of self, binding her in the future against the temptation to satisfy her human needs unfairly at the expense of the needs of others.[81]

Notes

1. I should like to thank Perry Anderson, Norman Geras, G. Cohen and John Roemer for comments on earlier versions without which this essay would be even less balanced than it is.

2. Two full-dress retrospectives on Althusser are available from T. Benton, *The Rise and Fall of Structuralist Marxism: Althusser and his Influence* (London, Macmillan, 1984); and A. Callinicos, *Althusser's Marxism* (London, Pluto Press, 1976).

3. A personal favourite, echoed on pp. 190-1, occurs in the following illustration both of Cohen's style and his argument that structure-preserving changes in an economy are conceivable: 'It is true that if [a] bridge changes, then there is a structure which changes, for the bridge is a structure. But the structure the bridge is is not the structure the bridge has' (G. Cohen, *Karl Marx's Theory of History: A Defence* (Oxford, Oxford University Press, 1978), p. 36).

4. The major works after Cohen's Karl Marx's *Theory of History* include A. Wood, *Karl Marx* (London, Routledge and Kegan Paul, 1981); J. Roemer, *A General Explanation of Exploitation and Class* (Cambridge, MA, Harvard University Press, 1982); J. Elster, *Making Sense of Marx* (Cambridge, Cambridge University Press, 1985); A. Przeworski, *Capitalism and Social Democracy* (Cambridge, Cambridge University Press, 1985); and E.O. Wright, *Classes* (London, Verso, 1985).

5. The intention of the present paper is to establish some preliminary bearings in the intellectual territory opened up by these writers, rather than attempt a comprehensive assessment. I will concentrate mainly on Cohen and Roemer's contributions, which seem to me central to this purpose. A fuller assessment, inevitably displaying a greater variety of views, would deal in much greater detail with the controversy surrounding methodological individualism, and questions of explanation, recent work in the labour theory of value, the debate on 'Marx and justice', the question of collective action and the political ramifications of the new approach.

6. For the definition of Western Marxism, and the most erudite expositions of its development see the periodic Dean's reports issued by P. Anderson, *Considerations on Western Marxism* (London, New Left Books, 1976); idem, *Arguments within English Marxism* (London, Verso, 1980); idem, *In the Tracks of Historical Materialism* (London, Verso, 1983). The verdict is nearly always 'promising, but could do better'.

7. Can it be a coincidence that this is happening at a time when capitalism itself has reverted to type? Although one approaches with some trepidation any work in which the words 'ludic' and 'veridical' may be found in the same sentence, Anderson's *Tracks* does not go far to explain the remarkable shift he highlights in the centre of gravity of Marxist theoretical culture from Latin Europe to northern Europe and North America (Cohen is a Canadian in Oxford via London; Elster is a Norwegian in Chicago after an apparently rather uncongenial stay in Paris; Roemer is in California, of all the unlikely places for socialist innovation, although I suppose it had to happen eventually). True to former inspirations, and former paradigms, Anderson is more concerned to theorize the absence in Paris than the presence in Los Angeles. This geo-intellectual context of the revival is another issue given inadequate coverage in the course of this paper.

8. 'Analytical Marxism' is the title that appears to have been chosen by the leading exponents themselves. 'Game-theoretic Marxism' occurs in S. Lash and J. Urry, 'The New Marxism of Collective Action: A Critical Analysis', *Sociology*, vol. 18, no. 1 (1984). 'Post-classical Marxism' is taken from Anderson's discussion of

Western European Marxism from 1918 to 1968 (*Tracks*, p. 15.) Of these terms, 'Game-theoretic Marxism' is too narrow because only part of the novelty of the approach is captured by it and only some of the findings of the theory are illuminatingly expressed in the technical vocabulary of game theory; Neo-classical Marxism is too pretentious and post-post-classical Marxism is too clumsy. Roemer's introduction of the term 'analytical Marxism' in J. Roemer, ed., *Analytical Marxism* (Cambridge, Cambridge University Press, 1986), pp. 1–7, stresses a common concern for 'logic, mathematics and model building' and an accompanying 'search for foundations'. The problem is that the non-economists only occasionally resort to formal mathematical models, and while the standards of logical exposition set by Cohen are indeed high, it would be presumptuous to regard them as distinctive. Equally, it is not the search for foundations, but the kind of foundations sought, that is distinctive (Althusser also searched for foundations). I think the salience of the rationality assumption in the search deserves headline recognition, and it is significant that Roemer does adopt the term ' "rational choice" Marxism' for his contribution to *Analytical Marxism*. There is nevertheless a spectrum of adherence to the rational choice paradigm which would find Roemer and the economists, Przeworski, Elster and van Parijs, at one end with Brenner; Wright and Cohen influenced but less clearly committed; followed by Geras (whose disavowal of the label I should record here); with Wood placed firmly at the opposite end of the spectrum. Allen Wood is in fact the clearest example of a writer who is an 'analytical' without being a 'rational choice' Marxist. But it is worth emphasizing that Wood is sharply at odds with nearly all the writers mentioned on a range of fundamental issues (for instance, the normative foundations of Marxism, sympathy with the Hegelian side of Marx). It is also fitting that, so far as I know, the patent on the term 'rational choice Marxism' belongs to Barry Hindess (see his 'Rational Choice Theory and the analysis of political action', *Economy and Society*, vol. 13, no. 3 (August 1984)), and that Hindess has begun a counter attack on its assumptions (see also idem, 'Actors and Social Relations' in M. Wardell, and S. Turner, eds, *Sociological Theory in Transition* (London, Allen & Unwin, 1985); and idem, ' "Interests" in Political Analysis' in J. Law, ed., *Power, Action and Belief: A New Sociology of Knowledge*, *Sociological Review* Monograph no. 32 (London Routledge and Kegan Paul, 1986)).

9. The intuition underlying the remark is this: a structure is a set of relations between the members of a set of elements. At the highest level of description, the elements of social structure are at most people, things and ideas (at most, depending on one's ontology). But these are also the elements which enter the description of action, so that actions seem to be structures with the same basis as the social structures allegedly distinct from actions.

10. I say 'almost certain' since it would be logically possible for productive forces to increase their level indefinitely but asymptotically to some level that stays within the compass of given relations of production.

11. A. Levine, and E.O. Wright, 'Rationality and Class Struggle', *New Left Review*, no. 123 (September–October 1980) pp. 47–68; G. Cohen, 'Reconsidering Historical Materialism', *Nomos*, vol. 26 (1983); J. Elster, 'Review of G.A. Cohen, *Karl Marx's Theory of History*', *Political Studies*, vol. 28 (1980); idem, 'Marxism, Functionalism and Game Theory', *Theory and Society*, vol. 11, no. 4, (July 1982) pp. 453-82; G. Cohen, 'Reply to Four Critics', *Analyse und Kritik* (1983); P. van Parijs, *Evolutionary Explanation in the Social Sciences* (Totowa, NJ, Rowman and Littlefield, 1981); J. Elster, 'A Paradigm for the Social Sciences (Review of van Parijs)' *Inquiry*, vol. 25 (1982), pp. 378-85; P. van Parijs, 'Marxism's Central Puzzle', p. 103; J. Elster, 'Historical Materialism and

Economic Backwardness', both in T. Ball and J. Farr, eds, *After Marx* (Cambridge, Cambridge University Press, 1984); R. Brenner 'The Social Basis of Economic Development' in Roemer, *Analytical Marxism*.

12. Cohen's decisive argument in *Karl Marx's Theory of History*, pp. 41–2, on this point is that the destruction of steam mills would have minor effects compared with the destruction of the knowledge of how to build and use them.

13. 'a description is social if and only if it entails an ascription to persons – specified or unspecified – of rights or powers *vis-à-vis* other men' (ibid., p. 94). But not 'other people'?! – a usage to which I will return.

14. 'The fact that we need the social point of view to discern the capitalist status of means of production or the slave status of a man does not mean that the means of production are not capital or the man not a slave. Each standpoint on a thing reveals a distinct set of properties, but the thing has all of them' (ibid., p. 91).

15. Doreen Massey says of her programme that 'the aim ... is to link two discussions – the one concerning production and social class, and the other concerning spatial organization. In relation to much previous analysis within geography, the argument is that what has been seen simply as the spatial distribution of employment is underlain by, and can be approached through, analysis of the geographical organization of the relations of production. In relation to the substantive social sciences the argument is that the social structure of the economy, the social relations of production, necessarily develop spatially and in a variety of forms. These forms we shall call *spatial structures of production*' (D. Massey, *Spatial Divisions of Labour* (London, Macmillan, 1984), p. 68 (emphasis in original)). Cohen, *Karl Marx's Theory of History*, p. 97, prefigured the connection between the new critical geography and rational choice Marxism in a brilliant, fleeting paragraph.

16. The alternative habit used to be most marked among Marxist sociologists in Erik Olin Wright, whose oft-cited characterization of social classes in *Class, Crisis and the State* (London, New Left Books, 1978) mapped the organization chart of the average American corporation onto society as a whole – the larger pyramid imitating the smaller. But Wright is still remarkable for being one of the few theorists to negotiate the transition from Althusserian to rational-choice Marxism. He was initially very sceptical, though appreciative, of Cohen's work, but seems to have fallen more into line after catching sight of Tony Giddens. Now he has made his peace with John Roemer's theory of class, though not before mounting a stout rearguard action on behalf of the old 'political' approach (power in the workplace) against the new 'economic' one (ownership relations and markets). See Levine and Wright, 'Rationality and Class Struggle', E.O. Wright, 'Giddens's Critique of Marxism', *New Left Review*, no. 138 (March–April 1983), pp. 11–36; idem, 'The Status of the Political in the Concept of Class Structure' *Politics and Society*, vol. 11, no. 3 (1982); and idem, *Classes*.

17. N. Geras, *Marx and Human Nature: Refutation of a Legend* (Verso, London, 1983), p. 107. For a succinct statement of Geras's position, see ibid., p. 68. For Cohen's statement of a position very similar to the one later elaborated by Geras, see Cohen, *Karl Marx's Theory of History*, p. 151.

18. See A. Carling, 'Forms of Value and the Logic of *Capital*', *Science and Society*, vol. 50, no. 1 (Spring 1986).

19. This division, and part of the terminology, bears the authority of Engels; see, for example, his *Speech at the Graveside of Karl Marx*, MESW, pp. 429–30. Cohen has said in 'Reconsidering Historical Materialism', p. 232, that 'Marx produced at least these four sets of ideas: a philosophical anthropology, a theory of history, an economics, and a vision of the society of the future'. I think that 'an economics' is a downgrading description of the special theory (only the theory of history counts

as a proper theory). It is symptomatic of the underestimation of the status of the special theory which is I believe the greatest weakness in Cohen's overall treatment of Marx.

20. This comment has in mind Elster's 'torch relay model of development' among a number of nations. See Elster, 'Historical Materialism and Economic Backwardness', p. 38.

21. This is the burden of Brenner's view of the transition to capitalism: it is only capitalist relations of production which have a systematic tendency to raise the level of development of the forces of production, so 'it becomes just about impossible to see how the sort of argument Cohen makes for the primacy of the productive forces can be sustained' (Brenner, 'The Social Basis of Economic Development', p. 47, n. 13).

22. 'How does production on the basis of exchange-value solely determined by labour-time lead to the result that the exchange-value of labour is less than the exchange-value of its product?' (*Critique of Political Economy*, cited in Cohen, *Karl Marx's Theory of History*, p. 43; cf. Roemer, *A General Explanation*, p. 185 Notice how the very form of this question makes it the grandparent of all attempts to understand how non-straightforward structure arises from straightforward agency, that is, how the particular puzzle which capitalism presented to Marx requires the sort of theory rational choice Marxism aspires to provide.

23. '[labour power], and not labour, is what the proletarian sells to the capitalist, who pays less for it than the value of what he is able to make it produce' (Cohen, *Karl Marx's Theory of History*, p. 43). See also J.E. Roemer, 'Should Marxists Be Interested in Exploitation?', *Philosophy and Public Affairs*, vol. 14, no. 1 (1985), pp. 30-65, p. 31 (reprinted in idem, *Analytical Marxism*, p. 261).

24. 'To make a fetish of something, or fetishize it, is to invest it with powers it does not in itself have' (Cohen, *Karl Marx's Theory of History*, p. 115). 'In commodity-producing societies there is a tendency to overlook the implicitly relational character of certain monadic predicates' (Elster, *Making Sense of Marx*, p. 96). On Marx's 'exaggeration': 'Economic agents do not invest commodities and instruments of production with the full panoply of mysterious powers that Marx describes in such detail. Money is indeed a mysterious entity, but only in part for the reasons brought out by Marx' (ibid., p. 99).

25. Cohen, *Karl Marx's Theory of History*, p. 115 and App. 1.

26. This comment trades on the existence of two orders of human need – for creativity and subsistence – and the two corresponding conceptions of labour which Cohen distinguishes in 'Reconsidering Historical Materialism'.

27. A recent example is J. Seabrook, *Landscapes of Poverty* (Oxford, Basil Blackwell, 1985), which combines a brilliantly observed evocation of contemporary life in Britain with an argument that the experience of poverty has shifted decisively from the external to the internalized landscapes of capitalism. If this is Orwell plus ideology, the contrast is overdrawn between the material and ideological landscapes.

28. The argument in the closing section is intended to show that these are independent criteria, that is, that egalitarianism cannot be seen merely as a historically conditioned response to scarcity. On the issues of whether Marx held values, what they were, and their importance for his theory, the range of positions may be represented by Elster, *Making Sense of Marx*, esp. ch. 4; and A. Wood, 'Marx and Equality' in Roemer, *Analytical Marxism*; with the most comprehensive appraisal of the debate given by N. Geras, 'The Controversy about Marx and Justice', *New Left Review*, no. 150 (March–April 1985), pp. 47–85. I will adopt the 'pro' side of the debate in what follows without further ado.

29. Roemer adopts Friday and Crusoe in 'Property Relations vs Surplus Value in

Marxian Exploitation', *Philosophy and Public Affairs*, vol. 11, no. 4 (Fall 1982), p. 299.

30. I assume that the level of development of the forces of production is always measured by (labour) productivity, but there are various possible definitions of productivity in the presence of constant capital, let alone other complications. The best procedure is to define productivity always as the inverse of unit value, so that productivity is well-defined whenever value is. In general, productivity will then be a vector quantity, which raises problems about the meaning of its 'level' for a multi-product economy. For relevant discussion (though not in quite these terms) see Cohen, *Karl Marx's Theory of History*, pp. 55–62.

31. It is, however, highly significant that the circuits of commodity production and exchange which are the qualitative basis of the discussion in *Capital* involve transaction sequences coinciding with those given by the equilibrium outcomes of Roemer's models. Marx's sequences are examined in A. Carling, 'Forms of Value and the Logic of *Capital*', *Science and Society*, vol. 50, no. 1 (Spring 1986).

32. The vocabulary of the social and the material is properly inserted here, since the outcomes bear a direct relation to the distribution of power. The relations are not social only by contrast with the initial situations of individual isolation on the two islands.

33. The 'slight adaption' of Roemer's opening statement of the two-person case in his *A General Explanation* is the provision of enough seedcorn to employ the whole population (two people) in the CI technology. Roemer makes the supply 'limited', in order to focus on the competitive outcome of extreme capitalism. It is also worth noting that Roemer consistently describes the models discussed in Part 1 of *A General Explanation* as relating to a 'pre-capitalist, subsistence economy' (Roemer, *A General Explanation*, p. 109). This is fair enough if the capitalist 'mode of production' is defined via the capitalist impulse for capital accumulation (cf. Cohen, *Karl Marx's Theory of History*, p. 81). It may be misleading if capitalism is considered sociologically in terms of its characteristic class structure and mode of exploitation, which do appear in the subsistence models of Part 1 of *A General Explanation*. I have used the term 'capitalist' freely in the account of the subsistence model above with the latter consideration in mind. (see also n. 38 below).

34. There are two routes to the greening of socialism from this point. One route concentrates directly on relations between the human and non-human worlds, and is out of sympathy with the classical emphasis on the 'mastery of nature'. The other looks at the non-human world as mediating human relations, especially between current and future generations. To say that current generations must not oppress the future by depriving the planet of non-renewable resources is fully consistent with the classical spirit, as I understand it.

35. Cf. Cohen's 'rough idea of exploitation, as a certain kind of lack of reciprocity' such that 'it is [unjust] exploitation to obtain something from someone without giving him anything in return' (G. Cohen, 'The Labour Theory of Value and the Concept of Exploitation' in I. Steedman, ed., *The Value Controversy* (London, Verso, 1981), p. 343). Elster's more refined dictionary definition is 'the asymmetrical notion of "taking unfair advantage of someone"' (J. Elster, 'Exploitation, Freedom and Justice', *Nomos*, vol. 26 (1983), p. 278).

36. If this sounds odd, recall the special definition of the social and translate: 'no return is owed to an exercise of power alone' or 'might is not right'. For Cohen's distinction, see his 'The Labour Theory of Value and the Concept of Exploitation', p. 219.

37. For the examples and further discussion, see A. Carling, 'Exploitation, Extortion and Oppression', *Political Studies*, vol. 35, no. 2 (June 1987), pp. 173–88. Wright

uses the term 'oppression' in a similiar sense in preference to Roemer's cumbersome 'Marxian unfairly treated', but Wright, *Classes*, pp. 74–7, implies that oppression is necessary for exploitation.

38. This point seems to mitigate the impact Nozick's celebrated Wilt Chamberlain argument has for the debate about Marxian exploitation. Chamberlain may be entitled to his wealth. He may not be entitled to use it in ways connected with capitalist market relations.

39. This is a mode of production in the sense of Cohen's 'economic structure' and not his mode of production in the sense of 'way of producing' (Cohen, *Karl Marx's Theory of History*, ch. 3). I have also used the term 'regime of production' as a synonym for the conventional 'mode of production'.

40. Cf. 'The proletarian may do anything he wishes with his labour power, short of violating the general laws of society, and nothing may be done with it without his contractual consent' (ibid., p. 66).

41. This reciprocal character of power will be difficult to 'think' in the social stratification paradigm, since the vertical metaphor tends to imply that 'power over' is an asymmetrical (unidirectional) relation. This is clear from F. Parkin, *Marxist Class Theory: A Bourgeois Critique* (London, Tavistock, 1979) in which the resistance offered by groups excluded from property is called 'usurpationary'. But there is no usurpation of bourgeois power when workers attempt to use the powers which define their own place in capitalist social relations: powers which run parallel with or exist on the same level as powers over means of production. A similar point applies to Althusserian notions of 'dominance'.

42. Given the agreement, it follows from the definition that each person has sacrificed some degree of power, since the maximum damage they might inflict has been reduced. Interestingly, the longer Friday works, the less power Crusoe enjoys over Friday, since Friday has a diminishing incentive to be exploited in the CI technology. It is natural to say that Crusoe does not have an interest in making use of his power to the full. This point may have wider application to the strategies of ruling classes.

43. This is the gist of an early exchange between Roemer and Wright, in which I have followed the Roemer line. For Wright's position, see his 'The Status of the Political in the Concept of Class Structure'; but note his frank retraction in *Classes*, p. 72: 'I now think Roemer is correct on this point'.

44. I have in mind the tendency of capitalist states to grant the formal 'right to strike' but to hedge this right around with such restrictions as to make the exercise of the right practically ineffective, above all, by maintaining capitalist access to an alternative labour supply. At some degree of restriction, probably surpassed in fascist regimes, the state would cease to be capitalist on this definition. A converse point would apply to restrictions on property rights.

45. 'Extent' rather than 'monopoly' in recognition of Giddens's amendment to Weber (A. Giddens, *The Nation State and Violence* (Cambridge, Polity Press, 1985), p. 20).

46. This point illustrates why the use of the term 'power' is often indexical, making reference to actors or resources excluded from some analysis of current concern.

47. Marx used this transition in 1 *Capital* to distinguish simple commodity production from capitalism, with respect both to class structure and motivational structure (the drive for accumulation). Roemer's basic model shows that the two aspects of the transition were inappropriately elided, since it has capitalist class structure and subsistence motivations. I missed this point in 'Forms of Value and the Logic of *Capital*'.

48. The Friday/Crusoe technology is strictly speaking non-Leontief, since there are two techniques for producing corn. But this will stand for a distinction between

products made using LI and CI techniques in the multi-product model.

49. 'in [the modal] definition, we do not consider an agent to be exploited if he *happens* to purchase a bundle of goods which embodies less labour time than he worked; he is only exploited if he could not feasibly have purchased a bundle of goods embodying as much labour time as he worked' (Roemer, *A General Explanation*, p. 135). A converse definition applies to an exploiter. Applications of the definition depend on an 'assumption of a large economy', since the supply of 'high-value' and 'low-value' goods must be large enough to absorb the revenues of any individual agent. The grey area always embraces the petty bourgeoisie (that is, those who optimize at self-employment). This conforms nicely with one of the traditional Marxist intuitions about their intermediate character. Elster, *Making Sense of Marx*, p. 173, gives the modal conception of class pride of place in his appreciation of Roemer's theory; cf. Cohen's modal worker: 'a proletarian must sell his labour-power in order to obtain his means of life' (Cohen, *Karl Marx's Theory of History*, p. 72).

50. The reason is that a CECP only holds if labour value is defined with respect to the profit-maximizing technologies rather than the whole technology set. But prices must be known before it can be ascertained which the profit-maximizing technologies are.

51. Roemer, *A General Explanation*, ch. 6.

52. There is no class decomposition in this case, because the actors (conceived as nations) are restricted to self-employment. But there is nevertheless a Wealth Exploitation Correspondence Principle – see ibid., App. 1.1; and idem, 'Unequal Exchange, Labour Migration and International Capital Flows: A Theoretical Synthesis' in P. Desai, ed., *Marxism, the Soviet Economy and Central Planning* (Cambridge, MA, MIT Press, 1983). This extension of the theory also motivates the nomination of Friday and Crusoe as the actors in the basic theory.

53. The 'credit classes' are pure lenders, mixed lenders, petty bourgeoisie, mixed borrowers and pure borrowers respectively (Roemer, *A General Explanation*, ch. 3).

54. The counter example occurs in ibid., pp. 234–5, and recurs more prominently with different numbers as Examples 1 and 2 in J.E. Roemer, 'Property Relations vs Surplus Value in Marxian Exploitation', *Philosophy and Public Affairs*, vol. 11, no. 4 (1982), p. 287 ff. The latter paper gives a résumé of all the important cases. Example 2b is Credit Market Island; 3 is the Friday/Crusoe case and 9 exhibits unequal exchange through trade.

55. Roemer, *A General Explanation*, pp. 194–5. 'if and' is deleted from the definition, together with a third 'dominance' condition, which Roemer includes in order to rule out a series of counter-examples involving the claims of the non-able bodied on the social product. The difficulty is that the dominance condition is not precisely stated. Roemer gives two interpretations of its meaning (ibid., pp. 195, 237), the second of which would imply that Crusoe does not exploit Friday and the first of which raises the general question of power in a way that I have tried to follow through in the previous section, but again without discriminating example from counter-example. In my view, the solution to this difficulty lies with the moral conditions for exploitation: it may be possible to represent the claims of the non-able bodied in terms of an unequal exchange with the able bodied, but even if so, the exchange is not unfair.

56. Elster has provided an example in which the two major conditions are satisfied, but there is no interaction between the exploiter and exploited (J. Elster, 'Roemer vs. Roemer', *Politics and Society*, vol. 11, no. 3 (1982), p. 367). To meet this case and subsequent to *A General Explanation*, Roemer substituted for the dominance condition another one designed to capture the interaction more precisely.

('Definition PR', condition 3 in 'Property Relations vs Surplus Value', p. 285 (the dominance condition is banished to footnote 12)). Elster replies that no set of counter-factual conditionals, however long, can ever capture the causal element in the intuition of exploitation. The story will run and run ... but not here.

57. An example is Roemer's 'non-subtle disagreement' between neo-classical proponents and Marxist opponents of capitalism (idem, *A General Explanation*, p. 206).

58. Roemer uses the term 'Marxian exploitation' to distinguish cases of surplus-value transfer which do not constitute capitalist exploitation under the general definition. In Elster's view the problem with the value approach is that it adopts too microscopic a perspective (*Making Sense of Marx*, p. 175 ff.). Parkin, *Marxist Class Theory*, p. 53, also had a sense of this point.

59. This point is made by Wright, *Classes*, pp. 77–8. The proposal has the additional merit of conforming to Cohen's definitions of the economic structures of feudalism and slavery (see Cohen, *Karl Marx's Theory of History*, p. 65).

60. See Roemer, *A General Explanation*, p. 243 (emphasis in original). Throughout his book, Roemer defines socialism via the nationalization of alienable assets, and develops a strong case against any alternative, and less operational, definition (see ibid., pp. 2–6). Both socialist exploitation and status exploitation exist in current socialist societies and 'are uncritically accepted' (ibid., p. 249). Although he thinks one or both forms may be socially necessary at the current historical stage, Roemer's openness in calling the relevant inequalities exploitative is an important example of the healthy directness with which Marxists of this persuasion are prepared to approach the societies of actually existing socialism without abandoning their sympathy for them.

61. I am grateful to P. Jowers for alerting me to Tawney's onion.

62. Elster's major contribution to rational choice Marxism lies in his treatment of the paradoxes and contradictions of collective rational action, applied to a wide variety of historical contexts (see esp. his *Making Sense of Marx*, chs 6–8). Przeworski has surveyed the valley that workers' organization must cross in the pursuit of socialism (*Capitalism and Social Democracy*; idem, 'Material Interests, Class Compromise and the Transition to Socialism', in Roemer, *Analytical Marxism*). Brenner and Taylor deal with the peasantry in the context of the transition to capitalism and modern revolutionary movements, respectively. For both writers, the strength of pre-existing peasant community is the crucial background variable of rational choice, inhibiting capitalist development (Brenner) or facilitating revolutionary mobilization (Taylor). (R. Brenner 'The Social Basis of Economic Development' in Roemer, *Analytical Marxism*; M. Taylor, 'Rationality and Revolutionary Collective Action' in idem, ed., *Rationality and Revolution* (Cambridge, Cambridge University Press, 1988).

63. This may be so even in the absence of socialist exploitation when 'socialistically legitimate returns to differential skills can become embodied as differential ownership of capital' (Roemer, *A General Explanation*, p. 261).

64. Cf. Pranab Bardhan's comment on the multiplicity of development paths in Roemer, *Analytical Marxism*, p. 73.

65. Roemer, *A General Explanation*, p. 243, 'note[s] a parallel' in which feudal and status exploitation are opposed to capitalist exploitation, because in the former examples property is derived from status, whereas capitalist status is derived from property.

66. This is the approach adopted in Wright's *Classes*, although it should be said that his credential assets (educational qualifications) and organization assets (formal position) are not quite Roemer's non-alienable assets and status, since credentials may involve a pure status ('cultural capital') component and formal position may include a skills component (knowledge of how to organize).

67.   M. Barrett, 'Weir and Wilson on Feminist Politics', *New Left Review*, no. 150 (March–April 1985), p. 146.
68.   J. Elster, *Ulysses and the Sirens* (Cambridge, Cambridge University Press, 1979); idem, *Sour Grapes* (Cambridge, Cambridge University Press, 1983).
69.   Cohen, 'The Labour Theory of Value', pp. 206, 223. Cohen also has the endearing and revealing habit of sometimes starting a sentence in resolutely non-sexist fashion and then sliding into the masculine by the end; see, for example, his 'Reconsidering Historical Materialism', p. 236: 'Why should a man or woman not find fulfilment in his or her work as a painter, conceived as his contribution to the society to which he belongs ...'.
70.   The most serious case is the following illustration indispensable for Elster's account in 'Roemer vs. Roemer', p. 365, of the distinction between exploitation and extortion: 'women are exploited by their employers if they get more rapid promotion by sexual favours, but are victims of extortion if they have to give these favours to obtain even the normal promotion'. This example is criticized at length in Carling, 'Exploitation, Extortion and Oppression', but I should also record my impression that sexist usage is on the decline among all those I complain of here.
71.   Cohen, 'Reconsidering Historical Materialism', p. 232.
72.   Such an omission from the otherwise encyclopaedic ambitions of Elster's *Making Sense of Marx* is also striking.
73.   Cohen, 'Reconsidering Historical Materialism', pp. 234–5, from which the preceding quotations are also taken. Cohen has acknowledged this point gracefully in a forthcoming collection of reprinted essays which includes ibid.
74.   The distinction between socialist and status exploitation has already taken Roemer outside historical materialism, since status, as distinct from non-alienable assets, is not a force of production whose level of development might be registered by the key theses of historical materialism.
75.   It is also worth emphasizing that the analytical distinction between 'sex' and 'gender' which was a basic achievement of second-wave feminist theory is parallel to Cohen's distinction between the 'material' and the 'social', and the feminist statement preceded the Marxist one.
76.   I take it that the defining characteristic of radical feminism is the completeness of the break with men thought necessary to bring this about. Wright discusses the counter-factual withdrawal options available to women, and expresses doubt whether women's labour in the home is exploited according to such a test, but his test explicitly leaves discrimination in the labour market in place! The empirical significance of the limitation may be judged from Wright, *Classes*, p. 129, n. 77.
77.   Cohen, 'Reconsidering Historical Materialism', p. 248, n. 10. I should like to acknowledge the rejoinder made by Cohen in the source material in n. 73, that my criticism of this quotation 'ride(s) roughshod over nuances' in its expression. In particular, I am not sure that anything offered in the rest of the paper is incompatible with Cohen's statement that 'racial exploitation is (largely) relegation to an exploited class because of race'. In soccer, the result between notes 73 and 77 would be a score draw.
78.   Wright's data on income distributions is interesting in this respect. The differential of mean incomes between his 'agreed upon' middle and working classes in each gender category is around 1.9. The differential between men and women in each class category is around 1.7 (see Wright, *Classes*, Table 5.15, p. 179). If, as Wright tends to do, one infers exploitation directly from income distributions (the inference may be incautious), it looks as if gender exploitation is just about as serious as asset exploitation for the situation of individuals in the United States today.
79.   I assume that rituals of this kind are especially characteristic of the behaviour of

men: towards women and towards other men. What is said here is intended to generalize beyond Northern Ireland, and beyond ethnic relationships.

80. This endorses the main argument of M. Taylor, *Community, Anarchy and Liberty* (Cambridge, Cambridge University Press, 1982). Cf. idem, *Anarchy and Co-operation* (Chichester, Wiley, 1976), ch. 7.

81. I owe the term and the concept 'formative commitment' to my friend and colleague David West's Ph.D. thesis, 'Nature, Society and the Will', University of Bradford (1983).

Index